A RECKONING

NEW PERSPECTIVES IN SOUTHEAST ASIAN STUDIES

A RECKONING

PHILIPPINE TRIALS OF JAPANESE WAR CRIMINALS

SHARON W. CHAMBERLAIN

THE UNIVERSITY OF WISCONSIN PRESS

The University of Wisconsin Press
1930 Monroe Street, 3rd Floor
Madison, Wisconsin 53711-2059
uwpress.wisc.edu

Gray's Inn House, 127 Clerkenwell Road
London EC1R 5DB, United Kingdom
eurospanbookstore.com

Printed in the United States of America

This book may be available in a digital edition.

Library of Congress Cataloging-in-Publication Data

Names: Chamberlain, Sharon W., author.
Title: A reckoning: Philippine trials of Japanese war criminals / Sharon W. Chamberlain.
Other titles: New perspectives in Southeast Asian studies.
Description: Madison, Wisconsin: The University of Wisconsin Press, [2019] | Series: New perspectives in Southeast Asian studies | Includes bibliographical references and index.
Identifiers: LCCN 2018018522 | ISBN 9780299318604 (cloth: alk. paper)
Subjects: LCSH: War crime trials—Philippines. | World War, 1939-1945—Atrocities—Philippines. | War criminals—Japan.
Classification: LCC KZ1183 .C43 2019 | DDC 364.1/3809599—dc23
LC record available at https://lccn.loc.gov/2018018522

Contents

Illustrations

Figures

Tables and Charts

Tables

Charts

Acknowledgments

This book would not have been possible without the support, encouragement, and extraordinary talents of so many friends and colleagues. It has been a long journey from the initial notion to explore the wartime experiences of Filipinos and Japanese who then faced one another in a postwar courtroom. Had it not been for Shawn McHale and Daqing Yang, I might never have pursued the issue of war crimes trials in the Philippines. I am immensely grateful to them for introducing me to such a rewarding area of research, as well as for their ongoing support.

The universe of scholars who have devoted attention to the subject of post–World War II war crimes in Asia is a relatively small one, and the subset of those who have focused particularly on war crimes in the Philippines is smaller still. Accordingly, the insights and encouragement I have gained from Ricardo Jose and Nagai Hitoshi have been much appreciated.

This book is based in large measure on research conducted at archival institutions in the Philippines, Japan, and the United States. The skilled staffs at the University of the Philippines, the National Library of the Philippines, the National Archives of the Philippines, the Diplomatic Record Office of Japan's Ministry of Foreign Affairs, the Japanese National Diet Library, and the US National Archives at College Park, Maryland, provided welcome support and guided me in my search for materials that I otherwise might have missed. I am also grateful for the institutional support of the History Department and the Sigur Center for Asian Studies of the George Washington University.

I am particularly indebted to Robert Cribb and Yuma Totani; their trenchant comments on earlier drafts of the manuscript have made the final work far better than it otherwise would have been. Others who have offered thoughtful suggestions and encouragement include Edward McCord, Mike Mochizuki, Sandra Wilson, Loretta Castaldi, Tim Curtis, Diane Kupelian, Paula Newberg, Andrea Pedolsky, Nicholas Smith, and Pierre Toureille.

The support of my family and friends has been invaluable. I am so grateful for the love and enthusiastic encouragement I have received from my sisters, Ann and Janice Chamberlain, and my brother-in-law, Mark Schwarz. Alice Donoghue, Sue Eby, and Anne Oliver have been unstinting in their support. I have cherished their friendship, which has extended across decades and continents. Many friends have listened patiently to my often rambling discussions of progress and setbacks—thanks in particular go to Joan Ablett, Cissie Coy, Deborah Katz, Al Schmidt, Kathy Schmidt, and Carole Shulman. And to all the members of my "Broadmoor family," who have followed my journey and cheered its completion, my sincere and heartfelt thanks.

Note on Japanese Usage

In the matter of Japanese names, I have employed Japanese usage, that is, the family name precedes the given name. Further, English-language records related to Japanese war crimes suspects occasionally misspelled the prisoners' names or confused family and given names, and these records invariably did not transliterate Japanese characters using macrons. Wherever possible, I have made the necessary corrections to achieve consistency, relying on available Japanese-language documents and memoirs to do so. Thus, for example, a citation to the transcript of the trial of Chushiro Kudo renders the name as Kudō Chūshirō. When in doubt, I have defaulted to the names as contained in the trial transcripts.

Moreover, in a very few instances I have maintained the usages common to traditional English transliterations, for example, Homma instead of Honma and *kempeitai* instead of *kenpeitai*. All translations are mine unless otherwise indicated.

Abbreviations

AFWESPAC	Army Forces Western Pacific
FEC	Far East Command
HMSO	Her Majesty's Stationery Office
JDRO	Japan Diplomatic Record Office, Tokyo
NACP	National Archives at College Park, Maryland
NAP	National Archives of the Philippines, Manila
NWCO	National War Crimes Office
PHILRYCOM	Philippines-Ryukyus Command
RG	Record Group
SCAP	Supreme Commander for the Allied Powers
UNWCC	United Nations War Crimes Commission
USAFFE	US Army Forces Far East

A RECKONING

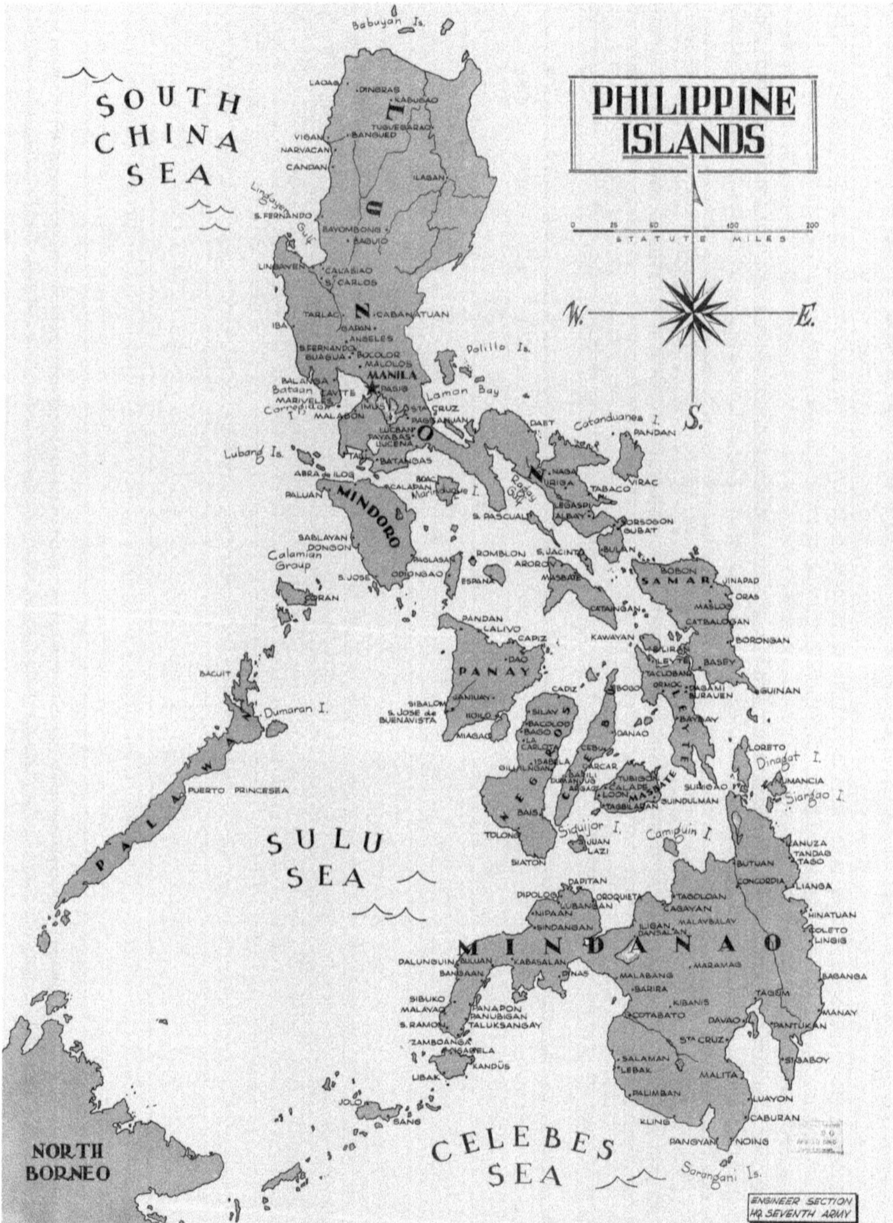

Map of the Philippines, February 1945 (Engineer Section / HQ Seventh Army, courtesy of the Geography and Map Division, Library of Congress)

Introduction

On May 14, 1998, an elderly Japanese man walked out of Ninoy Aquino International Airport and into the glaring sunshine of a stifling Manila afternoon. Fifty years ago, in the aftermath of World War II, a Philippine military tribunal had convicted Shirota Gintarō of war crimes and sentenced him to death. Now he was back, intent on revisiting the prison in Muntinlupa where he had been incarcerated for some five years before being granted a pardon in 1953.

On his journey back in time, Shirota and those from his hometown who accompanied him visited the hill near the prison where seventeen Japanese war criminals had been executed. There was no remaining trace of where the gallows had stood. As one of those present observed, "Everyone cried. The war had been over for six years when these young men lost their lives here, and one couldn't help but cry and cry at how pitiable they were."[1]

Shirota may have been on a personal pilgrimage of sorts, but it was not necessarily one of remorse or contrition. The writer who chronicled Shirota's return to the Philippines focused not on wartime brutalities but rather on the pathos and suffering of the Japanese with whom Shirota shared prison life. Shirota is portrayed as a victim of circumstances: he was convicted primarily by virtue of his association with the Japanese military police headquarters at Fort Santiago, a notorious place where Filipinos were tortured and killed. The Japanese committed atrocities in the Philippines, but Shirota and the other convicted war criminals in Muntinlupa were victims too, made to take responsibility for the crimes of others, including Japan's wartime leaders.[2]

It is not particularly surprising that Shirota would, even at this late date, return to the Philippines. Over the years, many Japanese veterans or their families have traveled overseas to the sites of battles and memorials to pay their respects to their dead comrades and loved ones. The Philippines has played host to a number of such memorials, including the Caliraya Memorial in Batangas

Province, completed in 1973—a project funded by the Japanese government with the approval of the Philippine government. Numerous private memorials have been constructed in the Philippines over the years, including a memorial stone near the site where Shirota's fellow soldiers were executed.[3] Instead, what seems unusual about Shirota's visit is the fact that he, a convicted war criminal, was personally invited to return by the mayor of Muntinlupa, the son of the prison superintendent who oversaw the welfare of the Japanese war criminals incarcerated there so many years ago. And he was not the first to return to the Philippines. In 1977 then president Ferdinand Marcos extended an invitation to Japanese veterans to visit the Philippines. Some of the war criminals did go back, although Shirota at the time could not bring himself to do so.[4]

In personalizing the impact of the war crimes trials held in the Philippines, one could just as easily point to the story of Segundo Lopez. He was called as a witness by the prosecution at the trial of Teramoto Tukuji (Tokuji) and testified to what he had seen and experienced during the Japanese occupation of his country. Lopez, a young Filipino farmer (likely about seventeen at the time of the events he described in his testimony), had occasion to learn some Japanese, and as a result, the mayor of his town had appointed him interpreter to the Japanese army garrison stationed there.

Lopez recounted that during his stint as an interpreter he had observed Teramoto, the garrison commander, order the torture and execution of multiple Filipino prisoners in separate incidents. He also personally witnessed the torture and beating of prisoners. Faced with this highly incriminating testimony, Teramoto's defense counsel tore into Lopez on cross-examination, hammering away at his admission that he had been an "agent" of the Japanese. The lawyer demanded to know why Lopez had done nothing to stop the abuse he had witnessed. Lopez responded that he had been powerless to do so. Shockingly, the next morning the prosecutor announced in court that Lopez had killed himself, unable to bear the stigma of implied collaboration. Lopez had left a suicide note in broken English suggesting that the lawyers had twisted his role as interpreter into that of spy or collaborator but that everything he had said was true. He begged the authorities to help his uncle return his body to his family and expressed his gratitude for getting to fly in an airplane to Manila to testify. The shaken defense counsel asked for and was granted an adjournment.[5]

Shirota was only one of more than 150 Japanese soldiers, sailors, and civilians tried by the Philippine government for war crimes, and Lopez was only one of many Filipinos who gave testimony or statements for those trials. A substantial number of the defendants were found guilty and sentenced to death, although ultimately only a few were executed. The remainder, as well as those serving term or life sentences, were pardoned as the result of a general amnesty granted by the Philippine president. The Filipinos who testified at the trials were left to get on with their lives as best they could. Over time, the trials faded from public memory.

The fates of the Japanese who committed or were suspected of committing atrocities, the scarred victims who survived the brutality, and those on both sides of the conflict who were touched less directly but not necessarily less acutely remind us that the story of the war crimes trials in the Philippines is first a chronicle of the experiences of individuals. Certainly for Filipinos who endured more than three years of enemy rule, the trials convened by the Philippine government offered them the chance to seek legal retribution for the abuses they suffered. The trials served an important role in documenting the suffering that individuals experienced during the Japanese occupation.

But the trials and their aftermath also held broader meaning for both the Philippines and Japan. For the Philippines, the responsibility for putting Japanese on trial became a vehicle for reinforcing the country's claims of sovereignty and status. This newly independent country (and former American colony) in Asia would be able to demonstrate, through its conduct of the legal trial proceedings, its worthiness to join the ranks of the civilized community of independent states, that is, the community of civilized *Western* states. And so the Philippine government committed itself to judicial proceedings intended to protect the rights of Japanese defendants while serving the ends of justice.

For Japan, the trials in the Philippines contributed to and eventually reinforced the perception that the trials in Asia had been unfair—a contemporaneous view that has gained staying power over the years. The trials have been faulted on various grounds: the selection of defendants was arbitrary, judges and prosecutors were not impartial, rules of evidence favored the prosecution, defendants lacked good representation, and those put on trial were lower-ranking soldiers only following orders, or, conversely, commanders were made to bear responsibility for crimes committed by their subordinates without their knowledge.[6]

These clashing views culminated in both sides devising and superimposing their own narratives onto the proceedings. Shirota's story actually illustrates two of these narratives quite well: a Japanese narrative of soldiers as innocent victims of wartime circumstances and a Filipino narrative of selfless generosity in eventually granting blanket pardons to those justly convicted of atrocities.[7] These constructed narratives served the immediate interests of specific groups.

Japanese families who sought the return of their loved ones could marshal broader societal support for amnesty—and thus increase pressure on the Japanese government to gain their release—by emphasizing the innocence of those unjustly imprisoned for crimes committed by others. Members of the Filipino elite could use a message of Christian forgiveness to try to moderate ordinary Filipinos' distaste for reengaging with Japan in the postwar era.

Indeed, once the trials had concluded, Filipinos came to embrace a narrative that combined their belief in a fair trial system with the acceptance of, or at least the acquiescence in, pardons for those Japanese convicted of war crimes as the act of a Christian, civilized nation. This reliance on a constructed narrative of justice tempered with mercy, coupled with a pragmatic understanding of the merits of eliminating barriers to a postwar bilateral relationship with Japan, allowed the Philippines to move forward. Despite the divergent narratives about Japanese culpability for war crimes that divided the two countries, Filipinos were able to look beyond the wartime brutality sufficiently to enable the Philippine government to resolve the fate of the war criminals. By doing so, the Philippines arguably serves as a model for both its handling of the judicial proceedings and its subsequent decision to deliberately put those proceedings behind it.

Nonetheless, to what extent the Philippines and Japan were able to move toward reconciliation in the postwar decades remains more difficult to ascertain, fraught with difficulties in defining what is meant by reconciliation and whether or how these definitions apply in formal country-to-country relations or the attitudes of individuals. But the war crimes trials convened by Filipinos removed one barrier to a path forward: a necessary but insufficient condition for overcoming or at least beginning to deal with the past. By the 1970s that past had receded enough for those convicted of atrocities to return to the land of their victims. Even so, there is a difference between "official" reconciliation between countries and that achievable between individuals. Those who, like Shirota, experienced the war firsthand continued to have—or at least to express—dissimilar memories and beliefs about what happened in the Philippines and the degree of personal reconciliation that had been achieved. Decades after the war ended, author Ishida Jintarō interviewed both Japanese soldiers who served in units responsible for mass civilian killings in places like Los Baños and Lipa and Filipino survivors of those massacres. The results are a striking mix of accusations and denials, remorse and forgiveness.[8]

A thorough examination of the war crimes trials that took place under Philippine auspices in the late 1940s offers both a window into the narrower issue of justice for individuals and an illumination of how the trials served broader goals and constituencies. A review of the Philippine government trials affords a unique opportunity to understand the brutality of the Japanese occupation from the vantage point of both the occupiers and the occupied; to interrogate the nature of justice through the scrutiny of both the process and the evidence presented; and to move beyond the trials themselves to an understanding of their broader postwar impact. Ultimately, this focus on the trials and their aftermath from the vantage point of the Philippines provides a basis for moving beyond the traditional East Asia–centric concentration on the trials and their nexus with issues of justice, memory, and reconciliation to a more nuanced and expansive interpretation of the meaning and impact of the trials throughout Asia.

Context: The Postwar Search for Justice and Historians' Assessments

The trials in the Philippines were part of a much larger story of suffering and the search for justice after World War II. Even before the end of the war in the Pacific, the United States and its allies had signaled their intent to hold Japan accountable for its wartime conduct; the Potsdam Declaration, issued in late July 1945, warned of the allies' intentions: "Stern justice shall be meted out to all war criminals, including those who have visited cruelties upon our prisoners."[9] To honor that promise, eleven allied countries (including the Philippines) put twenty-eight of Japan's military and civilian leaders on trial before the International Military Tribunal for the Far East, popularly known as the "Tokyo trial." The trial's charter, patterned after that of the Nuremberg tribunal, which was convened to try Germany's leaders but issued at the direction of Gen. Douglas MacArthur in his capacity as Supreme Commander for the Allied Powers, defined the categories of war crimes at issue and the rules governing the conduct of the proceedings. The trial's defendants were charged with Class A crimes—that is, the commission of crimes against peace as set forth in the charter—as well as responsibility for more conventional crimes. The Tokyo trial, held from May 1946 to November 1948, resulted in the convictions of twenty-five of the defendants, seven of whom were sentenced to death and executed in December 1948.[10]

The conduct of the Tokyo trial and the verdicts reached remain controversial to this day. At the center of much of the debate has been the question of the legitimacy of trying Japan's leaders for crimes against peace, that is, the pursuit of aggressive war. This, plus challenges to the trial on other grounds (violations of judicial conduct, the failure to hold the emperor accountable, flaws in rules of evidence), gave voice to the overall complaint that the trial represented nothing so much as "victors' justice." Recent scholarship continues to examine critical aspects of the Tokyo trial, providing more nuanced assessments of the trial's impact and shortcomings.[11]

Months before the Tokyo trial started, and continuing well beyond it, were the trials convened by individual Allied governments to try those accused of so-called Class B or C crimes. The Tokyo trial charter defined these categories of crimes as conventional war crimes and crimes against humanity, respectively, although in practice the distinction became blurred, and the trials are now commonly referred to as the B/C trials.[12] In over 2,300 trials conducted across Asia in more than fifty locales, some 5,700 Japanese were put on trial; around 4,500 were found guilty, and of these over 1,000 were sentenced to death.[13] These proceedings included, for example, trials convened by the British in Hong Kong and Singapore, the Dutch in Batavia, the French in Saigon, the Australians in Rabaul, and the Americans in Yokohama and Manila; they also included those by the Philippine government, also in Manila, that placed Shirota in the dock and Lopez in the witness box. The defendants in these trials ranged from general officers to privates and included some civilians; their alleged crimes ran the gamut from direct participation in the commission of atrocities to the overall failure to prevent them.

Compared with the international Tokyo tribunal, these national trials have historically received less attention among the English-language scholarly community.[14] One major exception has been the US trial of Gen. Yamashita Tomoyuki in the Philippines. That trial addressed the doctrine of command responsibility, that is, that commanders could be held accountable for the actions of their subordinates. Yamashita was charged with "permitting" members of his command to commit atrocities and was found guilty despite his insistence that he had been completely unaware of the acts committed. This standard of liability was subsequently applied in other trials, notably the Tokyo tribunal.[15]

Fortunately, a gratifying spurt of more recent works has made important contributions toward redressing the lack of sustained attention to the national trials, including assessments of trials in Hong Kong, China, and Australia and an overview of the Dutch trials in the Netherlands Indies. Two other studies offer broader comparative analyses of the trials in the Pacific theater: Yuma Totani's work focuses on trials of high-ranking Japanese officers in various national jurisdictions, while the authors of *Japanese War Criminals: The Politics of Justice after the Second World War* deal with both the trials and their aftermath. Scholars have also addressed aspects of the posttrial repatriation and release of the war criminals.[16]

These research efforts have tackled the content and context of the trials in various ways. A tendency to focus on single "important" trials (like Yamashita's) has been broadened to include more comprehensive assessments of the full complement of trials in particular jurisdictions. As a result we now have a better understanding of trial proceedings based in part on analyses of actual transcripts, leading to observations about the nature of prosecution cases, the types of evidence presented, the qualifications of attorneys for both prosecution and defense, and the like. The British-conducted trials in Hong Kong, for example, illustrate not just trial procedures but also key points of law raised by the proceedings. A comprehensive volume on the Australian trials addresses trials in specific locales but also examines a cross section of the trials' subject matter (e.g., trials of captured airmen) as well as the procedural and legal aspects of the proceedings.[17]

Certainly legal issues have tended to predominate in studies of these trials. In addition to the doctrine of command responsibility and its application, attention has focused on such issues as the caliber of admissible evidence and various defense strategies, including claims that defendants were only following orders or acting out of military necessity. Generally speaking, the proceedings conducted by the American, Australian, and British authorities sanctioned a broad interpretation of admissible evidence, allowing the introduction of sworn statements and other forms of hearsay that likely would have been inadmissible in their domestic court systems. And scholars have varied in assessing the potential impact of such evidence.[18]

Embedded in analyses of legal aspects of the trials are the more general issues of "fairness" and "justice." Were the trials conducted fairly (in procedural terms), and did they result in just outcomes for victims and alleged perpetrators? Those who have ventured an opinion on these questions have qualified their answers to varying degrees. One reviewer of the British trials in the Far East had few qualms about concluding that the trials displayed "a sensitivity to the rights of individual defendants which does credit to the humanity and even the chivalry" of those responsible for their conduct. In his view, this was in "stunning contrast to the wretched partisanship" displayed by Americans in their trial proceedings.[19] In their compendium, Australian scholars cited a number of factors that demonstrated the fairness of the Australian proceedings, among them the application of consistent procedures, the integrity and dedication of the officials involved, and the number of acquittals and/or successful overturning of guilty verdicts on appeal. In their view, the trials were "fair and just," albeit not without some problems (such as language difficulties or incidences of mass trials).[20] Alexander Zahar, in his analysis of the Hong Kong trials conducted by the British military, takes a less sanguine view, to judge from the various reservations he has about the conduct of the proceedings.[21] Alternatively, Sandra Wilson and colleagues suggest that the pursuit of definitive answers to the question of fairness is in some sense a fruitless exercise, given the complexity of wartime circumstances, the failure to hold Japan's accusers accountable for their own behavior, and the like.[22]

Finally, there have been efforts to situate the trials in Asia in a broader political or social context. In China the impact of the dissolution of Japan's wartime empire, the civil war between Jiang Jieshi's Nationalists and Mao Zedong's Communists and its consequences for Taiwan, and the political motivations of the two sides in addressing Japan's wartime behavior all inform Barak Kushner's examination of the war crimes trials convened on the Chinese mainland.[23] As regards the trials in Asia more generally, Wilson and her colleagues are at pains to stress the significance of political and social factors; they argue that while it would be wrong to conclude that "politics trumped justice" for war criminals, the complicated search for "justice" in procedural and/or substantive terms inevitably opened the door to political considerations.[24]

These areas of inquiry—the specific conduct of trial proceedings, matters of due process and just outcomes, and the overall domestic and geopolitical environment—have direct relevance to the study of trials conducted by the Philippine government. Still, these trials have received scant attention from English-language scholars, despite the fact that they were the only such proceedings convened by former colonial subjects in Southeast Asia.[25] Indigenous peoples in Burma, Malaya, Singapore, Indochina, and Indonesia had no such opportunity; it was the British, French, and Dutch who convened war crimes trials, ostensibly at least partly on these peoples' behalf.

But the Philippine government trials offer a rich field for exploring various facets of the war crimes trials: how a newly independent country approached issues of law and justice; how a people who suffered a harsh occupation balanced a thirst for vengeance against due process for alleged offenders; and how domestic considerations in an emerging Cold War world shaped policies dealing with the incarceration and pardoning of convicted war criminals. And in a comparative sense, the Philippine trials deviated in notable ways from the conduct of trials in other national jurisdictions—in the choice of defense lawyers, the critical dependence on eyewitness survivors, the significant use of local nationals as defense witnesses, and, perhaps most unexpected, the almost complete abandonment of a superior orders defense, that is, that those charged with crimes were only acting on the orders of their commanders and thus should not be held accountable. All of this suggests that an examination of the Philippine trials and their aftermath produces not just an important addition to the canon of war crimes trials assessments but a strikingly different perspective on the pursuit of justice after World War II.

But an analysis of these trials and their significance must first take into account the broader historical and social context in which they occurred. This becomes obvious with the posing of some key questions: How did the American colonial period shape Philippine jurisprudence, with attendant consequences for the conduct of the postwar trials? What was the nature of the prewar relations between Japan and the Philippines, and how might those relations have affected the postwar efforts to settle the fate of the war criminals? And how might the war and occupation have influenced the attitudes of ordinary Filipinos toward the Japanese who served in the Philippines?

Historical Contexts: The Colonial Era, Wartime Occupation, and Early Postwar Independence

For the roughly forty years prior to Japan's invasion of the Philippines in late 1941, the islands had been a US possession, the outcome of a decision by the Americans to seize control from Spain in the wake of the Spanish-American War in 1898. The early colonial administration was headed by an American governor-general, who also served as chair of an appointed lawmaking body (the Philippine Commission) that enacted a host of laws dealing with the civil service, education, taxation, and infrastructure.

The colonial administrators also fundamentally shaped the character of the Philippine judicial system that carried over into the postwar independent Philippines. That system embodied the fundamental principle of separation of powers, with an independently constituted judiciary comprised of the Supreme Court, courts of first instance (the trial courts), and justice of the peace courts (which generally handled minor civil cases). Early on, the Philippine legal system came to embrace the American concept of judicial review, with the right of the courts to challenge the constitutionality of statutes and executive orders.[26] The numbers of Americans who served as judges on both the Philippine Supreme Court and the courts of first instance helped, through their decisions, to shape the Philippine legal and judicial system. American lawyers licensed to practice in the Philippines, as well as the growing cadre of Filipino lawyers trained in the United States or in US law practices, reinforced the use of American legal principles and practices in Philippine courts. Wartime president Jose Laurel, who received his law degree from Yale, is but one example of the Filipino "lawyer-politicians" who predominated in the Philippine governing structure.[27] Court cases provided later precedents that Philippine military tribunals and trial reviewers drew upon in their adjudication of war crimes trials.

Over the years the United States took several steps to increase self-rule for its colony, culminating in the passage in 1934 of the Tydings-McDuffie Act, which provided for the establishment of a commonwealth and a ten-year transition period leading to full independence in 1946.[28] Preparations for the commonwealth involved a constitutional convention in the Philippines, a national plebiscite to ratify the constitution, the election of members to a national assembly, and the election of a president and vice president. Those posts were won by Manuel Quezon and Sergio Osmeña, respectively, both members of the existing Nacionalista Party, whose strength was such as to constitute essentially one-party rule during the commonwealth era. The Commonwealth of the Philippines was officially inaugurated on November 15, 1935.[29] This marked an era of increasing autonomy for the Philippines, with the United States primarily responsible for the foreign policy and defense of the islands.

The Philippines may have been a US colony and then commonwealth, but its geographic location in Southeast Asia rendered it of interest to the growing dominant power in Asia: Japan. Interactions between Japan and the Philippines have been traced back to early in the Spanish era, but the modern narrative of the bilateral relations between the two countries dates to the late nineteenth century, and it is characterized by a renewed Japanese interest in the Philippines and an influx of Japanese laborers and merchants.[30]

During the American colonial era, Japanese immigrants to the Philippines came to be concentrated in two main areas: Manila on the island of Luzon and Davao on Mindanao, the southernmost island. In 1903 there were fewer than one thousand Japanese in Manila; by 1930 that number had quadrupled and remained relatively steady in the following decade. The Japanese population in Davao had climbed from around 5,500 in 1900 to over 18,000 by 1940; the attraction of Davao stemmed from a desire to exploit Mindanao's rich natural resources, including hemp and iron ore. By the end of World War I, Japanese in the Philippines represented the single largest contingent of Japanese nationals in Southeast Asia.[31] After the outbreak of World War II in Asia and Japan's occupation of the Philippines, these Japanese residents were mobilized in support of the Japanese occupying forces.[32]

Characterizations of relations between Japan and the Philippines in the prewar years differ depending on context and emphasis. Tensions undoubtedly existed: attempts in the mid-1930s to curtail Japanese landholdings in Davao highlighted the conspicuous presence of Japanese there; Japanese believed (with some justification) that immigration restrictions enacted in 1940 were directed at them; and the generally deteriorating relations between Japan and the United States contributed to rising concerns in the Philippines about Japanese intentions after the Philippines gained independence.[33] Ricardo T. Jose has observed that in the commonwealth period many intellectuals worried about the Philippines' vulnerability to a Japanese takeover after independence; others, particularly in the military, regarded Japan with genuine apprehension.[34]

But other observers offer a more positive interpretation of the state of Japan-Philippine relations. Grant Goodman in particular has championed the view that relations between Japan and the Philippines were good and getting better throughout the decade of the 1930s, fueled by a mutual appreciation within the Japanese and Philippine governments about the potential vulnerability of a newly independent Philippines in Asia. Much of this goodwill has been attributed to Japanese efforts actively to cultivate members of the Filipino elite, especially in the years after the Philippines became a commonwealth.[35]

A small number of Filipinos were staunch Japanophiles. Benigno Ramos, leader of the Sakdal Party, which mounted an abortive uprising in 1935, had sought support from Japan (but with little success) and was actually in Japan at the time of the revolt.[36] Gen. Artemio Ricarte, a leader in the unsuccessful Philippine nationalist struggle against the Americans at the turn of the twentieth century, likewise turned to Japan and lived in exile there for many years, refusing to pledge allegiance to the American colonizers. Pio Duran, a professor of law at the University of the Philippines during the 1930s, advocated the advantages of alliance with and even annexation by Japan rather than continued domination by the United States.[37] (Duran later would champion the cause of convicted Japanese war criminals in the efforts to gain their release.)

Other members of the elite, epitomized by Jose Laurel, derived concrete benefits from their association and cordial relations with Japan. Laurel, as a lawyer in private practice, acquired a substantial clientele from among Japanese businessmen; others, including Duran, did the same. Manuel Quezon, arguably the most dominant politician in the commonwealth era, proved adept at balancing between the American and Japanese juggernauts; to signal his interest in maintaining friendly relations with Japan he himself developed a number of friendships with Japanese businessmen.[38]

This was the state of affairs as tensions rose between the United States and Japan in the late 1930s and into 1940. The generally deteriorating relationship contributed to rising concerns in the Philippines about Japanese intentions after the Philippines gained independence. By mid-1941, following the advance of Japanese troops into southern Indochina and the American freezing of Japanese assets in the United States, President Franklin D. Roosevelt took the additional step of recalling General MacArthur to active service. MacArthur, then serving as Philippine president Quezon's military advisor, was placed in command of the newly designated US Army Forces Far East, combining the Philippine army and all US army units in the Philippines.[39]

High-level talks between US and Japanese officials during the latter half of 1941 failed to avert war. The resulting surprise attack on Pearl Harbor on the morning of December 7 (local time) preceded only by hours the bombing of Clark Field in the Philippines. This was followed, later in December, by landings on the island of Luzon of units of Japan's Fourteenth Army under the command of Lt. Gen. Homma Masaharu. The combined American and Filipino forces were forced to fall back, unable to prevent the Japanese advance toward Manila. Members of MacArthur's headquarters and certain Philippine officials, among them President Quezon and Vice President Osmeña, fled to the island of Corregidor; MacArthur's troops retreated into the Bataan Peninsula. As the situation deteriorated, MacArthur received orders to leave for Australia; unable to hold out, the forces on Bataan surrendered in April 1946 and those on Corregidor in May.[40] At American urging, Quezon and Osmeña had already left the Philippines, making their way to the United States and establishing a government in exile in Washington, DC.

In early January 1942 soldiers of the Fourteenth Army occupied Manila. At that time, the army proclaimed the dissolution of American sovereignty, declared martial law, and established the Japanese Military Administration to oversee governance of the Philippines. To that end, and with the intent to use the existing prewar governmental machinery, the Japanese pressured members of the Philippine commonwealth government to cooperate, with the result that by the end of January the Philippine Executive Commission had been formally established, with Jorge Vargas as its chairman. Philippine political parties were dissolved, and a new, supraorganization was formed to take their place: the Kalibapi (Kapisanan sa Paglilingkod sa Bagong Pilipinas).[41]

Almost immediately after Japanese troops occupied Manila, Japanese prime minister Tōjō Hideki announced that the Japanese government intended to grant independence to the Philippines at some future date. By mid-1943 the Japanese government had decided to make good on that promise. Accordingly, the Japanese Military Administration instructed the Kalibapi to form the Preparatory Commission for Philippine Independence, which drew up a constitution for the new republic. That constitution conveyed broad powers to the chief executive, who was to be elected by a national assembly; the assembly itself was to comprise equal numbers of appointed members and those handpicked by the Kalibapi. Jose Laurel was named president of the republic.[42] Nonetheless, Philippine "independence" was a highly circumscribed affair; the country was still garrisoned by soldiers of the Fourteenth Army, and Philippine officials' freedom of action was significantly curtailed.

The Japanese occupation of the Philippines combined two overarching and ultimately competing objectives: to win Filipinos to the Japanese cause (and thereby wean them from their loyalty to Americans in particular and the West in general) and to ensure the security and stability of the islands in support of military objectives. Japanese propaganda efforts sought to convince Filipinos of their Asian identity and place in the new order, while at the same time the military administration attempted to eliminate American influence (by changing street names, requiring the teaching of Japanese, and the like) in favor of stressing Japan's moral superiority (through cultural exchanges and an emphasis on Japanese societal values). But these efforts ran aground, torpedoed by the ample evidence on the ground of Japanese disdain for and cruelty toward ordinary Filipinos and the failure of the Japanese leadership to effectively counter Filipinos' belief in America's promise of real independence.

The Japanese military situation had become increasingly precarious by 1944 as American successes in the Marianas and New Guinea foreshadowed the defeats to come. Having successfully argued for a retaking of the Philippines on the way to the Japanese main islands, MacArthur returned in October 1944 with an invasion force that landed on the island of Leyte. After mounting a fierce but ultimately unsuccessful defense, Japanese forces under Gen. Yamashita Tomoyuki fell back into the mountains on Luzon to await the arrival of the Americans. Yamashita had ordered one of his army commanders, Lt. Gen. Yokoyama Shizuo, to evacuate Manila, but the commander of the naval forces there had other ideas, and Yokoyama acquiesced, reinforcing the city's defenses with some of his own troops. The result was carnage, as US and Japanese forces engaged in heavy street fighting and Filipino civilians died in the crossfire and as a result of Japanese atrocities.[43]

Japan's defeat meant the return of the Americans and the reversion of the Philippines to commonwealth status. Sergio Osmeña, vice president of the commonwealth government at the beginning of the war, had succeeded to the presidency after the death of Quezon while still in exile. He returned with MacArthur to the Philippines in 1944. At war's end the timetable for full independence was also resumed, and Osmeña called the Philippine Congress into special session in June 1945. The Congress consisted of those who had won seats in the November 1941 elections, had survived the war, and were not in detention as suspect collaborators.[44] But Osmeña and his supporters found themselves outmaneuvered by challengers led by Manuel Roxas, who was elected Senate president.[45] At another special session, the Congress passed an elections law (signed into law by Osmeña in January 1946) that provided for general elections for president and vice president, senators whose terms had not expired, and all members of the lower house.

In the subsequent April 1946 elections, Roxas, running under the "liberal wing" of the Nacionalista Party, defeated Osmeña for the presidency; Elpidio Quirino won election to the vice presidency under the same banner. On July 4, 1946, Roxas, the last president of the commonwealth, became the first president of an independent Philippines.[46] Roxas died in office of a heart attack in mid-April 1948, leaving his vice president, Quirino, to serve out Roxas's term. Quirino was elected to his own term as president in 1949 but failed to win reelection in 1953. The rise of the Liberal Party (which formally split from the Nacionalistas after the elections) under Roxas and Quirino ushered in a period of essentially two-party rule in the Philippines, with the Nacionalista and Liberal Parties contesting for power at the presidential and congressional levels. But Philippine party politics during this period could hardly be characterized as stable—Filipino politicians could and did swap parties with apparent ease.[47]

One of the key dilemmas facing the Philippines in the early postwar months was how to deal with collaborators. During the occupation, members of the elite, including Jorge Vargas, Jose Laurel, Camilo Osias, and Benigno Aquino, had chosen to cooperate with the Japanese; those who joined the occupation government argued that they had no choice and, moreover, had been motivated by the desire to ameliorate as best they could the harshness of Japanese rule. On the opposing side were those who joined guerrilla units that mounted an armed resistance struggle against the enemy throughout the war. The remaining population occupied the uneasy middle ground—Filipinos of all social levels had to make hard choices about the extent of cooperation or resistance they could or would embrace to survive.

Ultimately, the Philippines created a special judicial process to deal with collaborators.[48] Commonwealth Act 682, enacted in September 1945, provided for the establishment of the People's Court to try Filipinos accused of treasonous collaboration with the enemy.[49] During its tenure, thousands of cases were filed with the People's Court, but the process of adjudicating them was slow and cumbersome. In the end, members of the Filipino elite who had cooperated with the Japanese authorities during the war paid no real political price for their actions. On January 29, 1948, President Roxas transmitted to the Congress for its concurrence a proclamation granting amnesty to Filipinos accused of political and economic collaboration. Those accused of taking up arms, engaging in espionage, or engaging in criminal activity for the purpose of aiding the enemy were excluded and continued to face trial for their actions.[50]

Of more direct import to the issue of the war crimes trials, the survival of certain members of the elite had consequences for individual Japanese as well as the eventual resolution of the entire issue. Men like Osias and Duran, to say nothing of Laurel and other postwar survivors, took a direct interest in and played an active role in working to gain the release of Japanese convicted of war crimes and incarcerated in the Philippines. Others, by their stance in ongoing reparations negotiations between Japan and the Philippines to redress the damage suffered during the war, had a concrete influence on the timing of the war criminals' release. The survival, indeed the flourishing, of such individuals arguably presaged—or at least helps explain—the relatively benign outcome for many of the war criminals.

The efforts to hold collaborators accountable for their wartime behavior and the ultimate decision to grant amnesty to the most high-profile offenders took place concurrently with US and then Philippine trials of Japanese war crimes suspects. Consequently, both sets of trials became part of the postwar experience that linked the Philippines and Japan; it was no accident that President Quirino granted pardons to convicted collaborators and war criminals in the same proclamation in mid-1953.[51]

The war crimes trials in the Philippines and elsewhere also took place amid the worsening relations between the United States and the Soviet Union. The resulting Cold War had undeniable repercussions for American policy toward Japan and the Philippines—in short, the United States became committed to, even driven by, the need to make sure that both Japan and the Philippines remained firmly in the non-Communist camp. American Cold War policy also ensured that the US government would retain an interest in strengthening bilateral relations between Japan and the Philippines, particularly economic ties. US government officials, although sensitive to the difficulties caused by Filipino animosity toward any contact with Japanese in the immediate postwar years, continued to push for expanded trade between the two countries.[52]

The US government also exerted pressure on the Philippines to accept the terms of a draft peace treaty for Japan. The main sticking point was payment for the damage inflicted during the Japanese occupation. Despite American urging, the Philippines refused to abandon the pursuit of reparations, and the final treaty did allow for a process by which the Philippines and Japan would enter into negotiations on appropriate compensation. Even though the Philippine government did sign the 1951 San Francisco peace treaty, the Senate failed to promptly ratify it, and the drawn-out reparations negotiations that followed did not result in an agreement until 1956.

Even so, Cold War politics do not appear to have played any significant role in the specific resolution of the war crimes issue between the Philippines and Japan. That is, the United States appears to have exercised little direct influence on the outcomes. President Quirino's administration dictated the pace and results of posttrial sentence reviews and decisions on executions and pardons, and such decisions were not always or necessarily in line with American policy decisions on the fate of war criminals in US custody.

Certain aspects of the Philippines' prewar and wartime history had significant impacts on the course and outcome of Philippine trials of Japanese war crimes suspects in the immediate postwar years. At its most basic, the American influence carried over into the conduct of the trials themselves. The resumption of American colonial rule, at least briefly, meant that the US government exerted considerable influence on the initial efforts to bring war criminals to justice in the Philippines. Further, the Philippines' legal and judicial responses to war crimes were shaped by its colonial experience: Philippine trial procedures, rules of evidence, and court rulings relied on American jurisprudence as well as the specific procedures adopted by US war crimes tribunals.

More profoundly, the survival of the Philippine elite power structure had enormous consequences for the postwar Philippines. Inevitably, that meant that members of the elite (including those with strong prewar ties to Japan) dictated not just war crimes policy but the economic and political interactions between Japan and the Philippines in the immediate postwar years. These Filipinos charted a course toward "reconciliation" with Japan, at least on state-to-state terms, even if ordinary Filipinos retained some ability to influence the pace of that rapprochement.

1

War Crimes during the Occupation

The Picture That Emerges from the Trials

The series of war crimes trials conducted in Manila, first by the United States and later by the newly independent Philippines, documented the myriad abuses committed by Japanese forces during their more than three years of occupation of the Philippine archipelago. By intent and necessity, these trials focused on atrocities for which evidence of culpability could be marshaled against individual defendants who had survived the war. The trials likewise largely depended on the accounts of victims who had also managed to survive. Trials of high-ranking defendants—generals and the like—tended to paint a broader picture of the scale or extent of Japanese brutality, while trials of lower-ranked soldiers or military police might focus on the torture or murder of members of a single family.

It is important to stress that the trial records cannot provide an unproblematic or full understanding of the nature of the Japanese occupation. That would require the broader context of the overall conduct of the war, the ensuing economic disruptions and political accommodations, and localized responses to both the Japanese presence and the emergence of Filipino collaborators and a guerrilla resistance. Instead, what the trial transcripts do offer is essentially a catalog of the kinds of atrocities that ordinary Filipinos suffered. Survivors and alleged perpetrators voiced their own perspectives on their experiences in a way that allows us to build a picture, albeit selective, of the nature and scope of crimes committed regardless of the proven guilt or innocence of specific individuals.

At their core, the US and Philippine trials documented the nature of the brutalities inflicted on both the civilian population and POWs.[1] Eyewitnesses, their stories given voice in the now fragile pages of decades-old trial transcripts, recounted the horrors experienced by ordinary Filipinos throughout the course

Civilian victims, Manila, February 1945 (Photo SWPA-Sig-C-45-13684, box 1993, UD 1358, RG 331, courtesy of the National Archives at College Park, MD)

of Japanese rule. Survivors recounted appalling stories of atrocities they had experienced or been forced to witness. Many described tortures that included beatings, electric shocks, cigarette burns, and the "water cure."[2] Others testified to being stabbed with bayonets and left for dead, fleeing from buildings set on fire or dynamited, and being raped. Some watched others being brutally tortured and killed. Frequently, these witnesses would be asked to show the scars of wounds inflicted on them—the lasting effects of beatings or bayonet stabbings. Some survivors described being rounded up in a "zona" (short for "zonification," the term employed to describe the tactic used by the Japanese military to gather up the populations of whole villages) and being paraded before a "magic eye" (a disguised or hidden informant who pointed out those suspected of guerrilla activities). Those so identified faced harsh interrogations, beatings, or worse.[3]

The trials also provide some sense of the tactical military situation in the Philippines and the ongoing efforts of commanders and their subordinates to maintain "peace and order" in precarious circumstances. Japanese soldiers spoke of battles fought with guerrillas and the increasingly dangerous conditions as the underground resistance grew increasingly emboldened. The evolution of the military situation in the Philippines is most broadly depicted in the proceedings against three of the top commanders in the Philippines, Fourteenth Army commanding generals Homma Masaharu, Kuroda Shigenori, and Yamashita Tomoyuki, whose command tenure spanned much of the occupation. (The fourth commander, Tanaka Shizuichi, committed suicide at the end of the war and thus could not be brought to account for what transpired during the period of his command.)[4]

The trials also hint at the complicated sets of loyalties that obtained for those compelled or willing to interact with the Japanese occupation forces. Some civilians, including postwar president Elpidio Quirino, supported Japanese defendants; others testified to their suffering at the hands of Japanese civilians and Filipino collaborators alike. Those born in the Philippines to Filipina mothers and Japanese fathers feared the soldiers who employed them and the guerrillas who might wreak vengeance on them. Witnesses included former "puppet" mayors and members of the Bureau of Constabulary (a Japanese-supported police auxiliary) whose claims to be secret guerrilla supporters did not always go unchallenged.[5] Collaborators admitted they had been or would be tried for treason. And even wartime guerrilla leaders might find themselves in the witness box refuting the claims of prosecution witnesses. The trials tell a story of ongoing hard choices, not always clear-cut.

The following narrative of specific war crimes perpetrated by Japanese forces in the Philippines during the occupation is roughly chronological, beginning with the initial landing of Japanese troops in late 1941, the surrender of American and Filipino forces in 1942, and the subsequent treatment of prisoners of war; efforts by the Japanese military police (Kempeitai) to stifle any resistance; the mounting pressures from guerrillas and the increasingly severe counterstrategies used to suppress them; the final fierce fighting and reprisals against the civilian population; and the postsurrender resistance of individual Japanese soldiers who found themselves unwilling or unable to accept Japan's defeat. An understanding of the nature and severity of the atrocities committed by the Japanese forces makes it possible to more fully appreciate Filipinos' thirst for retribution once the conflict ended.

Surrender and Aftermath: The Bataan Death March and Treatment of POWs

Japanese forces under the command of Lt. Gen. Homma Masaharu began landing on the main island of Luzon on December 10, 1941, following the successful air attacks on Clark Field and elsewhere in the immediate aftermath of the attack on Pearl Harbor. By Christmas Day, large numbers of troops were poised to move on Manila from both south and north of the capital. Recognizing the futility of a counterattack, General MacArthur declared Manila an open city, and his forces began the retreat to the Bataan Peninsula; he established his headquarters on the island of Corregidor.[6] Homma and his subordinates later recounted the unexpectedly long battle against these US Army Forces Far East (USAFFE) troops who had abandoned the defense of Manila and withdrawn into the Bataan Peninsula. Following the eventual surrender of American and Filipino soldiers on Bataan in April 1942, Homma then succeeded rather more quickly in obtaining the surrender of the remaining USAFFE forces, which were under the command of Lt. Gen. Jonathan Wainwright.[7]

After their surrender on Bataan, USAFFE troops were forced to march about sixty miles to San Fernando in Pampanga Province, a march infamously known as the Bataan Death March. As alleged by US prosecutors, it resulted in the deaths of about twelve hundred Americans; some sixteen thousand Filipinos were missing or dead.[8] Survivors recounted the punishments they were forced to endure along the march and the brutalities they had witnessed. One US corporal, questioned by an investigator, responded as follows:

Q: To your personal knowledge, about how many prisoners of war did you see die on that march?
A: I have seen 25 or 30 lying on the side of the road.
Q: Were they moving?
A: No.
Q: Were they breathing?
A: I don't know.
Q: To your personal knowledge, how many did you see get up and march?
A: About 10 Americans . . .
Q: Did you see some of the prisoners of war killed by the Japanese on that March?
A: Yes.
Q: Did you see any?
A: I actually witnessed one killing, but I heard of many others.[9]

A Filipino officer (Capt. Jose Lukban, who was later to figure prominently in the Philippine government trials) recounted his own experience as a POW on Mindanao. He and others had surrendered in May 1942 and been transported eventually to Camp Keithley, Lanao Province, a camp that housed both Filipino and American POWs. Lukban recounted an incident in July when four Americans had managed to escape the camp. In the aftermath, he saw three American officers carrying picks and shovels being led away by Japanese soldiers. The Americans were never seen again. Later he was told by a civilian Japanese interpreter that they had all been executed by bayonets, presumably in retaliation for the escapes.[10] Filipino and American POWs at Camp Keithley were shortly thereafter assembled and forced to march to another location some twenty-three miles from the camp. Both Lukban and another Filipino witness observed the killing of two Filipino soldiers along the way.[11]

It was Homma's contention that as overall commander of the Fourteenth Army, he had issued instructions for the proper treatment of prisoners. Under the circumstances it was imperative for staff to handle prisoners of war on their own initiative and without active supervision; any offenses committed by individual officers had occurred without Homma's consent or knowledge. Moreover, various circumstances beyond his control had contributed to the outcome: he had only assumed command of the Fourteenth Army one month prior to the invasion, leaving limited time for troop training and indoctrination; the campaign had been unexpectedly long and bitter, with higher than anticipated casualties from battle and disease; and the surrender of the Bataan forces had necessitated the care and feeding of undernourished and sick POWs. Homma explained that he had received reports on the poor physical condition of the prisoners, which he attributed to malaria and malnutrition. It was also his understanding that his officers were working to improve conditions. He stated that he had never heard the phrase "Bataan Death March" until after the end of the war.[12]

Those who survived the march to San Fernando were transported or made to walk to Camp O'Donnell in Tarlac Province, where they continued to face harsh conditions. One former POW described the crowded conditions at Camp O'Donnell in the early postsurrender days, when exhausted prisoners suffered from a lack of food and medical supplies and received no treatment for malaria, dysentery, or malnutrition. The so-called hospital was just a place where men went to die.[13] The camp commandant, Tsuneyoshi Yoshio, faced charges that he had failed to ensure that prisoners had adequate food, water, shelter, and medicine, thereby contributing to their sickness and suffering and further contributing to the deaths of more than one thousand POWs; that he had compelled these prisoners to work while sick and physically unfit; and that he had permitted his men to torture and kill prisoners.[14]

Numerous survivors of the camp spoke of their harsh treatment, ranging from insufficient food and medicine to the lack of sanitary conditions and resulting disease. Individuals also told of witnessing or hearing of the executions of prisoners for such things as being too near the camp fence or being found in possession of Japanese currency.[15] In his own defense, Tsuneyoshi explained that he had had no prior experience in managing a POW camp; he was overwhelmed by the seventy thousand prisoners who had arrived when he had been told to expect twenty thousand. Tsuneyoshi described his efforts to obtain greater supplies of food; expressed regrets for his "blunder" in not requisitioning clothing for the prisoners; and explained that he had delegated to his medical officer the responsibility for obtaining and distributing medicines and medical supplies. But he denied giving any orders to execute POWs who attempted to escape, nor was he aware of any prisoners bayoneted for approaching the camp fences. In the end, Tsuneyoshi was sentenced to life in prison.[16]

The conditions that obtained at Camp O'Donnell were not the exception, as amply documented in war crimes trials that dealt with conditions at other POW and civilian internment camps in the Philippines. For example, Lt. Gen. Kou Shiyoku was charged with allowing soldiers under his command to commit brutal atrocities against POWs and civilian internees in his capacity as commanding general of all such prisoners from March 1944 to January 1945. Specific charges levied against Kou included the mistreatment and neglect of prisoners at the Cabanatuan POW camp—lack of adequate quarters and medical care, withholding of food and supplies, brutal treatment of prisoners, and requiring forced labor—and similar abuses at other locales, including a POW camp in Davao, the Sakura Detached Hospital Camp at Fort McKinley, and the internment camps at Santo Tomas University, Los Baños, and Baguio.[17]

Numerous survivors of these camps described the abuses they had experienced or witnessed. US Army Col. John Ball testified that he and about 350 other sick prisoners had been ordered to leave the hospital at Sakura despite the fact that none were fit for duty; they were routinely given less than standard food rations. Rudolpho Parra, staff sergeant and medical corpsman, related his experiences while confined to the Cabanatuan camp. Food was scarce, malnutrition was common, and the Japanese in charge refused to provide medicine to treat rampant diarrhea and tuberculosis. The sick were still forced to work; they were like skeletons, and some would fall over from exhaustion and weakness. Raymond Knapp, an army major, told of frequent beatings of prisoners by camp guards, administered with rifle butts, iron pipes, ax handles, or any other handy implement. Many others confirmed these accounts and offered their own stories of abuse, as well as having witnessed the killing of one prisoner near the camp perimeter.[18]

Lt. Gen. Kou Shiyoku (*second from left*) as he was sentenced to death by an American tribunal (Photo SC-242569, courtesy of the National Archives at College Park, MD)

Kou's various defenses—that he did not have command responsibility over the troops committing the abuses; that he had never authorized or permitted beatings of POWs; and that as a Korean he had been marginalized and resented as a commander—proved unpersuasive. He was ultimately convicted and sentenced to death.[19]

Torture as a Means of Control: Fort Santiago and Kempeitai Abuses in the Philippines

Even before the extended siege of Bataan and Corregidor, Japanese troops had reached Manila in early January 1942, set up command operations, and begun to exert control. Almost at once, Manila residents were warned that their cooperation was expected and demanded. Any resistance to Japanese occupation would be met with harsh reprisals.[20] It was left to the Japanese military police to

Entrance to Fort Santiago after the shelling of Manila, February 1945 (Photo SC-374557, courtesy of the National Archives at College Park, MD)

enforce obedience. Fort Santiago, a prison dating to the Spanish colonial era, served as the headquarters of the Kempeitai; as such, it became synonymous with repression and brutality—the site of the interrogation, torture, and murder of countless Filipino civilians. The Kempeitai, leery of the loyalty Japan could command from Filipinos, almost at once began rounding up those who were suspected of guerrilla activity or who could be intimidated into turning informers. This pattern repeated itself throughout the islands as military police commanders and their men dealt with the perceived or actual threat of resistance from the local population.

Victims of Kempeitai abuses during the tenures of Lt. Col. Ohta Seiichi (Kempeitai commander in chief from January to September 1942) and Col. Nagahama Akira (commander in chief from October 1942 to January 1945) described their ordeals in detail in various court proceedings. Shockingly typical were the accounts of Filipino Joaquin Pardo De Tavera and American Joseph Garrick Eisenberg. De Tavera recounted how Japanese policemen roused him from bed early one morning, slapped him, and brought him to Fort Santiago, where he was placed in a cell. Over the course of two months he was investigated multiple times, suffering beatings and torture each time.[21] And he witnessed the abuse of others:

> I have seen children crying and being beaten up, and a child of fourteen years was put in my cell bleeding. One afternoon a whole family of Chinese, including the grandmother, were tied up on the bars of the cell with chains and in the morning they were all hanging from the chains. I don't know if they were dead or alive. It was continuous torture, physical and moral. If you have to admire torture, I admired it. They would never use the silent kind, it was always walking, yelling, beating, so you never knew what was going to happen to you. You never knew who was going to be taken out of the cell, and you never knew who was going to come back.[22]

Eisenberg had been captured by the Japanese at Bataan in April 1942 and was incarcerated at Fort Santiago as a prisoner of war until June. He was then transferred to a hospital in Manila; by November he had been reclassified as an internee and sent to internment camps for most of the remaining duration of the war. At Fort Santiago, Eisenberg was beaten frequently and heard or witnessed the beatings and torture of other prisoners. "It was a common practice to beat the prisoners across the kidneys and buttocks with some heavy implement, usually a heavy board or the flat of a shovel."[23]

Fermin Miyasaki, born in the Philippines to Japanese parents, was employed by the Kempeitai as an interpreter and later described the torture and killings he witnessed. In November 1944 he was asked by a Japanese officer to accompany twenty-seven prisoners to a cemetery in Manila. Upon arrival, he saw the prisoners blindfolded, taken one by one to a newly dug hole, and then decapitated. He also observed the torture of a woman who had been bound naked, hung by a rope from the ceiling, and burned with cigarettes. At Fort Santiago he saw prisoners beaten with pieces of wood or galvanized iron pipes. He heard screaming every day and bodies being carried away.[24]

One particularly gruesome incident took place at Fort Santiago during Nagahama's tenure in which more than four hundred Filipino prisoners died of suffocation—an incident notable for indifference to human suffering if not deliberate criminal intent. Japanese and Filipino accounts suggested that overcrowding in the cells, prisoner agitation over lack of water, and criminal indifference to the prisoners had all contributed to the fatal outcomes.[25]

Ohta and Nagahama both attempted to explain or excuse their actions. Ohta described his efforts to improve conditions at Fort Santiago, including the construction of a new cell block; stated that it was customary for the Japanese army to use "light" force in interrogations but that this was by no means torture; and insisted that if any torture occurred, it was contrary to his orders. Nagahama did ultimately take responsibility for the actions of his men but sought to explain the forces that had prevented him from executing a policy in which the object of arrests would be not punishment but admonition and education. He had not been strong enough to overcome the objections of those who opposed this policy. These opponents' (whom he did not name) advocacy of force and intimidation was reinforced by the growing strength of the guerrillas and the increasing hostility of the inhabitants owing to the wartime circumstances that forced the Japanese to live off the land. These efforts at mitigation proved fruitless; both men were found guilty and sentenced to death.[26]

Ongoing Efforts at "Peace and Order": Guerrilla Subjugation and Punitive Expeditions

Japan's initial military successes in overrunning Southeast Asia, coupled with the Allied powers' overall wartime strategy of balancing demands in the European and Pacific theaters, meant that the Philippines could not expect a quick or easy end to Japanese military occupation. Notwithstanding Japanese hopes of winning the support of Filipinos, the behavior of Japanese troops, coupled with the stubborn loyalty of many Filipinos to the departed Americans, led to the emergence of an underground resistance that embedded itself on islands throughout the Philippine archipelago. Fourteenth Army commanders were plagued with guerrilla resistance virtually from the outset of the occupation, a resistance that mounted in intensity as the war situation turned against the Japanese.[27] Trial transcripts are replete with descriptions of efforts to subdue guerrilla activity in campaigns taking place throughout the archipelago, including the islands of Cebu, Negros, Panay, Mindanao, and of course Luzon. If anything, the trials conducted in the Philippines showcase just how seriously the Japanese regarded guerrilla activity as a threat to their war operations.

Japanese troops of the Fourteenth Army, including Kempeitai units, were stationed at various locales. A particular municipality might have a garrison commanded by an army officer as well as one led by a Kempeitai commander, possibly augmented by members of the Bureau of Constabulary. Even so, the Japanese could hardly hope to achieve full control over the archipelago. One guerrilla commander estimated that of the one thousand or so municipalities in the Philippines at the time, the Japanese maintained garrisons in only two hundred; the remaining eight hundred were overtly or secretly controlled by the guerrillas.[28] As conditions worsened, Japanese troops would conduct operations designed to flush out guerrilla suspects or sympathizers. The transcripts of the trials of those brought to court over their alleged conduct introduce the language of "guerrilla subjugation" and "punitive expeditions." These were the shorthand efforts to describe the increasingly harsh treatment that Japanese troops meted out to the local populations as the war situation worsened and resistance to the occupation mounted in severity and volume.

The trials of Lt. Gen. Kōno Takeshi and some of his subordinates illustrate quite well the nature of these punitive expeditions. From May to October 1943 Kōno had been in command of all the Visayas, with particular focus on Panay, Guimaras, and Tablas Islands; in October Leyte and Samar were removed from his jurisdiction; and after July 1944 he was in charge of the western half of Negros and Panay Islands.[29] Various accounts describe Panay as a particular hotbed of guerrilla activity almost from the outset of the Japanese occupation, leading eventually to a decision to mount an aggressive antiguerrilla campaign beginning in the later half of 1943.[30]

According to prosecutors, Kōno's units stationed in Panay and Guimaras systematically engaged in expeditions from August 1943 to December 1944 intended to eliminate as many civilians as possible.[31] Tozuka Ryoichi, one of Kōno's direct subordinates, maintained that the expeditions that he and his men led were primarily aimed at capturing guerrilla commanders and their wireless transmitters. Neutralizing the threat from guerrillas would allow them to focus on the main objective of fighting the Americans. Tozuka insisted that the instructions he received from Kōno's headquarters were to capture guerrilla leaders but not to harm innocent civilians. In fact, he was to treat residents kindly in order to gain their cooperation. He denied any knowledge of torture or murder committed by his men—such acts were strictly forbidden.[32]

But local inhabitants refuted Tozuka's claims of benevolent treatment, describing how they had witnessed the capture and killing of many individuals.[33] Bernardita Naman, age fifteen, recounted how five Japanese came to her family's place of evacuation on Panay Island in January 1944 and discovered five rifles in the possession of a guerrilla who had been sleeping there (and who managed to run away). The Japanese questioned her family, then killed her parents, grandparents, aunt, and her four siblings, age two, four, six, and thirteen. She herself was "hacked" and bayoneted, surviving with wounds to her hand, head, and shoulder and the severing of her right hand.[34]

Augustin Dasas and Filomeno Cirineo were both seized by the Japanese during expeditions conducted on Panay in September 1943. Dasas was caught and taken to an area where he saw four dead bodies and two other people being killed. His hands were tied behind his back, and he was ordered to kneel. A

Japanese soldier "hacked" his neck twice, but he survived his injuries and fled. Cirineo had been captured and forced to accompany the Japanese soldiers for two months as a cargador, that is, a porter. At various barrios along the way, he saw groups of Filipino civilians, including women and children, tied and beheaded or bayoneted.[35]

One Japanese soldier who participated in these expeditions acknowledged the killings but claimed that he had only been following the orders of his superior officer, Captain Watanabe. When he was in a good humor Watanabe would spare the women and children, but when he was in a bad humor he ordered everyone killed.[36] Asked about his own involvement, the soldier responded as follows:

Q: Did you kill any children?
A: Children cannot be cut by a sword because their neck is too short.
Q: Did you kill any children?
A: I did not.
Q: Did you kill any women?
A: Yes, I did.[37]

Nonetheless, Kōno's defenders stressed the nature of the guerrilla threat that Japanese forces faced in the months preceding the anticipated arrival of US forces. Wachi Takaji, who had served as Fourteenth Army chief of staff, described the orders that had been sent to Kōno's headquarters to maintain peace and order in the Visayas, particularly Panay Island, where guerrilla activity was especially violent and extensive. It was the mission of the Fourteenth Army to defend the Philippines, but there were weak points in that defense. The Japanese anticipated that the Americans would strike at the "middle" (the five islands of Panay, Cebu, Bohol, Leyte, and Negros), and it was essential to deal with guerrilla activity. The orders to suppress the guerrillas left to Kōno's discretion how to go about this; Wachi denied that Kōno was ever ordered to kill unarmed men, women, or children or to torture or mistreat them.[38] Kōno himself insisted that when he took command of Panay Island, he had issued a standing order on the capture of guerrilla leaders and the destruction of their communications facilities, but at the same time and in later orders he also directed his men to "sympathize [with] and love the civilian residents." At no time did he order the brutal treatment or killing of noncombatant civilians, and he had taken all possible steps to prevent such killings.[39]

It was the trial of yet another of Kōno's subordinates that provided one of the more comprehensive discussions of the threat posed by guerrillas as seen from the perspective of the Japanese forces. Yamaguchi Masakazu, who had led punitive expeditions in the province of Negros Occidental from January 1943 to March 1945, faced Filipino survivors who recounted their suffering at the hands of his men. Manuel Batisla-ong, for example, told how he was rounded up and taken with some four hundred others to a church, where he and others were beaten. He later saw the bodies of three men who had been killed as guerrilla suspects.[40]

In response, Yamaguchi described a tactical situation that demanded action against guerrillas and spies. When he took charge of security in 1943, the strength of the "bandits" (the term Yamaguchi used interchangeably with "guerrillas") on the entire island exceeded fifteen thousand, and they were armed with automatic rifles. At their peak strength, the Japanese had only sixteen hundred men, and their principal weapons dated to the Russo-Japanese War of some forty years earlier. As the Japanese sought to secure vital points along the coast, they were increasingly harried by bandits who knew the terrain thoroughly and were assisted by civilians. Casualties mounted; in combat he lost the majority of his subordinates.[41] "It was as if we were fighting an apparition. They could see and knew about us, but we, in turn, did not know about them. If they were outnumbered, they mingled with the populace, but if they outnumbered us, they launched surprise attacks and caused casualties. These guerrillas were superior in strength and arms."[42] Yamaguchi condemned this type of guerrilla warfare as unfair and inhuman. He pleaded for understanding, arguing that he and his men had "fought these strong, cunning and barbarous guerrillas with our weak force for three years under difficult conditions, taking full precaution[s] to avoid casualties among the civilians."[43] He then expressed his deep regrets to the people of Negros who had suffered in spite of the precautions he had taken.[44]

End Game: The Battle for Manila and Mass Executions in Southern Luzon

The early months of 1945 both presaged the eventual end of the war in the Philippines and marked the period when the death toll of Filipino civilians at the hands of the Japanese armed forces reached into the thousands. Yamashita Tomoyuki, commander of the Fourteenth Area Army (formerly the Fourteenth Army), had originally planned for a decisive battle on Luzon, but various circumstances (including the disastrous decision, against Yamashita's recommendation, to counterattack the Allied invasion of Leyte in the central Philippines in October 1944) led to the eventual decision to mount a defensive campaign on Luzon. The strategy was to pin down as many US divisions as possible in order to slow their advance to the Japanese home islands. Yamashita ordered his forces concentrated in three areas: his own Shobu Army in northern Luzon in the area northeast and east of Lingayan Gulf, the Kembu Army in the area of Clark Field and the Bataan Peninsula, and the Shimbu Army defending all of southern Luzon and commanded by Lt. Gen. Yokoyama Shizuo. Yamashita instructed Yokoyama not to defend Manila but instead to pull his forces from the city. However, owing to the complicated command structure, which left Yokoyama with limited ability to direct the naval forces in the area (which remained in the city), the upshot was a brutal and destructive battle as US troops converged on the city and Japanese forces, their escape now blocked, fought to the death. On March 3, 1945, when the US commander reported that organized resistance in Manila had ceased, US casualties were reported as 1,000 killed and 5,500 wounded; the Japanese lost approximately 16,000 men. Much of the city had been destroyed, and the civilian death toll was staggering: upward of 100,000 Filipinos had lost their lives.[45]

The records of the Yamashita trial provide a good overview of the military situation that Japanese forces faced as the Americans began their fight to retake the Philippines, and Yokoyama's trial as well offers a picture of the destructive battle for Manila.[46] Less well known but equally riveting are the accounts of the widespread killings that took place in the provinces in southern Luzon in the early months of 1945, described by one prosecutor as "a reign of terror that has no equal, perhaps except in the experiences of the poor civilians in Europe with the Gestapo."[47] Various trial proceedings collectively provide a detailed picture of what the inhabitants of Batangas and Laguna Provinces suffered between January and March 1945 at the hands of the Japanese military units stationed there. Col. Fujishige Masatoshi and a number of his subordinates were charged with having undertaken a "widespread plan" to kill civilians and destroy property in Laguna and Batangas Provinces. It was alleged that over seven thousand civilians were murdered during the ensuing rampage.[48]

Fujishige commanded what was known as the Fuji Heidan (Group), the result of a January 1945 reorganization that threw together the Seventeenth Infantry Regiment (which had arrived in the Philippines in October 1944) and a number of smaller units. The Fuji Heidan reported to Yokoyama Shizuo (a direct subordinate of Yamashita), and its troops were stationed in various towns in southern Luzon. The main missions of the Fuji Heidan were to delay the American advance toward Manila and to deal aggressively with guerrilla attacks.

Sakata Yuzo, a former member of the Seventeenth Infantry Regiment, recounted that he had heard of orders issued by Fujishige in November 1944 and again in January 1945 on the need for an aggressive guerrilla subjugation campaign. It was Sakata's understanding that because all civilians had become guerrillas, all, including women and children, were to be killed. Sakata believed that neither of these orders was carried out immediately because the trigger was to be the landings of the Americans on Luzon, which had not yet occurred.[49] Ichimura Isao, one of Fujishige's direct subordinates, confirmed that his battalion had received orders from Fujishige in early 1945 to kill all who opposed the Japanese. The essence of the order was that since almost all civilians had become guerrillas, all must be "thoroughly subjugated." Although Ichimura denied his own participation, he acknowledged that the orders had been carried out.[50]

Several survivors recounted what they had endured during the Japanese onslaught in southern Luzon. Their stories are revelatory, not least because of the variety of ways the soldiers found to kill their victims. Pamfilo Umali, a resident of barrio Pusil in Lipa, Batangas Province, described how he and some seven hundred others had been rounded up by the Japanese and then taken in groups of four to six and "dumped" in either of two wells in the barrio:

Q: After you were in the well were there any shots fired or was anyone harmed after jumping into the well?
A: After we were down inside the well we were shot—or rather, they began shooting at us.
Q: How did you get out of the well?
A: A rope was lowered down to us by one of the women and then one by one we climbed out of the well.
Q: How many people climbed out of the well, as far as you know? . . .
A: We were seven that came out of the well, but the seventh died; only six of us came out alive. . . .
Q: What happened to the other 294 persons, or 293 persons who were dumped into the well with you?
A: They all died. . . .
Q: Why did you jump into the well?
A: Because I was afraid that I might be bayoneted, and I didn't want to die; so I preferred to jump inside the well.[51]

Other victims offered their own dramatic accounts of the brutal ways in which the Japanese military dealt with civilians, whether guerrilla suspects or noncombatants. In the municipality of Buaun, Batangas Province, the town crier summoned villagers to the church at the behest of Japanese soldiers, who had arrived in force in early February 1945. Mariano Alix and his family obeyed the summons; the women and children were then taken to a school building, while the men were separated into three groups of one hundred each. Japanese soldiers then took Alix's group to a house near the church and ordered the doors and windows locked. Then there was a flash and an explosion—the house had been dynamited. Alix was injured and lost consciousness. "When I opened my eyes, I found dead bodies and injured people moaning all around and some asking for help." He managed to escape, but many others died.[52]

Two women who survived a February 1945 attack on the residents of barrio Masbud in the municipality of Taal described how they hid with others in a ravine after hearing that Japanese soldiers had killed the people of another barrio. The arriving Japanese fired on them with a machine gun, threw grenades at them, and bayoneted others. Both women were wounded. That same month, in the town of Bay, Laguna Province, Jose Kariktan described how Japanese soldiers arrested and tortured him. He and others were then taken to a house and stabbed with bayonets; the Japanese then set fire to the house and left. He and a companion managed to loosen their bonds and flee.[53]

It was Uehara Zenichi, another of Fujishige's subordinates, who provided the most detailed rationale for what had transpired during these early months of 1945. Uehara explained that the main missions of the Fuji Heidan were to strike a heavy blow against the landing American forces, to destroy enemy communications, to make any counterattack by the larger Japanese force a success, and to resist American progress. By January the Americans had already landed on Mindoro (the island directly south of Luzon), and local Filipinos shared the belief that the US forces would head to Batangas next. Anti-Japanese activities increased accordingly. Guerrillas were gaining in strength, and there were reports of attacks on Japanese soldiers. At January meetings of Fuji Heidan commanders Fujishige spoke about the increasing intensity of guerrilla activities and the corresponding need for thorough and resolute suppression. At one of these meetings it was said that women who were armed should be considered guerrillas, but nothing was said about children. Fujishige issued a written order that all garrison unit commanders were to attack guerrillas at every opportunity; additional telephone orders were given in February to specific units. The suppression order did not contain any details as to how it should be carried out—that was left to the battalion commanders, since the situation with guerrillas differed in each locality. Uehara testified further that he had been surprised at reports of the numbers of guerrillas killed (450 in one report) and mentioned this to Fujishige, who expressed satisfaction. When Uehara recommended that orders be issued for the evacuation of civilians, Fujishige indicated he would consider it, and it was Uehara's belief that at some point Fujishige had agreed. Uehara noted that his own interpretation of guerrilla subjugation meant an

Victims of the wholesale killings in Lipa, February 1945 (Photo 41-51-1, box 1236, entry 143, RG 153, courtesy of the National Archives at College Park, MD)

attack on guerrillas—armed bandits and those who cooperated directly with the guerrillas and whose status was quite clear. He denied that the late January policy on guerrilla subjugation meant the massacre of people by bayoneting, shooting, or burning. He speculated that when Fujishige praised the first account of the killings without further investigation, this was misinterpreted as an endorsement of what had occurred, thereby encouraging other local commanders to proceed in a similar manner.[54]

Postsurrender: Stragglers and Resistance

In the aftermath of the US atomic bombings of Hiroshima and Nagasaki, Japanese emperor Hirohito proclaimed Japan's surrender on August 15. Throughout Japan's wartime empire, millions of soldiers and civilians found themselves stranded. Repatriation would take years, and many never made it home at all. In the Philippines the nature of the fierce fighting toward the end of the war and harsh physical conditions complicated efforts to determine accurately those who had survived the battlefield. This confusion, compounded, as Beatrice Trefalt notes, by a military ethos that rejected the very idea of surrender, contributed to the number of "stragglers" who sought to evade capture in the months and even years that followed Japan's formal surrender.[55]

One Philippine government war crimes trial in particular highlighted the desperate lengths to which some Japanese soldiers were willing to go to avoid surrender. Ainoda Hajime and his sixteen codefendants were charged with one or more of twenty-four counts of torture, murder, and cannibalism committed over the course of more than a year in the remote province of Bukidnon, on Mindanao. All these acts took place after Japan's surrender.[56]

The prosecution made much of the sensational aspects of the case. The defendants, the "desperate remnants" of the Japanese army, had waged war on defenseless men, women, and children and ignored the "gates of democracy" open to them. Instead, they had engaged not just in torture and murder but also in the butchering and consumption of their victims. Survivors and the Filipino soldiers who eventually arrested the alleged perpetrators offered their individual accounts of what they had experienced.[57]

A farmer described how in September 1945 he and his companions had gone to the cornfields, where they were surrounded by Japanese and tied up. These Japanese then took four of the men away. When the witness looked toward them, he saw his father being stabbed and heard the screams of the others. Eventually, when the Japanese slept, he and the others managed to escape. A young woman described how the Japanese came to her house in October 1945, tied her and her sister up, and took them both to the chicken house, some three yards from the house. From there they saw the Japanese kill their father, cut off one of his thighs, and cook and eat it. She further stated that the Japanese then raped her while she shouted and struggled. Two other witnesses—a grandfather and his grandson—related how they had been caught by five Japanese in March 1946 and brought to a house in barrio Culaman. The grandfather was tied up and hacked with a bolo; he then lost consciousness. When he came to, his grandson untied him, and they ran away. He saw the body of his wife—her head had been severed.[58]

A Filipino soldier whose patrol had captured the stragglers testified that their commander had admitted that he and his men had eaten human flesh. This was confirmed by the finding of kettles of human flesh and human bones at the stragglers' campsite. An American prosecutor who also questioned a number of the Japanese stated that he had obtained confessions from them, and in the end, the evidence presented was sufficient to persuade some of the men to plead guilty.[59]

The particularly sensational nature of this case reinforced the notion that the perpetrators seemingly found it impossible to admit defeat or envision any other option than their continued struggle to survive by whatever means necessary, including murder and cannibalism. In his confession, Ainoda, a doctor, admitted with no apparent sense of irony that he had been present when killings occurred but left them to others because by profession he was a "saver of life." His statement explaining what they had done was chilling: "Whenever possible, we avoided killing people by eating the bodies of people who died from illness or were killed in action or executed for crimes. I sincerely regret the deaths of Filipinos (soldiers and civilians) who were killed by our patrols, and if any other course had been open to us, these deaths may not have occurred."[60]

Another of the defendants, Tsuji Chōichi, later wrote a memoir of his experiences in the Philippines, recounting how he and his comrades hid in the jungles of Mindanao to avoid capture and what hardships they endured before they were forced to surrender. He never explicitly mentions the crimes with which he and his codefendants were charged, nor does he acknowledge that some pleaded guilty to charges of murder and cannibalism. He instead claims that they were unfairly blamed for the actions of others who had already been allowed to go home and had been the target of witnesses unfairly coached by the prosecution to identify them as the perpetrators. He concludes that the trial trampled on the dignity of the law and was more about making victims of the losers than about justice.[61]

Atrocities and the Thirst for Retribution

The suffering that individual Filipinos endured during the Japanese occupation was manifest from the accounts of those who had survived their ordeal. A report of the destruction of Manila in early 1945, accompanied by graphic pictures of murdered residents and accounts of indiscriminate killings, highlighted the brutality of the conflict: "Manila has been destroyed. The once proud city of the Far East is dead. Its churches, convents, and universities are piles of rubble, bombed and burned beyond recognition. Its civilian population has been raped and burned, starved and murdered, its women mutilated, its babies bayoneted."[62]

It is no wonder, then, that many Filipinos viewed the Japanese with anger and hatred in the early postwar years. Those feelings were reflected in commentaries by contemporaneous observers, in letters and editorials in the local papers, and in acts of revenge against Japanese prisoners of war. Hatred of the Japanese was visceral and expressed itself in periodic outbursts of rage often triggered by reports that Philippine officials were considering reengaging with Japan economically or that individual Japanese might visit the Philippines.

A *Philippines Free Press* columnist in 1949 described an incident in which young Filipinos in a nightclub, seeing a group of Japanese Americans, asked them to leave to avoid an incident. "It was an ugly thing to do, nasty, cheap. . . . But the act, though a dubious exhibition of courage, made it clear that many Filipinos cannot see any Japanese even today without seeing red."[63] That anger was reflected even more viscerally in a *Daily News* column that fairly dripped with rage at the very presence of three Japanese staying at a local hotel on a one-night layover. It used language quite reminiscent of the ways in which the Allies had dehumanized the enemy during the war with racist cartoons and images:

> Just imagine. Three chimps each lolling in a lush Manila Hotel bed. . . . If I had been hired to guide the Japs around, I would have taken them to a place in Tondo where some of the local thugs could take a good look at them. It would have been a most exciting time, both for the Nips and for the thugs. . . . I would have taken them also to a local nightclub. . . . There would have been a lot of broken glasses in consequence, but the three apes would remember the experience long and fondly, if they lived through it.[64]

These sentiments evoke the context in which the Philippine government a few years earlier had contemplated assuming responsibility for trials of Japanese war crimes suspects. Japanese atrocities and the hatred they fueled were at once the imperative for convening trials to gain justice for victims and a potential bar to achieving just outcomes. Both sides had qualms about the ability of Filipinos to look beyond their anger and conduct impartial proceedings. It was a challenge that the Philippine authorities were determined to meet; their chance came with the decision to transfer responsibility for trials from the United States to the Philippine government in 1947.

2

Rising to the Challenge

Assuming Responsibility for Trials

Philippine Commonwealth president Sergio Osmeña, wading ashore on Leyte with Gen. Douglas MacArthur in October 1944 as American forces began their battle to retake the Philippines, faced a daunting landscape.[1] Conditions in the war-torn islands were chaotic, and worse was to come: the fierce battle for Manila in early 1945 and Japanese reprisals against the civilian population in the surrounding areas produced a death toll in the hundreds of thousands and left the capital city in ruins. At the end of the war, Filipinos had to cope with the massive challenges of reconstruction, elite infighting for political control, and the incendiary question of what to do with collaborators. These dilemmas had by no means disappeared by the time the Philippines gained independence in July 1946, with Manuel Roxas as its first president.

And so the Philippines was, arguably, hardly in a position to assume immediate responsibility for bringing Japanese war criminals to justice, even had the United States been amenable. It was the Americans who took charge of the first set of trials. Filipinos supported US investigative and prosecutorial efforts, but it was not until a full year after independence that the Philippine government took over the prosecution of the remaining Japanese war crimes suspects. By that time, the framework for the trials had been firmly established, and the US tribunals served as important precedents for the Philippine government trials.

Nonetheless, in critical ways Filipino officials in charge of the trials had to make significant adjustments to the conduct of the proceedings. These officials had the power to materially affect the nature of the defense afforded Japanese war crimes suspects, with potential consequences for the kind of justice such defendants could expect. In taking over the trials, the Philippine authorities charted a course that built on the earlier American trials but also deviated from them in key ways, largely as a matter of necessity. These changes involved decisions on the kind of legal representation the Japanese were afforded and their access to evidence to support their defenses.

Creating the Infrastructure for War Crimes Trials

The United States and its allies had first signaled their commitment to prosecuting war crimes in response to reports of atrocities being committed in the European theater. In 1942 the Allies created the Inter-Allied Commission on the Punishment of War Crimes and in early 1943 issued the Declaration of St. James, which affirmed a commitment to punish those guilty of war crimes. These actions were followed later in 1943 by the establishment of the United Nations War Crimes Commission (UNWCC), which was given responsibility for collecting evidence of war crimes. At the urging of the Chinese member of the commission, the Far Eastern Sub-Commission was established and based in Chungking (Chongqing); its first meeting was held in November 1944.[2]

In reality, the burden of documenting atrocities and perpetrators fell to the individual UNWCC member states. In the United States, the War Department's War Crimes Office, organized in October 1944, served as the central agency for the collection of evidence of war crimes in all theaters.[3] It was supported by the War Crimes Branch, which was activated in the Pacific theater in April 1945. Shortly thereafter the War Crimes Investigation Detachment was set up in Manila for the purpose of collecting evidence of Japanese atrocities against POWs and American and Filipino civilians. In support of this effort, President Osmeña created the National War Crimes Office in August to collect evidence of war crimes and to work with US authorities to ensure the just punishment of those Japanese guilty of atrocities.[4] Members of the detachment, which included US and Philippine army personnel, fanned out across the Philippine islands to interview witnesses and obtain their sworn statements. The resulting case reports documented widespread atrocities and POW abuse and were used in support of eventual prosecutions of war crimes suspects.[5]

With Japan's surrender, the War Crimes Investigation Detachment became part of an organizational structure that had its central locus in occupied Japan. To oversee the US-led occupation, the US government named General MacArthur the Supreme Commander for the Allied Powers (SCAP); that acronym became synonymous with the burgeoning occupation machinery based in Tokyo. SCAP's various organizational components included the Legal Section, headed up by Col. Alva Carpenter; it was the Legal Section that assumed overall responsibility for developing general policies and procedures on war crimes, overseeing war crimes investigations, and supervising the prosecutions of war crimes suspects. In July 1946 the War Crimes Investigation Detachment was formally designated Legal Section Manila Branch and reported to SCAP Legal Section Tokyo.[6]

American Trials in the Philippines: Establishing Precedents

The regulations governing most of the US trials in the Philippines, issued by SCAP in December 1945, set forth the structure and conduct of the proceedings. These regulations authorized the establishment of military commissions and dictated their composition and how they were to function. They also spelled out the duties of prosecutors, the rights of the accused, and the use of witnesses and admissible evidence. Verdicts, which required a two-thirds vote of commission members, were subject to review and required approval of the convening authority before sentences could be carried out. All death sentences had to be confirmed by MacArthur himself. To address issues of fairness, the regulations stipulated that defendants be advised of all charges against them before trial, be represented by court-appointed or their own chosen counsel, and be permitted to present witnesses and evidence, as well as cross-examine prosecution witnesses.[7]

US authorities chose to divide responsibility for the trials conducted in Manila (as well as Yokohama).[8] For the Philippine trials, Army Forces Western Pacific (AFWESPAC) acted as convening authority in appointing military commissions and defense counsel, reviewing sentences, and maintaining custody of war crimes suspects.[9] The Manila Branch of SCAP Legal Section spearheaded investigations and the preparation of cases for trial. The commanding general of AFWESPAC reported to the commander of US Army Forces Far East (USAFFE), whereas Legal Section Manila Branch reported to Legal Section Tokyo.[10] Thus, the ultimate authority was still MacArthur either in his capacity as SCAP or as USAFFE (later Far East Command) commander. As explained in a later history of SCAP's role in the trials, "This policy of placing the military commissions and defense counsel under a separate command from that of investigation and prosecution set a precedent for the trial of accused war criminals, and proved most effectual in affording the defense freedom of action."[11]

The first and by far the most sensational of the trials conducted in Manila under US jurisdiction was the proceedings against Gen. Yamashita Tomoyuki. This trial, which resulted in his conviction and execution, pursued a theory of command responsibility wherein commanders could be held accountable for the actions of their subordinates even in the absence of direct knowledge of the crimes committed. It was MacArthur himself who in September 1945 instructed Lt. Gen. Wilhelm Styer, AFWESPAC commanding general, to proceed with the trial of Yamashita; MacArthur also approved the initial rules and regulations governing his trial.[12] Philippine press coverage of that trial bordered on the obsessive, as illustrated by the almost daily front-page stories offered by the *Manila Times*. On December 8, the day after Yamashita was found guilty, the *Times* ran his picture over the caption "DOOMED," and the article opined that the verdict constituted a "precedent in war criminology."[13]

Later analyses of the Yamashita trial have not been kind. The haste with which the trial began, its procedural failures, and, most critically, its interpretation of the individual criminal responsibility that Yamashita bore for the atrocities committed in the Philippines have all been seen as damaging weaknesses.[14]

Philippine historian Teodoro Agoncillo later acknowledged both the depth of hatred that led Filipinos, including himself, to celebrate the Yamashita verdict at the time it was rendered and his own later realization that emotion had triumphed over justice. His war diary "trembled with supreme hatred for the Japanese." But after many years of reflection and study, "I hung my head in shame for having refused then to wait for a more propitious and less emotional time for rendering an impartial judgment."[15]

Subsequent trials convened by the US military in the Philippines dealt with both the mistreatment of prisoners of war and atrocities committed against American and Filipino civilians. Between late 1945 and mid-1947, when the US trials ended, US military commissions had convened ninety-seven trials, convicted 90 percent of all defendants tried, and sentenced ninety-two to death. After appeals, sixty-nine were executed, all but two in the Philippines (the other two were repatriated to Japan and executed there). As the US trials concluded during the first half of 1947, war criminals convicted and sentenced to life or lesser terms were sent back to Japan to serve out their sentences in Sugamo Prison in Tokyo.[16]

Handover of Trials to the Philippine Government

Although the Philippines gained independence from the United States on July 4, 1946, the Philippine government did not assume formal responsibility for the conduct of war crimes trials until mid-1947, and the first trial under Philippine jurisdiction did not begin until August 1947.[17] Historian Philip Piccigallo has suggested that the delay can be attributed to the Philippine government's preoccupation with other more pressing matters, including how to deal with collaborators and address the threat posed by domestic insurgents—the Hukbalahap.[18]

By 1947, however, it is likely that the interests of both the United States and the Philippines were converging in favor of a handover, although the Philippine government had significant reservations about costs and logistics that had to be overcome. If, as a noted Japanese scholar of the trials has observed, President Roxas was eager to take over the trials, he was clever in displaying just enough reluctance to extract the maximum number of concessions from the United States.[19] For their part, the Americans might have wished to wind down their involvement once the more "important" cases had been tried, but a powerful, albeit less visible, motive was also at work. The US War Department had been embarrassed by accusations of mismanagement and incompetence in the handling of trials in Manila.

The US government began pressing the Philippines to take over as early as January 1947. At that time SCAP Legal Section outlined the goal of turning over the investigation and trial of war crimes suspects to the Philippine Republic and noted among anticipated problems the need to "convince" the Philippine government of its responsibilities and the "desirable effect" of properly publicizing such a transfer.[20] At roughly the same time, the War Department began to urge the early closing of the Manila office. Back in November 1946, US civilian defense attorneys posted to Manila had begun to complain about their working conditions, office mismanagement, and "farcical trials" that were "setting disgraceful precedents." These attorneys escalated their concerns to the commanding general of AFWESPAC, the secretary of war, and ultimately members of Congress. Army officials in Tokyo and Manila fiercely rebutted the accusations about the trials, insisting that they had been "eminently fair" from the outset. The War Department, despite offering some assurances of support, had a backchannel source in the person of a junior officer who had recently gone back to the Philippines to provide evidence against Japanese war crimes suspects (he had been a POW there during the war). He met with department officials on his return from Manila and provided a picture of an office in disarray, where "there seems to be a total state of disorganization in the prosecution and defense." In a later recap of the issue, the War Department noted its belief that "War Crimes Trials in Manila have not progressed satisfactorily."[21] (In its final close-out report, the local command in charge of the US trials seized the opportunity to even the score, charging that the failure of the War Department to adequately screen civilian attorneys had led to the posting in Manila of three habitual drunkards, a lawyer censured and dismissed for cause in one trial, and other "lesser incompetents."[22])

Clearly, the War Department had an incentive to hasten the transfer of responsibility for the trials to the Philippines. In early February 1947 Colonel

Carpenter, the SCAP Legal Section chief, met in Manila with Philippine government officials to discuss the transfer of pending war crimes cases involving Filipino nationals. Following that meeting, Filipino and US military officials agreed to prepare briefs in support of the use of Philippine military commissions to handle the trials, apparently to head off the suggestion that the trials be transferred to civilian jurisdiction. On March 12, 1947, the Philippine government formally accepted the US proposal to assume responsibility for war crimes trials.[23]

However, during subsequent meetings between Philippine government officials and SCAP Legal Section representatives, President Roxas made it clear, as reported by US officials, that "the financial condition of the Republic would not permit it to conduct a war crimes program, successfully and expeditiously, unless the United States provided the maximum of assistance." At an April 11, 1947, cabinet meeting attended by the Legal Section Manila Branch executive officer, Roxas proceeded to outline the specific assistance he had in mind. He asked that the US army retain custody of Japanese war crimes suspects and deliver them for trial as required; that the US army assume responsibility for the transfer to Japan and incarceration of those Japanese convicted and given less than death sentences; that the Philippine government be provided with Japanese interpreters and counsel to act as defense attorneys; that facilities and equipment (including buildings, office furniture, and motor vehicles) currently used by the Legal Section Manila Branch be loaned to the Philippine government for use in its war crimes trial program; and that Legal Section Manila Branch retain sufficient staff in the Philippines to advise the government on the conduct of the trials. On May 6, 1947, Legal Section chief Carpenter recommended that Roxas's demands be met, and by early July the necessary orders had been issued to accommodate virtually all of the Philippine government's requests. The Philippine government would assume responsibility for trying the remainder of Japanese war crimes suspects in the Philippines, and the US government would continue to provide some support.[24]

To implement the Philippine government's responsibilities, President Roxas issued Executive Order No. 68 on July 29, 1947.[25] EO 68 established the new National War Crimes Office (NWCO) under the jurisdiction of the judge advocate general of the Philippine army and tasked it with collecting evidence of war crimes, bringing about the "prompt" trial of the accused, and maintaining direct liaison with SCAP Legal Section. The NWCO, initially headed by Maj. Eleuterio Fojas (he was succeeded by Capt. Mariano Yenko Jr. after Fojas's death in June 1948), at the outset consisted principally of the Prosecution Division, led by Capt. Nicanor Maronilla-Seva, and the Administrative, Investigation-Apprehension, Records, and Interpretation and Translation Divisions, all also headed by Philippine military officers.[26]

The executive order also outlined the specific rules and regulations governing the conduct of the trials, which were closely patterned after those used by US military commissions. The commissions, to be convened under the authority of the president of the Philippines, would consist of a minimum of three members and render their verdicts by a two-thirds majority. All guilty verdicts and sentences would be reviewed, with the president having responsibility for confirming life or death sentences before they could be imposed. The rights of the accused would include the right to have advance notice of the charges and specifications against them, the right to be represented by counsel, the right to testify in their own behalf, and the right to have their counsel cross-examine adverse witnesses who appeared before the commission.

The official transfer of responsibility for the trials may have put the Philippines in charge, but the terms of that agreement ensured that the United States would continue to have a presence. SCAP Legal Section Manila Branch remained open (but without those pesky civilian defense lawyers), and US attorneys assigned to the office provided advice and guidance to the NWCO on policies and procedures related to the trials. This attention was particularly assiduous at the outset: before the first trial the branch's executive officer met with the secretary of justice, commission members, and the prosecution and defense; he subsequently conducted an orientation on the forthcoming arraignment of the defendant; and he then routinely attended the trial sessions. The Americans seemed particularly anxious that the defense was seen as effective. The head of Manila Branch noted with relief that the local press had commented favorably on the effectiveness of defense cross-examination.[27]

Those on the ground in Manila found it difficult to resist continued involvement. In September the head of Manila Branch advised Tokyo that he had "lectured" commission members of two forthcoming trials about such matters as rules of evidence and (rather condescendingly) found them to be quick-witted, "high type men." He also recounted an episode in which commission members had "fumbled" a ruling; he had "unobtrusively" passed a note to them suggesting a recess, which allowed them to resolve the issue.[28]

Perhaps in anticipation of the need to set some boundaries over the continued involvement of US personnel in the Philippine trials, SCAP Legal Section Tokyo had attempted to define the limits of US participation before the handover. Manila staff members were instructed in late May 1947 to defer to

NWCO chief Fojas on whether remaining outstanding cases were prosecutable.[29] (Moreover, Filipino prosecutors could and did bring cases against individuals previously cleared by American investigators. At least twenty-seven men who had been repatriated to Japan were later arrested based on information supplied by Philippine investigators and returned to the Philippines to stand trial.[30]) Tokyo issued a further warning in March 1948, instructing Manila staff to avoid becoming actively "embroiled" in helping the defense in Philippine cases. Legal Section Manila Branch firmly rejected the criticism, insisting that staff had simply been continuing to serve in a liaison capacity between the prosecution and defense.[31]

Resolving Structural Issues: Legal Representation and Evidence Admissibility

The rules governing the Philippine trials were clearly patterned after those used by the Americans, and the handover was further eased by the familiarity of a number of Filipino army officers with the process. These men had participated in investigative efforts from the start and had on occasion served as military commission members or prosecutors. For example, Gen. Basilio Valdes sat as a commission member in the trial of Homma Masaharu, while Manuel Lim (later Philippine solicitor general) served as one of the prosecutors in the same trial; in yet another case the prosecution was handled entirely by Filipino prosecutors.[32]

But the Philippines had to make two important adjustments that centered squarely on the issue of how to ensure that Japanese defendants were treated fairly. EO 68 had mandated certain safeguards to ensure due process for Japanese defendants. Key among them were defendants' right to legal representation and the ability to present evidence in their defense. In practice, achieving these safeguards posed significant challenges, and the results were not wholly consonant with the standards for conventional criminal trials.

Initially, two Filipino defense counsel represented the first Japanese defendant to face trial before a Philippine military commission. These counsel were considered "provisional," however, and acted for the defendant only until the arrival of Japanese lawyers. A group of ten attorneys had arrived in Manila by the end of August 1947. It was intended that these lawyers would take over the defense of all Japanese facing trial in Philippine tribunals.[33] (The logistical and expense arrangements for the assignment of both lawyers and interpreters preoccupied the American occupation officials for some months prior to the convening of the actual trials.[34])

The use of Japanese lawyers to defend Japanese war crimes suspects had been part of the agreement reached between the governments of the Philippines and the United States on the transfer of responsibility for conducting war crimes trials. This was consistent with the dispatch of Japanese attorneys and interpreters to support Allied trials in other venues; such personnel were under contract to the Japanese government, and their salaries were paid by that government. Nonetheless, this represented a departure from the US war crimes trials in the Philippines, where Japanese defendants had been generally represented by American counsel, although the applicable regulations allowed them to be represented by other counsel if they so chose. A number of former general officers being held in Manila had requested that Japanese attorneys be sent to assist US defense counsel, largely to minimize the language barrier.[35] The Americans in Manila had suggested that members of the US defense staff employed in the US trials would be willing to stay on. SCAP in Tokyo swiftly rejected the idea, noting that no US funds would be available for the hiring of attorneys. The work would have to be done by Japanese lawyers, unless the Philippine government was willing to bear the expense of alternatives.[36]

Japanese POWs facing trial in the Philippines had been leery from the start about the effectiveness of the defense they could expect in Philippine military tribunals. Former Lt. Gen. Yokoyama Shizuo, writing on behalf of Japanese POWs incarcerated in LUPOW (Luzon Prisoner of War) Prison Camp #1 in the Philippines, penned a series of letters and petitions to high-level officials in both Japan and the Philippines expressing their anxieties.[37] As early as April 10, 1947, even before the details on the transfer of the trials had been settled, Yokoyama wrote to MacArthur, President Roxas, and the commander in chief of the Philippines-Ryukyus Command in response to newspaper accounts that they would be tried by the Philippine government. He noted that it would be difficult, for "emotional and mercenary" reasons, to assign Filipinos as defense attorneys and accordingly urged that American defense counsel, joined by some Japanese lawyers, continue to represent Japanese defendants. This would ensure "fairer and juster trials."[38]

Yokoyama further noted in a petition to MacArthur on June 15, 1947, that he and his fellow POWs were "encouraged" that Japanese defense attorneys would be made available and also expressed the hope that the "most reliable American lawyers" might also be requested to assist in their defense. An earlier petition from the camp addressed to the SCAP Legal Section Tokyo noted that the possible participation of American defense lawyers "made every one of us extremely happy and assured" in light of the fact that Japanese lawyers, even if they did come to the Philippines, would be faced with the disadvantages of the language barrier, as well as an unfamiliarity with Anglo-American jurisprudence. Yet another petition to SCAP Legal Section Tokyo, dated April 18, 1947, explicitly noted the prisoners' "uneasiness and anxiety," commenting that "there is little probability that able Filipino lawyers will be available in the future trials because of emotional antipathy against the Japanese."[39] The judge advocate general of the Philippine army, in receipt of similar requests from Japanese defendants for the appointment of American counsel but having made no financial provision for such an accommodation, sought and received an opinion from Legal Section Manila Branch that international law required only the provision of qualified counsel, which the Japanese lawyers were deemed to be by virtue of their selection by the Japanese government.[40]

As it turned out, the use of Japanese lawyers did not last long. Of the group of ten attorneys who arrived in Manila in August 1947, all but one had been sent back to Japan by the end of the year. The immediate catalyst appears to have been the reported bad behavior of some of the attorneys, dramatically covered in the local press. In one well-publicized incident, it was reported in late November that Captain Maronilla-Seva, head of the NWCO Prosecution Division, had been attacked, thrown to the floor, and kicked by several Japanese. At the time, according to news reports, Maronilla-Seva had been attempting to explain to the Japanese defense attorneys his refusal to agree to a postponement of a trial. A spokesman for the Japanese group later denied Maronilla-Seva's accusation that the defense was deliberately faking the illness of the accused to gain a postponement of the trial. Editorial opinion in the Philippine press was blistering. The *Manila Post* of November 22 argued that the Japanese who "ganged up [on] and mauled" Maronilla-Seva should themselves be prosecuted, while the *Liberty News* of the same day suggested that the attack represented "the collective efforts of the Japs who were quite intent in adding another victim to the number of Jap atrocities."[41]

The rocky position of Japanese lawyers had been highlighted a few days earlier in the trial of Nakamura Hideichi and his codefendants. According to the *Manila Chronicle*, defense attorney Tanamura Shigenobu had been attempting to cross-examine a prosecution witness when he became exasperated with the repeated objections of the prosecutor, all of which were sustained by the military commission. "Irked by the attitude of the commission, the Japanese counsel, trembling with anger, hastily gathered his papers on the table, dumped them into his portfolio and announced that if such was the kind of treatment accorded the defense, he would resign as counsel. He hinted that the defense was not getting a fair trial in the case at bar."[42]

The actual trial transcript paints a less sensational picture but does indicate that Tanamura was frustrated with commission rulings and was suggesting a change in defense counsel. Tanamura was granted a recess, but the commission president rejected the notion that the commission was favoring the prosecution. He noted that in fact the reverse was true: every effort was being made to help the defense attorney, given his inexperience with such cases, but in this instance the witness had been subject to cross-examination for nearly two weeks, and counsel had repeatedly asked immaterial and irrelevant questions. After the recess, Tanamura continued his questioning but was replaced as defense counsel on December 8.[43]

The US Embassy in Manila reported that a Filipino committee had investigated the Maronilla-Seva incident on behalf of the Philippine government and recommended that the Japanese lawyers be sent back to Japan. Responsibility for the defense of Japanese war crimes suspects would be assumed by Philippine army lawyers. The Defense Panel, headed by Capt. Pedro Serran, was established within the NWCO, and its lawyers included Capt. Jose G. Lukban and Capt. Artemio Alejo, professional lawyers as well as army officers.[44] In four ongoing trials, Filipino counsel replaced the Japanese counsel. (In fact, Filipino attorneys had from the beginning been assigned to all the trials, presumably to provide guidance to the Japanese attorneys, and in some instances had taken over the questioning of witnesses or had raised objections to prosecution questions.)[45] At the first trial in which a Japanese defendant was defended from the outset by Filipino counsel, the commission president rather defensively noted that "to my mind, the interests of the accused had never been served better than when a Japanese accused is defended by a Filipino attorney" and further commented on the skills of defense counsel Serran, notwithstanding Serran's war service as a guerrilla and his reluctance to serve as a defense attorney. (The commission thereupon found the accused guilty and sentenced him to death.)[46]

The initial reaction among the Japanese war crimes suspects to the use of Filipinos as defense counsel was consternation. In another petition to SCAP Legal Section Tokyo dated January 3, 1948 (with a similar petition addressed to the president of the Philippines), Yokoyama noted that it was a "most regrettable affair" that the Japanese lawyers had been recalled to Japan and pleaded for the appointment of other Japanese counsel, "not for the direct purpose of defending the accused but for the purpose of legal liaison between the accused and Filipino defense counsel because we have had great difficulty conveying our ideas of the cases and to explain the matters legally and logically so that the lawyers can understand the cases in issue readily as to points of importance."[47] Yokoyama's plea for the posting of Japanese lawyers in a liaison capacity appears to have been accepted. In a lengthy report on the trials prepared in May 1949, the Japanese Foreign Ministry noted that at that time three Japanese lawyers had been posted to Manila.[48]

In the end, it appears that the Japanese became more than resigned, even accepting, of the Filipino lawyers assigned to defend them. By August 1948 the Japanese POWs were actually complaining about the then single remaining Japanese defense attorney, Masutani Hideo. Legal Section Manila Branch reported that the dissatisfaction stemmed from "a complete lack of confidence in Japanese defense lawyers as contrasted with Filipinos acting in that capacity" and suggested that Masutani's abrupt and forthright manner had offended the Japanese prisoners.[49] A few years after his conviction, former Lt. Gen. Kuroda Shigenori commented that the Japanese lawyers had suffered from several disadvantages, among them unfamiliarity with Anglo-Saxon law and a reliance on interpreters that prevented timely or effective cross-examination.[50] (The transcripts confirm that Japanese defense counsel in the early trials had issues with witnesses answering questions before they could be translated and counsel had a chance to object.[51])

The head of SCAP Legal Section Manila Branch had also expressed concern with the qualifications of the Japanese attorneys, noting that most of them could not speak English and, given the unfamiliarity of all but one of them with war crimes proceedings, it would be necessary to hold a "school" for both defense counsel and interpreters at the start of the Philippine trials.[52] In a rather remarkable display of disdain for the Japanese defense counsel, the Filipino lawyer assigned to the defense in one trial sought permission from the commission to continue the examination of a witness in order to "ask some two or three questions which have been miserably missed" by the Japanese counsel.[53] Certainly, the Japanese lawyers themselves were not unaware of their limitations. In his summation in the trial of Kodama Yoshiaki, his counsel noted that they were "not familiar with the trial in the American way" and therefore were less competent than the prosecution.[54] In another case, the Japanese defense attorney noted a second major drawback: it was too dangerous for him to travel around Manila seeking witnesses for the defense.[55]

Individual Japanese war criminals commented favorably on the competence and dedication of the Filipino defense lawyers. For example, at the close of his trial Matsuzaki Hideichi thanked his defense counsel for having overcome their natural antipathy toward Japanese and having "nobly defended" his cause.[56] Likewise, defendant Matsuta Junzō spoke of the uneasiness and anxiety that accompanied the dismissal of the Japanese attorneys, which were soon replaced by the "full reliance, confidence, and deep trust" in their Filipino replacements.[57]

General Yokoyama's wife, presumably on his behalf, observed in 1952 that Filipino lawyers "overcame their emotions and defended [the war criminals] zealously" and had also visited the prison to comfort those who had been convicted.[58] Long after the trials were over and he had been released, Satō Sō, who had received a life sentence, thanked his Filipino attorney in the preface to his memoirs, convinced that the lawyer's "devotion" (*nessei*) at Satō's trial had saved him from the death penalty.[59] The Japanese Foreign Ministry reached its own conclusion that the Filipino defense lawyers were "zealous and capable" (*nesshin yūnō*) and that Capt. Pedro Serran, chief of the defense team, was an "extremely able and honest lawyer." The Filipino lawyers, "contrary to expectations," had exerted themselves despite the pressures of Philippine public opinion.[60]

One rather remarkable exchange serves to illustrate the extent to which Japanese prisoners were willing to assert their confidence in their Filipino defense counsel. Former Maj. Harada Shimpei, along with three of his subordinates, had pleaded guilty to their roles in the torture and killing of a number of Filipino civilians; just before their sentences were pronounced, they all expressed their gratitude to their defense counsel, Lieutenant Perez. Harada, however, who had received a death sentence, subsequently charged in petitions to the sentence review board and President Quirino that he had been pressured by Perez into offering a guilty plea despite his innocence. Moreover, his counsel "compelled [him] to testify falsely" as part of his plea. Not surprisingly, the head of the Philippine Defense Panel, Captain Serran, rejected Harada's charges as unfounded.[61] But it was Japanese prisoners themselves—the more than one hundred war crimes suspects still awaiting trial—who voiced the strongest defense of Perez in a letter to the Defense Panel office:

> We have been informed that some portion of the content of the petition submitted to His Excellency, the Republic of the Philippines, by Major Harada was contrary to what we always entertain. . . . That petition was written and submitted on the sole discretion of Major Harada as an individual and it represents in no way whatever the opinion of other war criminal suspects. . . . For the past nine months, Lt. Peres [*sic*] has been exerting all his efforts in the defense of alleged war criminals. His indefatigable fight to uphold justice is what everyone [*sic*] of us is very familiar with. Not only are we grateful for his unyielding efforts for our cause, but we also place absolute confidence and trust in him as our defense counsel.[62]

In one odd instance, a defendant successfully insisted on representing himself midway through his trial. Maj. Gen. Hayashi Yoshihide and Maj. Gen.

Kawaguchi Kiyotake had been charged with ordering the death of Jose Abad Santos, chief justice of the Supreme Court, for his refusal to cooperate with the Japanese occupation forces.[63] Both generals had been represented initially by Filipino defense counsel Jose Lukban, but as the trial progressed Lukban asked that he be removed as counsel for one of the defendants, arguing that he perceived a conflict of interest in continuing to represent both men. The commission agreed, and another lawyer was named to represent Hayashi. When the prosecution rested its case, Lukban requested that the proceedings be postponed because he believed Kawaguchi was suffering from paranoia. Kawaguchi then insisted on dismissing Lukban as his counsel and representing himself. The drama continued: The commission refused to commit Kawaguchi to a hospital for observation; Lukban asked to be removed from the case; and Kawaguchi's codefendant then asked that Lukban represent him (a request the commission denied). Lukban left the court, and the trial continued. The curtain finally came down when Kawaguchi took the stand and pleaded guilty to the charge against him. (Hayashi maintained his not-guilty plea and was convicted and sentenced to life in prison.)[64]

The assignment of capable interpreters and translators was an important corollary to assuring an adequate defense for Japanese war crimes suspects, and this too initially proved challenging. In accordance with the terms of the transfer arrangements worked out between the US and Japanese governments, ten interpreters had been sent to Manila along with the Japanese lawyers in August 1947. But the initial reaction to the performance of some was mixed at best. Legal Section Manila Branch commented in early October on the poor ratings given some of the interpreters and very quickly thereafter reached the conclusion that four were incompetent and needed to be replaced. And in early January 1948 former general Yokoyama complained that most of the official court interpreters were incompetent and urged that the Japanese government send personal interpreters for the accused to address the anticipated greater translation burden with the assumption of defense responsibilities by Filipino army officers.[65] Indeed, once Filipino lawyers took over the defense, commissions dispensed with the routine translation of all the proceedings into Japanese, instead relying on personal interpreters for the defendants.[66]

By June 1948 there was more of a consensus that the interpreters were performing their duties effectively. And while it is difficult to ascertain the skill levels of those posted to Manila in the early months, the résumés of at least some of those who arrived later indicate both a command of English and prior experience with war crimes proceedings. For example, one such interpreter arriving in Manila in early 1949 had been born in the United States, attended school there for several years, and later served as interpreter for the war crimes court in Singapore and been named the chief interpreter for the Malayan war crimes court. Another of these interpreters had a similar background: he attended grammar school in Hawai'i, and his employment history included stints as an interpreter for both the Singapore and Hong Kong war crimes trials conducted by the British military.[67]

Finding competent interpreters was only part of the story; retention was also an issue. The US government had agreed to assume the costs of transporting the interpreters to Manila and housing and feeding them at army installations; NWCO was responsible for providing personal allowances. As contract employees of the Japanese government, the interpreters' salaries were paid by that government to their relatives at home. By mid-1948 the Japanese personnel in Manila were petitioning Legal Section Manila Branch for help in persuading the Japanese government to raise their salaries, because with rising inflation in Japan, their families were having difficulty making ends meet. Legal Section Manila Branch supported the petition, noting that the lives of these Japanese employees were necessarily restricted in Manila and it was important to boost morale to ensure their continued effectiveness.[68] Staffing levels continued to be of concern; Kuroda Shigenori, who represented the prisoners, and the chief of the Japanese Interpreters' Group both signed a letter to MacArthur in November 1948 stating the need for ten interpreters and five translators, given an increasing workload that involved not just translation of trial proceedings but also interpretation of meetings with counsel and translation of mail and petitions arriving from Japan. SCAP Legal Section also recognized the need for additional support. In a December 1948 memo the chief of the Legal Section noted that sixteen interpreters were then posted to Manila, but seven would be returning to Japan at the end of the year; he recommended that six interpreters be sent to replace them, and this recommendation was acted upon.[69]

Providing effective legal counsel and finding and retaining competent interpreters were not the only problems that required resolution. Also at issue were the rights of the accused to obtain and use evidence in their defense. Executive Order No. 68, which was patterned after the regulations used in the American trials, directed the military commissions to apply rules of evidence "with the greatest liberality" and expressly allowed the use of affidavits, diaries, sworn or unsworn statements, or any documents or reports deemed useful regardless of provenance.

The leeway afforded by EO 68 allowed prosecutors to present affidavits in lieu of witnesses. It also meant that US occupation officials could curtail the sending of witnesses from Japan to testify at the trials. Concerns over logistics and expense had led to increasing resistance by the US authorities in Tokyo to the idea of sending defense witnesses (generally former Japanese military personnel who had served with those on trial in Manila) from Japan to testify to an alibi or the good character of the accused. This reluctance had manifested itself quite early: in September 1947 Legal Section Tokyo advised that significant reductions in ocean transport between Japan and the Philippines would make it impossible to schedule trials in Manila with any certainty that witnesses from Japan would be present. Unless the Philippine government was prepared to pay plane fare for witnesses and then claim reimbursement at a future peace conference, routine availability of witnesses was highly unlikely.[70] In late 1948 Legal Section Manila Branch reminded the chief of the Philippine Defense Panel of the circumstances: the only ships traveling to the Philippines from Japan were commercial transports and LSTs (landing ship, tank) under the control of the US navy but operated by Japanese crews. The latter did not operate on any set schedule. In any event, no Japanese witness could travel to Manila unless the Philippine government advanced the money for passage or the witness had dollar credits outside Japan to fund the voyage.[71]

As a result, attorneys for Kudō Chūshirō, the first defendant put on trial, failed in their efforts to have all but one of their witnesses sent from Japan, instead relying on the testimony of other POWs and excerpts from earlier American trials. The commission rejected the request of the defense for a postponement to await possible affidavits from witnesses in Japan, noting that, judging from the witness questionnaire, any such statements would be merely corroborative of the witness who had already testified.[72] In another early case, the prosecution agreed to enter into stipulations with the defense on what certain defense witnesses would say had they been allowed to testify in person—a compromise not entirely satisfactory to either side. The prosecutor cautioned that his agreement with the introduction of these stipulations did not in any way mean that he accepted the truth of such statements—in fact, quite the contrary. And the defendant in his final remarks to the commission lamented his inability to present affidavits and written testimonies from those who served with him.[73]

The case of Nakano Shizuo highlights the potential consequences of the decision to curtail witness travel to the Philippines, albeit for reasons that did not relate to expense. In that trial, US authorities refused to send a potentially key witness (his superior officer) despite the insistence of Nakano's defense counsel that the witness's testimony was absolutely critical to the defense. In this instance, the head of Legal Section Manila Branch appeared in court to explain that the witness was unavailable because he was already serving a life sentence in Sugamo Prison; sending Japanese defense lawyers to Tokyo to question him was not an option either, because at that time no Japanese national was allowed to enter

Sugamo. (The American went on to note that the witness's testimony might not be helpful, since he was now claiming that an injury suffered in Manila had caused a loss of memory. The prosecutor chimed in that bringing the witness to Manila to testify would not help the defense, because if his testimony differed from that at his own trial, the commission wouldn't believe him anyway.)[74] Nakano was convicted and given the death penalty.

Notwithstanding the rather cavalier dismissal of Nakano's request to have his commanding officer testify in person, Filipino and American officials were not unmindful that a failure to allow defendants access to the testimony of witnesses viewed as crucial to their defense could represent a breach of the tenets of due process promised in EO 68. With the sending of witnesses increasingly highly problematic, the idea emerged of taking witness statements in Tokyo and transmitting them to counsel for use in the trials. This strategy took shape initially as a result of a suggestion by Japanese defense counsel in September 1947 (before their return home) that one of them be allowed to return to Japan to obtain witness statements for a variety of cases—a more effective procedure than relying on the submission of questions from Manila. Legal Section Tokyo deemed the request "logical" but feared that it would be abused by Japanese seeking to return to Japan for personal reasons. By September 25 Tokyo had accepted the idea of a defense attorney returning to Japan to conduct interrogations, but Philippine NWCO chief Fojas raised the ante by proposing that an investigation section be permanently established in Tokyo, with defense staff in Manila submitting questions and the resulting statements forwarded back from Tokyo for use in the trials. By early October Legal Section Tokyo had reported that its chief, Colonel Carpenter, had concurred with Major Fojas that some sort of investigation staff should be set up in Tokyo under the supervision of Legal Section.[75]

Then a glitch occurred. On October 31, 1947, Legal Section Manila Branch, relying on assurances that Carpenter had approved the concept, submitted a detailed implementation plan based on conversations among the Defense Panel, NWCO, and Manila Branch. The plan envisioned the establishment of a commission in Tokyo. The commission would consist of one or more Japanese attorneys to be transferred from Manila; one or more Philippine army officers to take depositions for prosecution witnesses and to cross-examine defense witnesses; and an officer from Legal Section Tokyo to serve as president of the commission and coordinate operations. This proposal apparently went far beyond what SCAP had envisioned, and the response was swift. In early November Legal Section Tokyo rejected the plan, principally on the grounds that it had no staff available to serve on such a commission and that it would create a bad precedent for other Allied governments, which might then seek similar support.[76]

Finally, a compromise was reached, possibly as a result of continued pressure from Philippine government officials. On December 15, 1947, NWCO chief Fojas advised Legal Section Manila Branch that he and the judge advocate general of the Philippine National Defense Forces wished to travel to Tokyo in January 1948 to confer with Colonel Carpenter on the establishment of an investigative panel in Tokyo to facilitate the taking of statements from Japanese prosecution and defense witnesses. As a result of that visit and conferences with Japanese government representatives, it was agreed that the panel would be established and would consist of three Japanese lawyers, two interpreters, two clerk-typists, and one Philippine army officer. Capt. Ambrosio Dollete of the Philippine judge advocate general's staff was subsequently assigned as the first Philippine officer detailed to the newly constituted Philippine War Crimes Investigation and Coordination Panel, established in Tokyo.[77] Even without formal authorization, some sort of defense office had begun functioning in Tokyo by January 1948. Two of the original attorneys sent to Manila, Ogura Kiyoshi and Nakamura Kazunori, having returned to Japan by the end of 1947, drafted reports in January and February outlining their plans to begin work and requesting equipment and support for the "Tokyo Branch, Manila War Crimes Defense Office."[78] Nonetheless, the panel's functions were not what those on the ground in Manila had originally envisioned. There would be no depositions with the opportunity for cross-examination, and the evidence obtained from witnesses would be in the form of affidavits.

The Philippine National War Crimes Office took one additional step intended to help the defense. Fojas relaxed the rule, enforced during the American trials, that the defense would not have access to investigation reports. Under the operating procedures established in August 1947, Legal Section Manila Branch agreed to scrutinize such reports, note anything "remotely favorable" to the defense, and submit such items to the NWCO. With NWCO approval, these items would then be turned over to the defense. The head of the branch commented that this process was intended to serve the interests of fairness and avoid, where possible, obtaining affidavits from Japan when equivalent affidavits and testimony were already contained in such investigation reports.[79]

The men awaiting trial in the Philippines were not happy with the decision to preclude their ability to call witnesses from Japan.[80] In a January 3, 1948, petition, former general Yokoyama conveyed the prisoners' dissatisfaction with the strategy of obtaining statements in lieu of sending witnesses from Japan, which they had been "obliged to agree to despite the right of the accused" as provided for in Executive Order No. 68. Acknowledging that they had no say in the policy decision itself, Yokoyama urged that the process be improved to ensure the speedy and thorough preparation of necessary statements. The Japanese government also voiced concerns: its Central Liaison Office (set up to provide coordination between the US occupation authorities and Japanese government offices) sent a memo to GHQ/SCAP on November 7, 1947, noting that the use of affidavits prepared in Japan for the defense might prejudice the proceedings, given that prosecution witnesses were freely available to testify at the trials.[81] (Conversely, the Americans had speculated that the defense could be persuaded to accept affidavits, as it would avoid their witnesses being subjected to cross-examination by the prosecution.[82])

Potential Consequences of the Transfer to the Philippines

The Philippine government appeared willing and able to assume responsibility for the conduct of the war crimes trials in Manila, given continued access to US matériel and guidance. Regardless of American attitudes about the ability of Filipinos to assume responsibility for the trials, the fact is that after forty years of colonial experience, there was an existing infrastructure of legal principles and practices that served the newly independent country well. Moreover, the Philippine government was able to draw from a cadre of trained lawyers that included those who had participated actively in the development and prosecution of the US trials in Manila.

Nonetheless, the transition from US to Philippine tribunals did not mean complete continuity with the former. In two key structural aspects of the trials—legal representation and witness testimony—the Philippine government had to find workable solutions that balanced the interests of the accused against practical considerations like costs and logistics. Initially uncomfortable with how both issues were resolved, the Japanese prisoners came to respect the efforts of Filipino defense attorneys on their behalf. The use of affidavits in lieu of bringing witnesses to Manila to testify, however, remained a sore point. Although the Japanese Foreign Ministry was able to comment in mid-1949 that the lawyers—both Filipino and Japanese—assigned to manage the affidavit process were performing their duties fairly and capably, the prisoners themselves were not convinced.[83] In a private (later published) letter dated March 10, 1950, Yokoyama observed that it was very painful for the defendants not to be able to summon their superior officers or subordinates to Manila to testify on their behalf.[84]

The inability to freely choose lawyers to represent them and the decision to use hearsay evidence (statements/affidavits) in place of actual witnesses might seem to be prima facie evidence of the Philippine government's failure to ensure fair trials for Japanese defendants. The key, of course, is to what extent the solutions that were contrived—the use of Filipino defense attorneys and the use of affidavits in lieu of transporting witnesses from Japan to give testimony in court—materially affected the ability of defendants to mount an effective defense. In practice, the decision to fire the Japanese attorneys and substitute Filipino defense counsel proved the better choice. The Japanese lawyers who took on the earliest cases struggled to overcome their unfamiliarity with American law and their language limitations and were well aware of their deficiencies. Moreover, those Japanese represented by Filipino counsel did not believe they suffered as a result. Even if we dismiss defendants' statements made during the trials as self-serving or less than candid, the subsequent observations of the Japanese Foreign Ministry and defendants like Satō Sō suggest an overall satisfaction with the caliber of defense representation.

The use of affidavits remains more problematic. As Richard Minear and others have pointed out, the use of affidavits and other forms of hearsay evidence, while permissible under the regulations governing the war crimes trials, represented a clear departure from the norms of US law.[85] The solution first proposed by those in Manila—the establishment of a structure in Tokyo that would allow for the questioning of witnesses in the presence of both prosecution and defense representatives with the opportunity for cross-examination—would have addressed the main problem. But that option was essentially vetoed by the American occupation authorities. So the question remains: Did the use of affidavits in the Philippine government trials materially or adversely affect the outcomes? Answering that question requires a careful review of the actual trial proceedings.

3

The Trials

Questions of Guilt and Innocence

Kudō Chūshirō, "tall, thin-lipped and balding," entered an improvised courtroom on the grounds of a Manila school on August 1, 1947. The room was packed with spectators and newsmen. The accused, in a "firm, almost angry voice hissed a 'not guilty' plea" to charges of having ordered and permitted his men to torture and kill large numbers of civilians in the town of Bay, Laguna Province, in February 1945.[1] And so began the first trial of a Japanese defendant by a Philippine military tribunal. The last trial ended in December 1949. During the intervening years, observers of these courtroom proceedings would see ordinary people bearing witness to the horrors they claimed were perpetrated by the defendants; they would hear from the accused who insisted on their innocence. It would be up to the judges to weigh the evidence presented and to determine, in each case, guilt or innocence.

It is precisely the outcomes in these trials, without much detailed scrutiny then or later, that have fed into broader judgments about the overall quality of justice rendered by Allied governments in the years after World War II. The transcripts of the Philippine government trials, preserved in archives in the Philippines and the United States, afford the opportunity to interrogate the proceedings with an eye to addressing two key questions: How did the trials comport with understood procedural safeguards to ensure fair trials, and how was the evidence weighed to ensure just outcomes? The transcripts allow us to scrutinize the quality of the prosecution and defense cases, the nature of the evidence presented, and the determinations of the judges. All these elements collectively allow judgments about the kind of justice obtained in Philippine courtrooms.

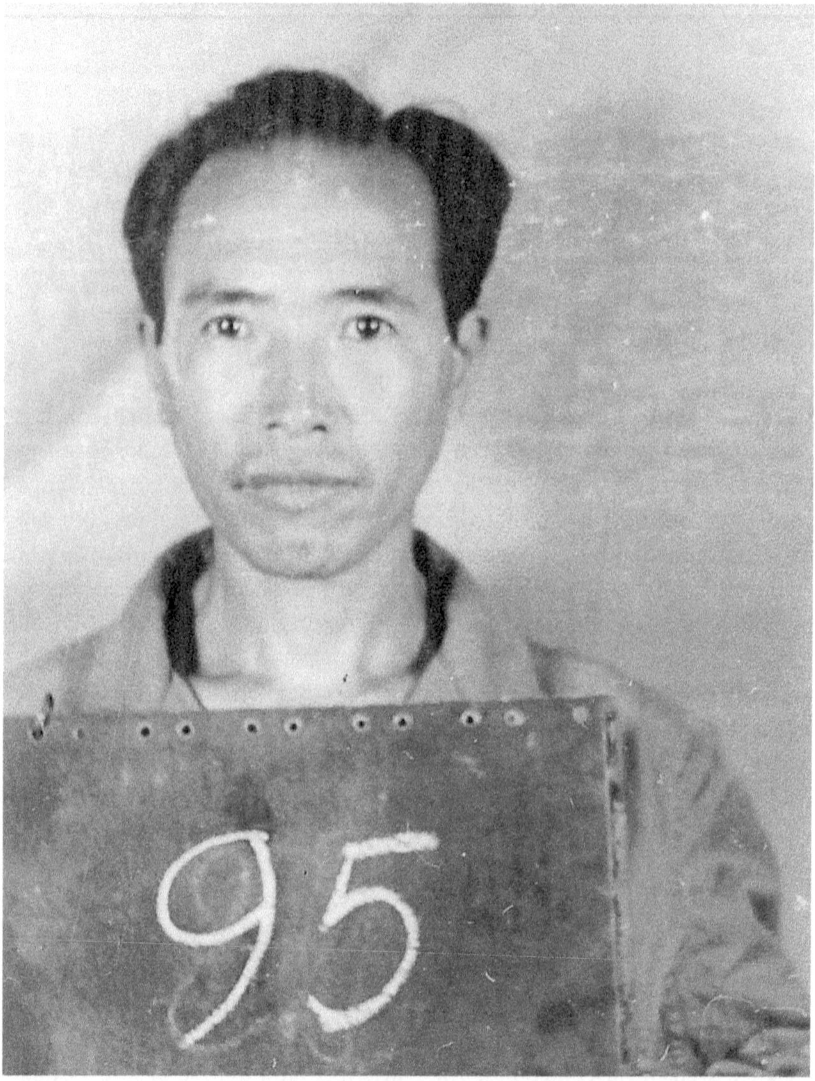

Kudō Chūshirō, the first Japanese to be tried by the Philippine government (Photo 95, box 1346, UD 1266, RG 331, courtesy of the National Archives at College Park, MD)

Trials: Defendants, Demographics, and Outcomes

The Philippine government ultimately charged 155 defendants with war crimes in 73 separate trials.[2] As the US government prepared to turn over responsibility for the trials, it had estimated that some four to five hundred Japanese suspects remained incarcerated in POW camps awaiting the resolution of their status.[3] As investigations proceeded, those cleared of involvement in war crimes were repatriated, while others were recalled from Japan to stand trial, resulting in the final tally of 155 defendants. The Philippine National War Crimes Office had planned to bring charges against at least eight additional defendants in association with the trials, but these prospective defendants were never arraigned for a variety of reasons (illness, suicide, insanity, or, in one instance, escape). In the case of one suspect, the military commission determined that his arraignment could not proceed because no interpreter could be found—the man was Okinawan, and his command of Japanese was insufficient to ensure a fair trial.[4] (The NWCO was still pushing for a separate trial for the Okinawan in late 1949 but apparently was unsuccessful in its appeals to obtain an interpreter before the trials ended.[5])

Philippine prosecutors tried cases involving alleged crimes committed in over twenty provinces on islands throughout the Philippines, from Luzon in the north to Mindanao in the south. The bulk of the cases involved from one to three defendants, but there were a few trials where the numbers were greater: one notorious case involved seventeen defendants charged with various crimes—rape, torture, murder, and, most sensationally, cannibalism—committed after Japan had surrendered (see chapter 1). Nonetheless, none of the trials came close to matching the numbers of defendants reported in some other national jurisdictions.[6]

Most trials involved atrocities (overwhelmingly the most serious crimes of murder, torture, and/or rape) committed against "unarmed noncombatant" Filipino civilians, although some of the victims were described as Chinese, and in a very few cases the government brought charges of unlawful acts committed against POWs or guerrillas, for example, execution without trial. One trial that involved charges of atrocities against American POWs and internees as well as Filipino civilians (*Philippines v. Kuroda Shigenori*) was split into American and Philippine phases, and the former was handled by an American prosecutor.[7] Although conventional wisdom has it that most atrocities were committed by Japanese troops in the final desperate months of the war—and indeed this was the period when large-scale killings occurred—some 40 percent of the Philippine cases involved at least some charges for incidents that occurred between December 1941 and June 1944.

Table 1. Military defendants by service and rank

Rank	Army	Navy	Total	% of total
Flag officers	5	1	6	4
Field grade officers	9	4	13	9
Junior officers	41	13	54	37
Warrant officers	13	0	13	9
Noncommissioned officers	33	1	34	23
Enlisted	27	0	27	18
Total	**128**	**19**	**147**[a]	**100**

[a]Excludes eight civilians tried for war crimes.

The Japanese military defendants ranged in rank from general to private, with more than one-third junior officers—captains and lieutenants. Table 1 shows the breakdown of the defendants by service and military rank.[8]

Most of the defendants served in the army, typically in infantry divisions or in the Japanese military police (Kempeitai); one-fourth of the accused were affiliated with the latter. Three cases featured navy personnel: one with a single defendant, Rear Adm. Furuse Takasue; another involving fifteen of his subordinates; and the third two naval officers accused of atrocities in Mindanao.[9] Some, especially the higher-ranking officers, were career military, but the majority had been inducted during the course of the war, and they either were sent directly to the Philippines or had served first in another theater such as China or Manchuria.

The Philippine government also tried eight Japanese civilians for war crimes. Japanese had begun immigrating to the Philippines in larger numbers at the turn of the century, and by the 1940s sizeable Japanese communities existed in Manila as well as Davao on the island of Mindanao.[10] It was from their ranks that the Japanese military recruited individuals as interpreters, guides, and informal liaisons between the Japanese forces and the local inhabitants. Some paid a price for their conduct or allegiances after the war.[11] In one such trial, prosecutors accused Takahashi Sadakichi, a Japanese civilian attached to the Kempeitai garrison in Quezon City, of torturing and murdering Filipinos: "We propose to prove that [the accused], who came to the Philippines to earn a living many years before the outbreak of the War, and who, throughout his stay in this country was never molested in his peaceful existence, drunk with power, singled out individuals who had been his neighbors, for the purpose of subjecting

Table 2. Philippine war crimes cases and verdicts

Cases	Number arraigned	Verdicts				
		Dismissed/ suspended	Death	Life	Term	Not guilty
73	155[a]	6	79	31	28	11

[a]The total includes two defendants who were each arraigned twice in different cases.

them to indescribable torture and unlawful deprivation of life."[12] Takahashi was found guilty and sentenced to hang; the sentence was later commuted to life in prison.[13]

Table 2 provides summary data on the numbers of cases, defendants, and verdicts rendered. Verdicts were reached for 149 of the 155 defendants arraigned on one or more counts of specific crimes. The charges were dismissed or cases suspended for the other six, in some instances because prosecutors determined they lacked the evidence to proceed. (For example, charges had been brought against Fukutake Kazuo on the basis of an earlier American investigation report, but the case fell apart once the prosecutors had a chance to interview the victims and other witnesses and concluded they could not prove the defendant's guilt beyond a reasonable doubt.[14])

Twenty-two of the 155 Japanese arraigned for trial pleaded guilty either at their arraignment or during the course of their trials. Ten of these defendants explicitly stated that they had committed the crimes on the direct orders of their superior officers.[15] An officer who pleaded guilty stated that he had ordered the killing of civilians because it was his duty to maintain order and that by doing so he was "contributing to win the war." One of his subordinates, described as a mestizo with a Japanese father and Filipina mother, claimed that he had been forced to serve in a civilian capacity and had obeyed orders to kill because he feared punishment if he did not do so. Yet another of the Japanese who pleaded guilty expressed his "deepest apology" to his victims.[16]

An analysis of the verdicts and sentences indicates that conviction rates were relatively consistent across the officer and enlisted ranks, but middle-ranking officers fared far worse in terms of the punishments levied, a finding that appears somewhat inconsistent with the outcomes in trials in other national jurisdictions.[17] Flag and field-grade officers combined had an 84 percent chance of being convicted and were sentenced to death 37 percent of the time. In contrast, less senior officers and noncommissioned officers collectively stood an 89 percent chance of conviction, and over 60 percent were sentenced to death. Enlisted ranks had the highest conviction rate (93 percent) but were sentenced to death at about the same rate as generals and colonels (36 percent). The higher death sentence rates for lower-ranking officers may be a function of the evidence presented of their direct complicity in the ordering or commission of atrocities (see the discussion on criminal liability below).

Structure and Characteristics of the Trials

While data help in weighing some potential criticisms of the trials—that, for example, they were unfairly tilted toward lower-ranking officers or indiscriminately brought to trial those incapable of defending themselves—such information alone cannot effectively address the issue of how well the Philippines prosecuted crimes against alleged perpetrators. An examination of the structural and procedural aspects of the Philippine trials illuminates just how seriously the principal actors—judges, prosecutors, and defense attorneys—approached their assigned roles and with what strategies. This tells us much about the overall conduct of the trials and what broader critiques may or may not be sustainable.

The Philippine war crimes trials were convened before military commissions comprising three to five military officers who served as judges; the highest-ranking officer was named commission president.[18] As dictated by Executive Order No. 68, these commission members heard evidence and rendered verdicts by a two-thirds majority. One "especially qualified" member was designated the law member and issued rulings on the admissibility of evidence in the event of challenges from either the prosecution or the defense. The president of the Philippines, or his authorized representative, had wide latitude in appointing commission members, who had only to be deemed "competent" to serve and have no personal interest, prejudice, or direct involvement in the case at hand. Formal challenges to the composition of the commissions were quite rare, except in two instances.[19] Prior to his being sworn in as a member of the commission to hear the case of Lt. Gen. Yokoyama Shizuo, Col. Jose Gonzales Roxas (a doctor) stipulated that he "did not wish to be instrumental" in imposing a death penalty on the accused should he be found guilty. As a result, the prosecutor challenged his appointment, and Roxas's swearing in was deferred; ultimately, he was not seated as a commission member. In a second case, a commission member stepped down after the defense counsel challenged the panel members to disclose their prior incarceration, if any, in a POW camp that had been run by the accused.[20]

Commission members did not just issue procedural rulings or limit themselves to rendering verdicts. In fact, they saw themselves as extraordinarily empowered by the terms of their mandate, a point of view that one commission president articulated explicitly and unapologetically: "The Commission has been created to determine and to find out whether the accused as they stand charged are guilty or innocent. It is not for us to quibble over the intricacies of the law, inasmuch as the Executive Order gives ample power and great latitude to the Commission so that it may arrive at a just decision, and that is our duty here."[21]

Accordingly, it was quite usual for various commission members to take an active role in the questioning of witnesses—probing for inconsistencies or clarifying the precise nature of a witness's recollections—sometimes to the point of eliciting objections from the prosecutor or the defense attorney that the questioning had gone too far.[22] On one occasion, commission members toured the site of alleged atrocities (Fort Santiago, the notorious locale of Kempeitai interrogations) accompanied by the defendant in order to question him on the facilities, the location of prisoner cells, and the like. In a second case, a commission member insisted on testing a witness's identification of the accused by grouping him with other Japanese in similar clothing and placing them all some distance away, whereupon the witness successfully picked out the accused from this ad hoc lineup.[23] In a few instances, individual commission members were replaced during the course of a trial. In practice, commission members were not bound to attend every trial session, and there were instances (not routine) where individual members missed a session and had the obligation to "catch up" with what had transpired in their absence. This was not true in the case of the law member, however; on the rare occasions when he could not be present, the trial was invariably postponed, because his presence was deemed essential to the proceedings.[24]

All the trials began with the arraignment of the defendants—acceptance of pleas and confirmation that they had received copies of the charges against them. The defendants were arraigned on the general charge of violating the laws and customs of war. They also faced one or more detailed "specifications" (counts) describing the particular crimes that the prosecution would seek to prove to substantiate the overall charge. Without exception, these involved charges of rape, torture, and/or murder, although in rare instances there might be additional lesser charges such as destruction of property.

Prosecutors sought to provide as much specificity as possible concerning the locations, dates, and victims of the alleged atrocities. To illustrate, one of the four specifications that prosecutors levied against defendant Inamura Rokujonō read as follows:

> In that Rokujono Inamura, formerly a warrant officer in the Imperial Japanese Army, did, at or near Aparri, Cagayan, Philippines, during the months of August and September 1944, while a state of war existed between the United States of America, its allies and dependencies, including the Philippines, and Japan, willfully and unlawfully order, direct and permit members of the Japanese Armed Forces then under his command, to brutally torture and maltreat, and participate in the torture and maltreatment of Abelardo Gantaliseo, Jesus Gorospe, Antonio Liban, Lorenzo Martinez, Hospicio Quajas, Adolfo Umangan and Longfellow Umangan, all unarmed, noncombatant Filipino civilians, in violation of the laws and customs of war.[25]

As the above example suggests, specifications contained wording that captured the nature of each defendant's alleged role or level of culpability—combinations of "ordering," "directing," "permitting," "participating in," or the "willful failure to discharge duties." For our purposes, these can be grouped into three general categories of involvement: (1) "participation" (defendants accused of at least one specification of actually committing the atrocities, either torture, rape, or murder); (2) "ordering/directing" (those defendants accused of being physically present at the scene of atrocities and ordering their subordinates to commit them and/or being directly tied to issuing such orders); and (3) "permitting" or "willful failure to discharge duties" (implying a more indirect link between the defendant and the atrocities committed).

In the Philippine trials, the overwhelming majority of the specifications involved a direct and close level of involvement by the accused. More than three-quarters of the Japanese defendants were accused of at least one specification of actual participation, and over 90 percent were alleged to have either participated in or directly ordered atrocities. This leaves only a handful of defendants who were charged solely with more general responsibility for the actions of their men. Lieutenant General Kuroda, for example, faced the overall charge that he did "unlawfully disregard and fail to discharge his duties as such commander [of the Imperial Japanese Forces in the Philippines] to control the operations of members of his command, permitting them to commit brutal atrocities and other high crimes against noncombatant civilians and prisoners of the Imperial Japanese Forces, in violation of the laws and customs of war."[26]

Once the defendants had been arraigned, the trials followed a set pattern, one familiar to observers of American criminal trials. First, the prosecution presented its case, usually beginning with a brief opening statement laying out the charges and highlighting the evidence to be presented. Prosecutors offered four main types of evidence: the testimony of eyewitnesses, the testimony of

Chart 1. Types of evidence presented against the defendants

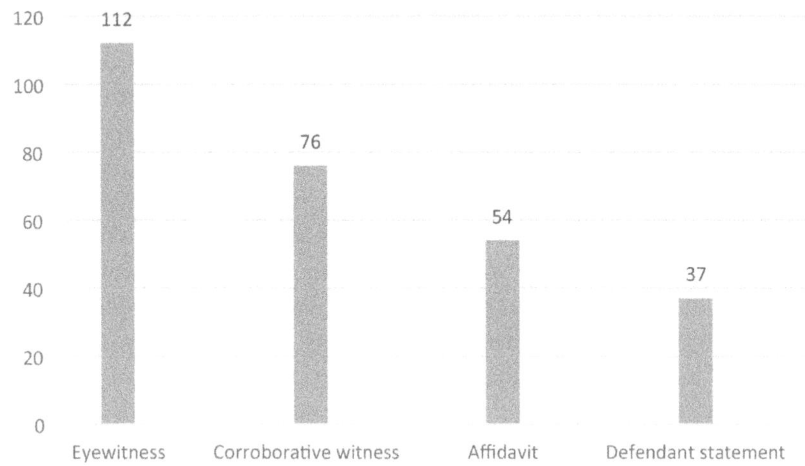

corroborative witnesses, statements made by the defendants themselves in earlier interrogations, and/or affidavits from those who did not appear to testify in person. Chart 1 shows the types of evidence used against each of the 133 defendants who entered not-guilty pleas:

Clearly, prosecutors relied heavily on the testimony of eyewitnesses to make their cases. Of the 133 defendants who pleaded not guilty, 112 (84 percent) faced their accusers, either survivors of atrocities or those who had witnessed them. A Japanese interpreter present at many of the trials later confirmed the often decisive impact of dramatic eyewitness identifications of defendants: "For example, an old woman, or perhaps a young woman with a baby, would come to court and take the witness stand. The baby is crying, and while the woman herself is crying, she looks at the defendant's seat and points a finger, saying, 'That man did it!'"[27] The criticality of eyewitness testimony can be deduced another way: in its absence, five defendants were found not guilty, and another five had their cases dismissed.[28] Only ten defendants were found guilty without the testimony of eyewitnesses, and six of these had made statements incriminating themselves and their codefendants that they did not challenge in court. (The remaining four acknowledged an incident during which a civilian was killed but suggested they had acted in self-defense.)

Many Filipinos came forward to testify to what they had seen and been forced to suffer at the hands of the Japanese military. Emotions ran high, and some witnesses could not control their anger. A woman described as the Chinese widow of a man killed in Fort Santiago by members of the Kempeitai and who had herself been tortured identified the defendants and then told the court, "Will you allow me, I want to hit them now," a remark that created a furor in the gallery.[29] Others found the experience of testifying against Japanese defendants understandably intimidating; one witness, asked by the prosecutor to approach the defendant and touch him on the shoulder for identification purposes, hesitated, saying, "Suppose he kick me, sir?"[30] Even so, the transcripts only rarely convey the emotions felt by the participants in those few instances where a prosecutor would note for the record that a witness was crying or overcome.

Prosecutors' reliance on witnesses (as distinct from documents such as affidavits) to prove their cases is quite striking and is indicative of the nature of the charges typically levied against defendants, that is, that they committed or ordered atrocities against local inhabitants. In comparison, Allied trials that focused on POW abuses tended to rely on affidavits rather than witnesses, while those involving crimes against local peoples tended also to rely on witness testimony.[31]

After the prosecution finished presenting its case, it was the turn of the defense. The evidence offered by defense attorneys consisted primarily of the accounts of the defendants themselves who testified to alibis or mistaken identifications, corroborative witnesses (both Japanese and Filipino), and affidavits (most often obtained in Japan and used to support an alibi or provide evidence of good character). Over 80 percent of the defendants testified in their own behalf, apparently unusual when compared with the pattern established in other trials in Asia where defendants were reportedly more reluctant to take the stand.[32] Some of the defendants in the Philippine trials offered evidence of illness to show they could not have committed the atrocities of which they were accused. Others in testimony or affidavits sought to show that their units had been assigned elsewhere; therefore, they could not have been responsible.[33]

The defenses mounted by Japanese defendants in the Philippine trials were particularly unusual for their failure to rely on a claim of following superior orders. It has been a conventional criticism of the trials in Asia that they unfairly penalized lower-ranking soldiers for having no choice but to follow the orders of their superior officers. This suggests that such a defense, whether or not successful, was a common occurrence in these trials. Indeed, this appears to have been the case in the trials conducted by the Americans in Manila and the British in Hong Kong and Singapore. Bing Bing Jia cites a number of instances in which defendants in Hong Kong offered the defense of following superior orders, with or without the added claim of duress; likewise, defense attorneys raised the superior orders defense at almost every trial conducted in Singapore.

There were similar instances of US trials in Manila in which such a defense was pursued.[34]

But this was emphatically not true in the trials conducted by the Philippine government. It was quite rare for Japanese defendants who pleaded not guilty to choose to make their cases on the grounds of following the orders of their superiors (or, for that matter, acting in response to military necessity). Instead, most defendants opted to maintain their complete innocence, apparently in the belief that denying any involvement constituted their best chance of an acquittal or for the simple reason that it was, in fact, the truth.

It is possible that Filipino defense counsel made it clear to their clients that a defense of following superior orders would not save them. Certainly, the Philippine executive order governing the trials explicitly rejected obedience to superior orders as a legitimate defense, although it did acknowledge that it could be considered a mitigating factor during sentencing. (This was in line with the position of other Allied governments, including the United States, that a plea of following superior orders could not in itself be the basis for escaping criminal liability altogether.)[35] And these defendants would have been well aware that those previously tried by American tribunals in Manila who had claimed such a defense had not fared well.[36]

Thus the general rejection of such a defense may have arisen from the conviction among the defendants that a strategy of relying on claims of innocence or an alibi would serve them better than claims of duress, wartime circumstances, or fear of the consequences of failing to obey orders. But in their private musings, some of the accused did discuss their strong belief that such considerations did and should matter. Lieutenant General Yokoyama noted in a letter that some of his fellow prisoners argued that it was the fault of the Japanese military system that made it impossible to avoid committing the crimes, or they had done the best they could under the circumstances, or they had been victims of a peculiarly wartime psychological situation. Likewise, defendant Owari Saburō in a letter to his wife emphasized that soldiers could not of their own free will defy the orders of their superior officers. The legality of such orders, considered to be the direct orders of the emperor himself, would be impossible to question.[37]

If the Philippines cases were unusual for this rejection of a defense of following superior orders, it might be argued that they were even more surprising for a significant reliance on the testimony and affidavits of Filipino witnesses in support of the defense. Given the nature of the Japanese occupation, it could easily be assumed that Filipinos would be eager to testify to the suffering they had experienced and certainly unwilling to come forward to testify on behalf of Japanese defendants. Indeed, many Filipinos were reluctant to testify or offer assistance to those defending Japanese accused of atrocities. In August 1947, back at the start of the first trials conducted by the Philippine government, SCAP officials scoffed at the very idea that any Filipino witnesses could be found to support defendants—it would be a waste of money to send out field investigators in search of them.[38] Likewise, an American civilian attorney who served as a defense counsel during the US trials observed that "it was a rare day" when any Filipino was willing to assist in a Japanese defendant's case. In another instance, a defense attorney carefully kept from one of his witnesses the fact that his testimony was intended to support the accused; the witness, who thought he was testifying against a Filipino collaborator, stated he never would have participated had he known he was potentially helping a Japanese soldier.[39]

And yet quite a few Filipinos did testify on behalf of defendants, and not merely on matters of fact or to provide routine information. In fact, the defense produced Filipino witnesses or their affidavits in support of more than forty defendants. In several instances, Filipinos testified to the good character of the accused. In a case involving three Japanese members of the Kempeitai accused of responsibility for the death by suffocation of over four hundred Filipino prisoners in Fort Santiago, Mrs. Luz de Reyes testified that one of the defendants, Lt. Kita Heiji, had helped gain permission for her to visit her son in prison, ensured that her son had medical attention when he was sick, and brought her family food. The prosecution attempted to soften the impact of her testimony by suggesting that Kita had only been motivated by propaganda considerations, but the witness held her ground.[40]

Even more striking is the case of Matsuzaki Hideichi, former army major and commander of the San Fernando Kempeitai, who was accused of ordering his men to torture Filipinos, including POW Fred Ruiz Castro (the postwar Philippine judge advocate general), and to torture and kill over sixty other Filipino and American POWs. Castro testified that Matsuzaki had slapped and kicked him and had him subjected to the water cure and other torture. To counter the testimony of Castro and other prosecution witnesses, the defense turned to witnesses like Manila police chief Antonio Torres and jai alai manager Timoteo Evangelista, who testified to the sympathetic character of Matsuzaki and his responsiveness to appeals for help in releasing incarcerated Filipinos. To cap these efforts, the defense submitted as an exhibit a letter from President Elpidio Quirino in which he related his family's successful appeals to Matsuzaki to have him released from prison. Quirino said his family had praised the defendant as "invariably helpful and sympathetic to me and other Filipinos I know who had occasion to seek his assistance in their difficulties during the occupation." The combined weight of this testimony would appear to have had some effect: Matsuzaki was convicted and ultimately sentenced to twenty years at hard labor—a relatively light punishment in view of the sentences in other cases.[41]

In a few cases, towns submitted petitions in favor of the accused. In the case of Shimizu Hisamitsu and Uemura Masao, for example, Philippine senator Ramon Torres not only testified for Shimizu but also, at the request of defense counsel, took the lead in obtaining signatures on a petition from the townspeople of Bago, Negros Occidental Province. The petition, signed by over three hundred people, attested to Shimizu's efforts to help Filipinos, thus sparing them from "more than their share of the unhappiness, misery, bereavement and ruin that come in the wake of war." In this case, the prosecution attempted to discredit the petition by hinting at the possibility of forged signatures and claiming that it represented the views of a minority, the "higher level" among the inhabitants. Senator Torres countered that he was only expressing popular sentiment with regard to the accused.[42]

The most logical—or at least most common—reason offered to explain the willingness of individual Filipinos to testify for Japanese defendants was gratitude. Prosecutors on occasion tried to suggest that it was only members of the elite who testified for Japanese defendants out of an obligation for favors received.[43] Thus, Filipinos who might have appealed to Japanese officers for leniency for themselves or their relatives during the war might have felt constrained to offer support to these same officers facing war crimes charges in the war's aftermath.

Wartime allegiances complicated other cases as well. In one striking instance, witnesses seemingly found themselves forced to choose between support for a Japanese defendant and a hated member of the Philippine constabulary. Prosecution witnesses testified that the defendant, Taninaka Katsuyoshi, the commanding officer of an army garrison on Samar, had commanded a firing squad (comprising both Japanese soldiers and constabulary men) that had executed three Filipinos. Defense witnesses testified that it was the head of the local constabulary, Bernardo Pablo, who had given the order to fire; Taninaka was kind to the inhabitants, whereas Pablo was cruel. In the end, the commission found the prosecution witnesses more credible and sentenced Taninaka to death but, perhaps with a slight nod to the defense (or with a fine-tuned sense of irony), directed that Taninaka be executed by firing squad ("death by musketry") rather than the far more usual sentence of death by hanging.[44]

During the presentation of the prosecution's case, the defense had the opportunity to cross-examine the witnesses, and of course vice-versa. Given the extensive reliance on witness testimony by both sides, the trials had the feel of old-fashioned courtroom dramas, with prosecutors and defense attorneys clashing in their efforts to portray the other side's witnesses as mistaken or lying. This quite frequently led to what seems, on reading the transcripts, the interminable cross-examinations of witnesses on minute details of their stories, presumably to discover inconsistencies that might tip the balance toward discrediting their testimony. In the case against Nakano Shizuo, for example, the prosecutor pounced on the defendant's testimony at trial that he was thirty-seven years old because it contradicted his pretrial statement that he was thirty-six. The defendant tried to explain that the discrepancy resulted from the different way in which Japanese reckoned age, but the prosecutor maintained that this was a test of the defendant's credibility.[45] In another case, defense counsel questioned a prosecution witness on the number of wheels on the truck carrying him and others who had been arrested by the Japanese.[46] In a third case, the defense went to great lengths to challenge one witness's testimony that a house where thirteen victims had been killed had stairs made of bamboo instead of wood.[47] It is hard to believe that such efforts carried any real weight with the commissions, but counsel all too often persevered in such questioning.

Some strategies, however, served the interests of the prosecution or defense much better. Prosecutors often attempted to paint Japanese witnesses—particularly those who served with the accused—as propounding rehearsed stories concocted to protect their colleagues. Defense counsel frequently relied for witnesses on those Japanese under suspicion or already convicted of war crimes, precisely because they were the most readily available witnesses. Consequently, their testimony offered a ready-made basis for challenge by the prosecution on credibility grounds. The confinement of Japanese suspects in the same POW camp, it was argued, afforded them ample opportunity to devise fake alibis for one another. Prosecutors also, wherever possible, introduced earlier statements taken from the accused to highlight inconsistencies with their subsequent trial testimony.[48]

Prosecutors also found it particularly useful to attack the credibility of Filipino defense witnesses by questioning them on their dealings with the Japanese during the war. In the case of Nakamura Fumio, an army sergeant charged with the torture or killing of Filipino civilians in several incidents, the defense produced a number of Filipino witnesses who testified that the defendant was being confused with another Nakamura, a member of the Kempeitai who had been the perpetrator of the atrocities. In cross-examination, the prosecutor showed that many of these witnesses had been accused or convicted of collaboration. One such witness, who had testified that he knew both Nakamuras and had been present when the Kempeitai Nakamura had arrested one of the men the accused was charged with torturing, admitted that he had been sentenced to life in prison as a collaborator. The end result: the commission sentenced the defendant to life.[49] Although the commission did not provide a rationale for its verdict, clearly it rejected the defense witness testimony as not credible. (Conversely, the panel that reviewed this case after trial apparently did find the defense witnesses more persuasive than the prosecution witnesses and recommended that the verdict be overturned; see chapter 4.)

For their part, defense attorneys tried to challenge the testimony of prosecution witnesses in creative ways. In one case involving several defendants, Tsuji Chōichi agreed to change seats with one of his codefendants during the course of their trial in the hopes of rattling a prosecution witness. It worked—that defendant was acquitted.[50] In another trial, defendant Satō Sō donned glasses during the prosecution's case to tempt witnesses into pointing to them as an identifying feature while later testifying that he had never worn glasses during the war. His attorney also presented the results of an eye test that purported to show that Satō did not need to wear glasses. He too was acquitted of the two specifications involving eyewitness testimony of his role in the atrocities, although he was convicted of a third. (Satō may well have outwitted the prosecution: his "mug shot" taken at Sugamo Prison in Tokyo while awaiting transfer to the Philippines clearly shows him wearing glasses, and a list of his belongings contains a reference to an eyeglasses case.)[51]

In some cases where rape was alleged, defense attorneys would attempt to discredit the victims by suggesting that their stories were not credible or that they had in some way acquiesced. For example, after one witness testified that the defendant had struck her, ripped her clothes off, and raped her, the defense counsel asked her if she had experienced "pleasurable feelings" during the attack. (The questioning by commission members was hardly less distasteful; one suggested to the witness that if she had really tried to resist, the attacker would have been frustrated in his attempts to consummate the rape.)[52]

Once the prosecution and defense had rested their cases, and after the presentation of any rebuttal witnesses or evidence, each side had the opportunity to make a closing argument. Commission members then adjourned to consider the evidence. At least one if not more days elapsed between closing arguments and the commissions' decisions (contrasted with more than one American trial in which commission members reconvened to announce their verdicts within two hours or less after the conclusion of the trial proceedings).[53] Philippine commissions also provided rationales for their decisions in over a third of the cases, a percentage that likewise compares favorably with the trial judgments issued by their US counterparts.

Overall, the Philippine trials were complicated by a number of variables. To afford both prosecution and defense sufficient time to line up witnesses or obtain affidavits, trials could last weeks or months—conditions in the Philippines made it difficult to find, or to make readily available, certain witnesses. The process of requesting and obtaining affidavits from witnesses in Japan could be time-consuming as well. Language barriers added another layer of complexity. Witnesses testified in a multiplicity of languages, including Tagalog, Visayan, Ilocano, Igorot, Ibanag, Spanish, and of course Japanese and English. Interpreters were required to translate each witness's testimony into English, the official language of the trials. And it was not unusual for witnesses to be illiterate or nearly so, which added to the painstaking nature of the proceedings; indeed, one prosecutor characterized his witnesses as "poor ignorant children of the soil."[54]

Nonetheless, the transcripts suggest that despite these challenges, prosecutors and defense attorneys pursued their respective assignments rigorously, and commission members actively weighed in on matters of law and fact. This is not to suggest that the trials were perfect—the transcripts also point to some failures of process or irregularities. On at least two occasions it was alleged or shown that prospective prosecution witnesses had been seen in the courtroom prior to giving their own testimony, and in another case the commission was disturbed at the news that a defense attorney gathering affidavits in the field had failed to be present when the affiants had signed the documents.[55] Moreover, in two cases involving multiple defendants, the commission allowed or insisted that witnesses try again to identify defendants when they failed to do so on the first try.[56] (In these instances, the eventual outcomes were mixed, with one defendant found not guilty of the relevant specification and the other guilty.) More disturbing, the outcome in one particular trial appeared on its face to be so blatantly in contravention of the evidence presented as to suggest bias—so suggestive that the subsequent review board had no hesitation in recommending that the guilty verdict be overturned (see chapter 4).[57]

Weighing the Evidence: Perjury and Hearsay

Commission members tasked with determining the fate of Japanese defendants had to weigh the quality of the evidence presented and assess its probative value. Generally speaking, commissions were not challenged with any particularly novel or difficult legal issues; rather, outcomes for individual defendants turned on how well the prosecution showed, or the defense rebutted, the actual involvement of the accused in the crimes committed. Two challenges the commissions faced in weighing the evidence had to do with assessing the veracity of witnesses and determining the admissibility and value of hearsay evidence.

As we have seen, in the Philippine cases it was the testimony of witnesses that mattered most, not documents and certainly not the kind of forensic evidence that exists today but was unheard-of at that time. Unsurprisingly, commission members were often presented with competing versions of events, and the transcripts make clear that both prosecution and defense witnesses were capable of lying, for understandable reasons. Filipino prosecution witnesses could be motivated by revenge for specific wrongs or a more generalized hatred of all Japanese—that was certainly a belief widely held by the Japanese on trial. Filipino defense witnesses, accused collaborators or not, might have been influenced by a sense of obligation to the Japanese for whom they testified. Japanese witnesses had a powerful motive to save themselves or their comrades from death sentences, and prosecutors frequently charged that the standard defense strategy was to claim an alibi or mistaken identity, or to blame someone else, preferably someone already dead.[58] A number of later accounts by Japanese who served in the war describe their efforts to develop stories that would minimize either their own or their comrades' vulnerability to prosecution and conviction.[59]

Specific examples illustrate the dilemma commissions faced in assessing the relative merits of the versions of the evidence presented by the prosecution and defense. In one case, Filipino prosecution and defense witnesses directly contradicted each other. In the case of Matsuda Ichiji, Vicente Tatishi, and Fujii Suehirō, the defendants, all civilian Japanese (Matsuda and Fujii were immigrants, while Tatishi identified himself as a mestizo with a Japanese father and Filipina mother), were accused of killing four Filipino civilians in Davao City, Mindanao, in late 1941.[60] Tatishi and Fujii were further charged with ransacking the house of another (the widow of one of those killed). The key prosecution witness, Napoleon Zapanta, testified that on December 28, 1941, he had been tied up in a building of the Tibungco Lumber Office, where he witnessed the arrival of four other Filipinos, who were later joined by Japanese soldiers and all three of the accused. The four Filipinos were taken to the wharf; he heard shots and saw Fujii and Tatishi firing at the prisoners, while Matsuda appeared to be giving orders. The bodies were dumped in the sea. In contradiction of Zapanta's testimony, a defense witness testified that he had fled to the mountains with the coming of the Japanese and had seen Zapanta there from December 20, 1941, to January 12, 1942, so Zapanta could not have been where he said he was on December 28, 1941. Two other Filipino defense witnesses testified that they had seen Vicente Tatishi at a cockfight in another locale on the afternoon of December 28, giving him an alibi. The commission found all three defendants not guilty of the murder charge, citing the prosecution witness as not credible, but it did find Tatishi and Fujii guilty of the lesser charge, describing the evidence as "palpable and convincing."[61]

Japanese witnesses also lied, and for those on trial the stakes could not have been higher. For example, during his trial on multiple charges of ordering and participating in the torture and killing of civilians, Morishita Tsuneo attempted to defend himself against some of the charges by deflecting responsibility for the deaths to his subordinate, Lt. Doi Kunio. Morishita, convicted and sentenced to death, later recanted that testimony in the trial of Doi, who had been repatriated to Japan but brought back to face charges. Morishita, under the mistaken impression that Doi had been killed during the war, presumably thought that Doi could be safely blamed for the killings. Doi in turn was found guilty of some of the charges against him and sentenced to twenty years.[62]

Another Japanese war criminal admitted after his conviction that he had lied to try to protect his codefendants. Satō Ichirō, a second lieutenant, had pleaded guilty to the charge that he had ordered and participated in the massacre of fifteen hundred civilians in Batangas Province in March 1945 but had testified that his subordinates Nemoto Takeji and Onoyama Masaichi were innocent. His gesture was in vain; all three were convicted and sentenced to death. Later, Satō acknowledged that he had tried to shield Nemoto and Onoyama. He explained that because superior officers (who did not survive the war) had ordered the killings, it was not a crime for subordinates to obey those orders, and he had attempted to accept the entire responsibility for his company's actions. It was not just Satō who lied; several former members of the unit who had already been cleared and repatriated provided affidavits swearing that Nemoto and Onoyama had not been involved—a rather striking example of wholesale collusion in an effort to protect their comrades.[63]

In addition to weighing the credibility of witnesses, commissions also had to consider the value to be assigned to hearsay evidence. One of the criticisms of the Tokyo trial of Japan's leaders—and, by extension, the subsequent trials of other war crimes suspects—has been the use of such evidence. The Philippine government executive order establishing rules for the trials allowed the introduction of any evidence that in the opinion of the commission would "have probative value in the mind of a reasonable man." This explicitly included affidavits as well as diaries, letters, and copies of documents if originals were not available. These kinds of evidence are considered hearsay, that is, statements made outside the court that are repeated in court to establish the truth of such statements. This would include the testimony of a witness who repeated something he had been told by someone else.

There are reasons why hearsay evidence is problematic and generally disallowed in criminal cases. It precludes the defendant from confronting witnesses against him and having them subject to cross-examination; its accuracy cannot be tested in court; and it prevents judges (in these cases, commission members) from weighing the credibility of those from whom statements were taken.[64]

Both the prosecution and defense in the Philippine trials used hearsay evidence. Prosecutors introduced statements from some witnesses when for reasons of scheduling or availability they could not attend the trials. And of course the defense relied in many instances on affidavits in lieu of actual witnesses as a matter of necessity, given the process negotiated between the Philippines and the US military in Tokyo. In one case, the prosecutor offered a general defense of hearsay evidence, arguing that "this is a military court where there is greater latitude of accepting evidence even rumors; even hearsay evidence should be admitted so that we can facilitate the ascertaining of what is true."[65] But in another case, the defense highlighted the pitfalls of hearsay evidence, noting that it should only be admitted when it did not prejudice the fundamental rights of the accused; to do otherwise would deny the defendant due process of law and represent "a mockery."[66]

A strategy did exist for navigating such pitfalls: as discussed in chapter 2, the taking of depositions would have avoided a major drawback of affidavits: the inability to cross-examine witnesses to test their credibility. But that option had essentially been foreclosed by the American occupation authorities at least as it applied to potential witnesses in Japan. Nonetheless, it was actually exercised in a Philippine trial. In one unprecedented instance, the prosecution and defense agreed to conduct a deposition of a Filipino witness who was unable to appear at the scheduled trial; that is, the prosecution questioned this witness in the presence of defense counsel, who had the opportunity to cross-examine the witness, and the results were subsequently made part of the trial record. Also present at the deposition were the commission law member and all the defendants.[67] In a second case, however, the defense refused to be party to a deposition, arguing that even this process prejudiced the interests of the defense because it did not allow all commission members to ask questions or weigh the demeanor of the witness. As a result, the prosecution simply introduced the statement of the witness.[68]

The use of hearsay evidence at the trials in the form of sworn statements was common. A careful reading of the trial transcripts reveals the introduction of another form of hearsay as well: witnesses who testified to what someone else had told them. This too was allowed by the commissions. For example, Tone Seiichi had been charged with torturing one Filipino and ordering the death of that victim and two others. A key witness testified to personally seeing the execution of the first Filipino but simply relayed what he had heard from someone else about the deaths of the two others. Over the objection of defense counsel, the commission permitted all of his testimony.[69]

In his closing argument in a second case, the attorney for Teramoto Tukuji (Tokuji) distinguished between affidavits and secondhand testimony and offered a strong denunciation of the latter and its damaging potential:

> The next technicality of the law that I should like to bring to the attention of the Commission and that is, the issue on hearsay evidence. When I say hearsay evidence, I do not mean to say the affidavits, depositions or other signed documents. What I mean is the testimony of witnesses, who testified on matters which are related to him by another person and such matters have been testified to here on oral testimony. I submit that this kind of hearsay evidence is not admissible in any court whether it is a military tribunal or civilian court. . . . [To allow such testimony is to] establish a very dangerous precedent.[70]

Commissions generally chose to ignore the distinction between hearsay in the form of affidavits and hearsay in the form of testimony given in court when ruling on admissibility. Invariably, such evidence was admitted for "whatever probative value it may have," notwithstanding the objections of either the prosecution or the defense. In other words, commissions adhered to the broad permission granted under Executive Order No. 68 to allow the introduction of anything deemed possibly relevant to the case at hand.

Given this expansive interpretation of admissible evidence, the key question is, What impact did it have? There is in fact some evidence that commissions were wary, if not outright dismissive, of various forms of hearsay evidence in reaching their verdicts. For example, in the Tone case cited above, the defendant was found not guilty of the specification that depended solely on hearsay. Likewise, the commission sitting in judgment of Shimamura Katsuji explained its not-guilty verdict by focusing on the improbability of the uncorroborated testimony of the one eyewitness against him. The judges explicitly discounted the testimony of other witnesses who merely related what they had been told by the eyewitness. Finally, the commission in Kobayashi Kesaki's trial found him not guilty of the charge of ordering, permitting, and participating in the execution of ten Filipino prisoners without trial. Much of the prosecution's case depended on hearsay testimony, records of earlier trials, and a previous statement of the accused; the defense cross-examination focused on highlighting that no witnesses had direct knowledge of Kobayashi's involvement in the deaths. Although the commission provided no rationale, clearly it found such evidence insufficient to support a guilty verdict.[71]

Still, it would be imprudent to conclude that the inclusion of affidavits or other hearsay evidence had no impact on the commissions' decisions. Rather, the significance of such evidence likely depended on the overall strength of the prosecution's case. In short, if the prosecution was able to present eyewitnesses who directly tied the defendants to the crimes, and if these witnesses were seen as believable by the commissions after the defense had the opportunity to cross-examine them, then the admission of secondhand testimony and the submission of any number of affidavits from the defense arguably would not have carried much weight or materially affected the outcome. And if the witnesses who provided affidavits for the defense had been allowed to appear in court, they would have been subject to cross-examination. The downside risk in these instances would have been a relevant factor, although it cannot be ruled out that such witnesses might have weakened the credibility of prosecution witnesses.[72] Conversely, commissions in other cases where the credibility of prosecution witnesses was an issue likely relied more heavily on the sum total of the evidence, including affidavits.

Commission Judgments: Assessing Criminal Liability

Conclusions about the justice rendered in Philippine courtrooms rest not just on process but also on outcomes, that is, the judgments of the military commissions and their bases for determining the evidence necessary to establish individual criminal liability. Philippine trial commissions offered rationales for their verdicts in over a third of the cases. These explanations, coupled with the changes commissions made to individual specifications in rendering their decisions and in some cases the sentences they handed down, allow for some informed judgments about what drove their verdicts, specifically, the extent to which eyewitness testimony, the doctrine of command responsibility, and the defenses of superior orders and military necessity may have factored into decisions about criminal liability.

Given the nature of the charges brought by prosecutors, commissions dealt most often with defendants accused of actually committing atrocities. In these instances, judgments on liability invariably depended on the relative value assigned to eyewitness testimony placing the defendants at the scenes of the crimes as weighed against a defense of alibi or mistaken identity. As it turned out, commissions consistently relied on existing legal precedents dictating that credible eyewitness testimony trumped claims of alibi. The outcome in the case against defendants Nemoto Takeji and Onoyama Masaichi (cited above) demonstrates this quite clearly. Several survivors of the March 1945 Batangas massacre testified that both men had stabbed or bayoneted victims. To counter this eyewitness testimony against the defendants, their commander testified that they had not been present. A second Japanese soldier (a defendant in a separate trial) testified that Nemoto's unit had been stationed elsewhere and had not been involved. Both Onoyama and Nemoto denied participation. In issuing its guilty verdict against the two, the commission rejected their alibi defense, citing a Philippine Supreme Court ruling (in a case completely unrelated to the war crimes trials) that "oral evidence of alibi is so easily manufactured and usually so unreliable that it can rarely be given credence."[73]

Other cases offer further elaboration of the legal bases for privileging eyewitness testimony over claims of alibi. For example, the prosecutor in the trial of Ogawa Somin and his codefendants (most of the charges dealt with the killing of noncombatants) was at pains to cite a variety of legal precedents for prioritizing the testimony of eyewitnesses, among them prior judicial determinations that "an alibi must be proved by positive, clear and satisfactory evidence"; "when the defendants are identified by the witnesses for the prosecution by clear, explicit and positive testimony, the alibi will not be credited"; and "an alibi cannot stand and prevail over clear and convincing testimony of credible witnesses."[74]

Of course, the key to invoking these legal precedents remained the credibility of eyewitnesses. Commissions could and did discount the testimony of prosecution eyewitnesses as not believable, leading to not-guilty verdicts for individual specifications or for all charges. In fact, six of the eleven defendants found not guilty at trial faced one or more eyewitnesses who testified to their culpability. In each case, commissions rejected such testimony in coming to the conclusion that the prosecution had not proved its case. In the trial of Kurasawa Tooru, for example, prosecutors produced several witnesses who testified to the defendant's role in directing his subordinates to kill hundreds of civilians on Ponson Island in December 1944. But the defense countered by showing that the witnesses had contradicted their own earlier sworn statements; this successful challenge to the witnesses' credibility led the commission to find Kurasawa not guilty, notwithstanding what appears to be a rather implausible claim of noninvolvement on the part of the defendant.[75]

Culpability arising from command responsibility—that is, a theory of liability wherein commanders at any organizational level can be held accountable for the criminal conduct of their subordinates—was also a significant aspect of the Philippine trials, but it is necessary to distinguish between those (mostly less senior) officers charged with "ordering and directing" their subordinates to commit crimes and those (usually higher-ranking) officers charged with the "willful failure" to control their subordinates and/or "permitting" them to commit atrocities. In essence, the distinction here is between those charged with a positive or direct contribution to criminal activities (which could be considered accomplice liability) and those charged with acts of omission, that is, the failure to act.[76]

The great majority of the command responsibility trials were of the former type, and as such the commissions again relied on eyewitness testimony to establish the culpability of the officers charged. For example, Kudō Chūshirō, it will be remembered, had been accused of ordering his men to kill civilians in the town of Bay in early 1945. Kudō's defense was that he had not been present in Bay that day and that another soldier (already convicted by an American tribunal) was solely responsible. In rendering its guilty verdict, the commission focused on the witness testimony placing Kudō at the scene and the weaknesses in his alibi defense; presumably, the judges also accepted the eyewitness testimony offered by the prosecution that Kudō both was an officer (by virtue of having worn a saber) and had shouted in Japanese before soldiers began beating and bayoneting civilians, thus demonstrating "ordering." In another case, the commission appears to have concluded (there was no rationale provided) that the five defendants were guilty by virtue of the evidence (mainly eyewitness testimony) showing that they were all officers who appeared to be in charge at the scene of the atrocities they were charged with ordering, directing, and permitting their men to commit.[77]

A key logic that tended to prevail was that evidence showing the presence of an officer during the commission of atrocities constituted a sufficient basis for at least some liability regardless of any specific evidence of "ordering" or "directing." Essentially, officers actually on the scene during the commission of crimes by their subordinates possessed the requisite knowledge of the crimes and were vulnerable to prosecution if they took no steps to prevent them.

Various trials highlighted this notion of liability stemming from sufficient evidence of an officer's presence even if it could not be proven that he had any role in ordering atrocities or, for that matter, participating in them. First Lt. Doi Kunio had been charged with direct participation in the torture of Filipino civilians and the killing of others. For the latter specification, the prosecution produced two witnesses who testified to seeing Doi arrive at the site where the victims were killed; Doi denied involvement, and his superior officer (Morishita) recanted his earlier testimony in his own trial that Doi had done the killings as ordered. The commission concluded that the evidence did not show that Doi had taken any part in the actual killings, nor was there evidence that he had ordered the soldiers to bayonet the victims. But the commission did not want to relieve Doi of all responsibility and so modified the description of the defendant's role: because the evidence showed that he had been the only officer present at the scene, it could be "safely inferred" that he had "tolerated" the killings because he took no steps to prevent them. Consequently, the commission reworded the specification to find Doi guilty of "tolerat[ing] the killing of" the named victims.[78] In two other cases, the commissions altered original specifications to find defendants Omura Yasuo and Matsuzaki Hideichi guilty of "not preventing" or "failing to prevent" crimes instead of ordering, directing, or permitting them.[79] In all three instances, the commissions appear to have grounded their verdicts in the belief that the defendants had the knowledge and the power to intervene but chose not to do so. (Just what impact these findings had on the sentences these three defendants received is difficult to determine, given that they were also found guilty of other counts; nonetheless, none was sentenced to death.)

Another case highlights a commission's judgment regarding liability when the defendant was present at the scene but his command status was in question. Nakano Shizuo had been charged with three counts of ordering and permitting soldiers under his command to torture or kill civilians. Although the commission did not provide a rationale for its verdict, it clearly wrestled with Nakano's exact role. Before rendering judgment, the commission took the unusual step of asking the prosecution and defense to submit briefs on the issue of whether the defendant would be liable if he was present at the crime scenes simply as the highest commissioned officer there rather than in command. The prosecution argued that Nakano was liable because he took a "consenting part" in the atrocities; that is, he was present and had the power and authority to prevent them but had failed to do so. Even granting that the soldiers who killed the victims had been part of another unit, Nakano still had command and control of these soldiers by virtue of his role as a ranking officer of the Kempeitai and the fact that the unit in question had been placed under the command of Nakano's superior officer. The defense, however, maintained that even if Nakano had been present, he had no authority to order or forbid the acts of another unit even if he had wanted to do so. Simply being a higher-commissioned officer was insufficient to make him legally responsible for the crimes. Without comment, the commission sided with the prosecution: it deleted the reference to "under his command" from the specifications but still found him guilty and sentenced him to death.[80] This would appear to conform to a theory of liability based on a judgment about Nakano's de facto (as opposed to de jure) authority over the soldiers committing the crimes.[81]

Establishing criminal liability in the cases cited above was made easier because prosecutors could rely on eyewitnesses to demonstrate that the defendants had actual knowledge of the crimes committed by their men (and by their presence at the very least had countenanced them). Proving criminal liability in the handful of cases where the defendants were more removed from the commission of the crimes was more challenging for prosecutors, who needed to establish that the accused had (or should have had) knowledge of and the authority to prevent or punish abuses but had failed to do so. The trials of two generals fall into this category; prosecutors in these cases tended to follow the path laid out in the earlier US trial of Gen. Yamashita Tomoyuki.[82] It is the trials of lower-ranking defendants that offer less frequently explored examples of how commissions weighed liability under varying circumstances.

Fujita Takefumi had been charged with three counts of permitting his soldiers to torture and mistreat civilians and a fourth alleging that the torture had contributed to the eventual deaths of two individuals after they were later transferred to Fort Santiago. In his opening statement, the prosecutor explicitly stated that this was a case of command responsibility. The defendant (a captain) had not directly participated in the crimes but, rather, had "knowingly and maliciously" permitted them. The prosecution's evidence consisted of the testimony of survivors who described their arrest and torture by Japanese soldiers and the prior statements of the accused and another Japanese officer on Fujita's role as commander of the Manila north sector of the Kempeitai and the substation most directly involved. Some of the witnesses described being brought before Fujita after their mistreatment and before being transported elsewhere. The defense countered that soldiers from another unit, not the Kempeitai, were responsible for the abuses; that there was no clear evidence that the victims had ever been under the custody of the Kempeitai; and finally that Fujita had no responsibility for any misconduct at Fort Santiago that led to prisoners' deaths.[83]

The commission was persuaded by the evidence that it was Fujita's subordinates who were responsible for the arrests and torture of various Filipino civilians; even granting that other units were also involved, they did so at the direction of the Kempeitai substation that reported to Fujita. Accordingly, the commission convicted Fujita of all four counts against him, although it did modify the last count to absolve him of any responsibility for the subsequent deaths at Fort Santiago. He was sentenced to life in prison.[84] In this instance, the commission appears to have been satisfied that, first, Fujita had command over those responsible for the crimes and, second, he had knowledge of the abuses. That the victims identified Fujita as the officer to whom they were taken after their torture appears to have been the key element establishing such knowledge.

In a second case, the main question at issue was the nature and extent of each defendant's organizational responsibility in relationship to the alleged crimes. Defendants Lt. Kita Heiji, 2nd Lt. Isobe Kōzō, and Warrant Officer Saitō

War crimes suspect Saitō Takao pointing out the entrance to the cell where more than four hundred Filipino prisoners suffocated to death while in detention in Fort Santiago (Photo SC-246854, courtesy of the National Archives at College Park, MD)

Takao, members of the Kempeitai, were charged with a single count of willfully disregarding and failing to discharge their duties at Fort Santiago, thereby permitting, allowing, and directing those under their command to mistreat prisoners, which in turn led to the death by suffocation of 450 prisoners in custody.[85] Prosecutors argued that Kita was responsible because he was in charge of prisoner facilities, Saitō because he was in charge of the cells where the prisoners died, and Isobe because as a doctor he was responsible for the health and sanitary conditions of prisoners. Survivors testified to their mistreatment, the conditions in the cells, and having seen Saitō and/or Kita appear to be in charge during the period of their incarceration. One witness testified to having seen Saitō and two guards at some point around the time of the suffocation. Another witness testified that she had been mistreated (although not by any of the defendants) and had seen all three during her incarceration—she saw Kita and Saitō making inspections and Isobe when she had passed by his clinic on-site. The prosecution also introduced affidavits from two Japanese Kempeitai officers describing the chain of command at Fort Santiago and the duties of the three defendants; both placed more direct responsibility on Saitō for what had happened.[86]

The main defense arguments were that another officer (Capt. Yanase Shoichi, one of the affiants mentioned above) was most directly responsible for the deaths and that none of the defendants had either the responsibility or the authority to prevent the abuses. Kita testified that he was unaware of the suffocation until after the fact. He also claimed that he had seen signs of beatings at Fort Santiago and had appealed to his commanding officer, but to no avail. He maintained that it was Yanase, over whom he had no authority, who was responsible for the arrest and investigation of guerrilla suspects. Saitō testified that he reported to Yanase, who was in charge of prisoner detention, and had tried to ease overcrowding in the cells, but Yanase had disagreed. He further stated that he believed the cause of the mass suffocation was the result of overcrowding with the arrival of new prisoners and that he had no involvement in the arrest and detention of prisoners. Isobe testified that he had been transferred to another location in October 1944 but returned to Fort Santiago to treat prisoners at a dispensary there. He was not allowed to treat prisoners in their cells and had no ability or authority to improve conditions in the cells, although he had on one occasion tried to suggest ways to improve the prisoners' lot.[87]

In its written summation, the defense argued that the evidence presented did not show that the defendants were guilty either of direct involvement in the deaths or by virtue of a failure to act. The prosecution had not met the necessary burden of proof:

> If the accused are charged with an act, the prosecution must prove that the accused by overt acts ordered, directed or permitted soldiers under their command to mistreat and torture the 450 prisoners. If they are charged with omission, the prosecution must prove that the three accused had command responsibility in the alleged atrocities. In the latter case the prosecution must prove the following elements of command responsibility: (1) existence of a power or duty to prevent or suppress the atrocious act; (2) actual or constructive knowledge by the accused of the act complained of; and (3) negligence in the failure to suppress the act.[88]

The prosecution countered with a summation that focused on the tortures inflicted on prisoners incarcerated in Fort Santiago, the deplorable conditions in the cells, and the lack of food and water or medical attention. It was the prosecution's contention that Kita and Saitō were guilty of overt acts in the deaths of the prisoners and Isobe of an act of omission in failing to care for the prisoners.[89]

The commission rendered a judgment that indicated its willingness to distinguish degrees of liability among the defendants and to place the greatest liability on the defendant viewed as most directly involved. Kita, in charge of facilities, did bear some responsibility for the suffering of prisoners, while Saitō as chief of the guards had been in the best position to alleviate their suffering but instead had ignored their cries for water and had allowed the cell doors to be closed airtight. Accordingly, the commission found Kita guilty, but only of "willful failure" rather than of directing or permitting the deaths, and it sentenced him to seventeen years. Saitō was found guilty of the specification as originally worded and sentenced to death. In Isobe's case, the commission found insufficient grounds to hold him accountable for the conditions of the prisoners and therefore acquitted him.[90]

As has been previously noted, defendants, whether charged with participation or command responsibility, almost always resorted to a defense of alibi or denial of responsibility. Only very rarely did commissions deal with defenses of superior orders or military necessity where the defendants actually acknowledged some involvement. Attorneys offered a defense of superior orders in just two of the trials where the defendants pleaded not guilty, one involving multiple defendants and the other a high-ranking general. The latter trial also invoked military necessity (as did one additional trial).

In the first of the superior orders cases, fifteen naval officers were accused of ordering and/or participating in mass killings (or in the case of one defendant, rape) in the municipality of Infanta, Tayabas Province, during the months of March and April 1945. The prosecution produced numerous eyewitness survivors who identified all but one of the defendants as the perpetrators with varying degrees of certainty (the case against one defendant was eventually dismissed for lack of evidence). The defense countered with a broad resort to a superior orders defense coupled with alibi defenses for individual defendants.[91]

The defense produced as its first witness Rear Adm. Furuse Takasue, who testified that as commander of the Furuse unit in Infanta, all the defendants had been his subordinates. Furuse, who had already pleaded guilty at his own trial, testified that he had issued orders to his unit's second battalion to conduct a punitive expedition against the inhabitants in the area after the Americans had landed and guerrilla activities had increased. He further stated that his officers had no choice but to obey his orders, and as their commanding officer he took full responsibility for their actions. At the same time, Furuse also went out of his way to offer alibis for as many of the defendants as he could.[92]

The first line of defense for virtually all of the accused was denial: they testified that they had no involvement in the punitive expedition or the killing of civilians. Some stated that they had other assignments, while others claimed to have been ill. Two of the more senior officers—Lt. Cdr. Ogawa Somin and Lt. Cdr. Mineo Shisuhiko—acknowledged involvement in the transmittal of Furuse's order to dispose of the inhabitants but otherwise denied any responsibility. Mineo testified that he had been present at the meeting when Furuse gave the order and had subsequently carried it to Ogawa, but he denied the charges against him that he had actually been a participant in the subsequent killings. Ogawa, the commander of the second battalion that was tasked with carrying out Furuse's order, acknowledged receiving the order but testified that he had vigorously protested it and had no choice but to instruct various companies to carry it out. Oddly, Ogawa was never charged with any command responsibility for the killings but only a single count of rape, which he denied.[93]

A third defendant, Nakamata Tomisaburō, a company commander in the second battalion, also admitted that he had received the order but explained that he had simply shown it to a platoon commander and directed him to seek clarification from battalion headquarters. He insisted that he had not given any orders to the platoon. The order came from Furuse headquarters, and as a junior officer he was not authorized or empowered to prevent its execution. He further denied any involvement in the charges against him that he had in fact ordered and permitted his men to kill civilians. Finally, another defendant, Kuahara Tetsuo, testified that he had been away from his company headquarters engaging the enemy and only learned on his return from the front of the Furuse order, which in his absence had been handled by his subordinate.[94]

In its summation, the defense argued that in the Japanese army and navy, military subordinates were under no obligation to question the orders of their superiors and in fact were taught to count on the legitimacy of those orders. Obedience to superior orders must be prompt and implicit, especially in the presence of the enemy. Still, the heart of the defense was attacks on the credibility of the prosecution witnesses who placed the defendants at the sites where the killings took place.[95]

Without explanation, the commission found all the defendants guilty of at least one of the specifications against them, and all were sentenced to death—even Ogawa, who faced a single rape charge.[96] Ogawa's sentence suggests that commission members were not unmindful of the command role he played and punished him for it. Although the defense did raise the issue of superior orders, it seemed in practice oddly disconnected from the actual conduct of the case. Basically, the prosecution ignored the superior orders defense and instead concentrated on presenting eyewitness testimony placing the defendants at the crime scenes. Likewise, the defense focused more on the standard defenses of alibi and denial. In short, both sides appeared to take refuge in the far more common strategies showcased in the Philippine trials rather than directly argue for or rebut a superior orders defense on the merits.

A much more straightforward superior orders defense surfaced in the trial of Maj. Gen. Masuoka Kensichi, who had been indicted on a single count of ordering the execution of spies in addition to the command responsibility charges he faced. His defense for the spy count rested on the dual claims of superior orders and military necessity. Testifying in his own defense, Masuoka acknowledged the execution of twelve Filipinos but explained that he had acted on the orders of his superior officer, Yamashita Tomoyuki, commander of the Fourteenth Area Army. He testified that those executed were spies, he had consulted with Yamashita on how to proceed, and Yamashita had told him the army could not hold a trial but that the Kempeitai should investigate the matter in as close to a trial proceeding as possible. Masuoka further testified that he was told by Yamashita's chief of staff to regard Yamashita's instructions as an order. Masuoka also couched the decision as a matter of military necessity: a trial of the spies had not been possible under the circumstances, given the war situation and the lack of army staff to conduct a trial. Instead, Masuoka directed his subordinates to form a committee of at least three Japanese officers to examine each prisoner's alleged offense and make recommendations accordingly. The commission rejected Masuoka's claims, finding that it was the defendant, not Yamashita, who had issued the direct order on dealing with the spies and that the procedures followed by the defendant were not close enough to a trial to satisfy international law. Nonetheless, the commission appeared to recognize the partial legitimacy of the claim of military necessity in citing certain mitigating factors, among them the critical war situation and the offense of espionage. Masuoka received a sentence of ten years.[97]

There was only one other case in which the accused introduced military necessity as a defense.[98] Satō Sō had been charged in part with ordering his men to kill approximately 150 unarmed noncombatant civilian men, women, and children in Cagayan Province in July 1945. In his defense, Satō testified that on the day in question he and his men were attacked by men brandishing bolos and were forced to counterattack to protect themselves. In other words, Satō and his men had fended off a guerrilla attack and were justified in their response.

Satō also made much of the fact that a US investigation had previously cleared him and his subordinates. Commission members accepted parts of Satō's account, deleting the description of the victims as unarmed civilians and reducing their number to thirty. Nonetheless, the commission still reasoned that Satō remained culpable because his soldiers were in no real danger from men armed only with inferior weapons. The right course of action would have been to arrest, investigate, and try the guerrillas. Satō received a life sentence.[99] Satō's conviction was upheld by a subsequent review board, but with one board member dissenting on the grounds that Satō had in fact been responding to military necessity (see chapter 4).

In the Masuoka and Satō trials, the underlying rationale for their guilty verdicts stemmed from a provision in military regulations that "unauthorized belligerents" (interpreted to include spies and guerrillas), while subject to harsh punishment, could not be summarily executed. Philippine prosecutors appear to have followed the US rules in place at the time; *War Department Basic Field Manual: Rules of Land Warfare, FM 27-10* stipulated that "if captured, [unauthorized belligerents] have no right to be treated as prisoners of war. They may not, however, after being captured, be summarily put to death or otherwise punished, but may be brought to trial before a military commission or other tribunal, which may sentence them to death or such other punishment as it may consider proper."[100]

Defense counsel in the Philippines were never really able to capitalize on the presumed different status to be accorded guerrillas under the rules of land warfare because they could not overcome the argument that guerrilla suspects or spies nonetheless had to be granted a trial before punishment. When defense counsel tried to elicit testimony from witnesses that victims were in fact guerrillas, prosecutors invariably sought to counter this with testimony that no trials had been afforded suspects before summary punishment. It is true that commissions did on occasion adjust specifications to describe victims as guerrilla suspects rather than noncombatant civilians, but this did not necessarily result in less severe sentences.[101]

An Overall Assessment

Given the nature of the proceedings and the judgments rendered, what then are we to make of the overall conduct of the trials in the Philippines? Undoubtedly, the Philippine trials presented a challenging landscape for both prosecution and defense. Prosecution witnesses were, not infrequently, uneducated, poor, or easily confused; the nature of the proceedings required translations in many languages; both sides had concerns over the use of hearsay (which was, nevertheless, employed by both); and the war produced conflicting loyalties and motivations for lying. Japanese defendants often marshaled an impressive array of affidavits from fellow soldiers to support their alibi defenses, but this was countered by eyewitness testimony, which frequently carried greater weight as a matter of law.

This topography makes absolute judgments about the conduct of the trials based on a reading of the transcripts or case files a somewhat problematic exercise. But some observations are possible. Not all of the generalizations about the unfairness of the trials in Asia pass muster when applied to the Philippine government trials. The Philippine authorities did not select defendants arbitrarily based on rank or lack thereof; instead, prosecutors demonstrated a willingness to pursue charges against general officers (Generals Kuroda, Hayashi, and Kawaguchi were recalled from Japan to stand trial) and also cleared a substantial number of lower-ranking subordinates. The available evidence suggests that the National War Crimes Office screened potential cases and cleared many more suspects than it ultimately tried. (Ironically, some defendants bemoaned the results of investigations that they claimed allowed guilty parties to return to Japan while they were left holding the bag.) A system that refused to indict those who appeared mentally ill or unable to communicate (the Okinawan suspect) can hardly be seen as railroading suspects into court. Moreover, there were times when prosecutors recommended dismissal of individual specifications or even whole cases when the evidence proved too weak. It is true that mid- and lower-ranking officers tended to receive harsher punishments relative to either senior officers or the enlisted ranks, but this was not a function of a failure of a superior orders defense but rather the apparent inclination of the judges to place more responsibility on those officers found to be actually on-site directing atrocities.

The Philippine government trials were notable—and in some respects distinguishable from other Allied trials—in important ways. The vast majority of the defendants had the opportunity to face their accusers and subject them to cross-examination. These cross-examinations were, after an abortive early reliance on Japanese lawyers, conducted by Filipino defense counsel familiar with Anglo-American jurisprudence and courtroom procedure. These lawyers had the added advantage of being more easily able to seek out witnesses for the defense and were manifestly successful in so doing, judging from the numbers of Filipinos who did testify on behalf of the accused. A high proportion (80 percent) of the defendants chose to testify in their own defense. Only a few of the trials had more than five defendants, and none reached the numbers attained in other jurisdictions. Finally, at least some judges displayed a rather healthy skepticism of hearsay.

Still, the various procedures and safeguards did not necessarily guarantee just outcomes. Certainly, proponents and detractors could point to specific trials that for them epitomized their disparate judgments about the fairness of the verdicts. The case against Nakamura Hideichi and his twelve codefendants became a cause célèbre in Japan, with observers convinced that at least half those charged were innocent. Those familiar with the trial of Teramoto Tukuji (Tokuji) would no doubt point to the preponderance of evidence and credible witnesses substantiating the defendant's culpability. And both sides could draw comfort from the case against Kurasawa Tooru, which showcased demonstrably perjured testimony from prosecution witnesses, the gritty efforts of defense counsel to bring to light the flaws in the prosecution's case, and the acquittal handed down by judges who, even given the improbable nature of the defendant's story, could not find him guilty beyond a reasonable doubt on the evidence presented.

The trial commissions' determinations of criminal liability rested overwhelmingly on the credibility to be assigned to eyewitness testimony. Legal precedents that privileged such testimony over claims of alibi represented an evidentiary "bias" that many defendants struggled to overcome. This placed enormous weight on both the role of the judges who were tasked with weighing the evidence and the skills of defense attorneys in challenging prosecution witnesses. On the one hand, all the members of the military commissions served in the Philippine armed forces; most presumably had no legal training, and they therefore relied on the single law member assigned to each trial. On the other hand, key safeguards did exist, including the ability of defense counsel to question commission appointments, the caliber of defense representation in protecting defendants' interests, and, perhaps equally important, a postsentence review process that could and did question the sufficiency of evidence on which commissions reached their verdicts. The trials were not perfect, but an examination of all (not just selective) cases belies the contention that all the trials were fatally flawed or that defendants were routinely convicted on the basis of weak or manufactured evidence.

Finally, and perhaps most obvious, context matters. Any critique of the Philippine trials must recognize the historical circumstances in which they occurred. These were military tribunals, not civilian proceedings, and they were conducted in the aftermath of a war that created practical and logistical difficulties. The midcentury confidence in the reliability of eyewitness testimony has since given way to a better appreciation of the fallibility of witnesses to remember and replay traumatic experiences and accurately identify perpetrators. And a style of defense that sought to discredit prosecution witnesses—notably, suggestions that rape victims enjoyed the experience—is simply cringe-inducing today.

Questions of guilt or innocence did not end with the judgments at the trials. Those convicted would have the opportunity to have their verdicts and sentences reviewed. In theory at least, any miscarriages of justice could be found and mitigated by that postsentence review process.

4

Awaiting Their Fate

Sentence Reviews, Reprieves, and Executions

For most of the Japanese convicted of war crimes, the future seemed bleak. Facing execution or life sentences, they were remanded to a prison outside Manila to await the review of their sentences. This process offered the chance to appeal and, perhaps, the possibility of redemption. Some were vindicated; three others had been executed by the end of 1948. A very few received presidential pardons. As time passed, the governmental review process slowed, although it retained its painstaking attention to detail. In Japan, after the attention riveted on the earlier US trials of Yamashita and Homma, press and public attention stilled. This was a time when the prisoners in the Philippines saw themselves as the "forgotten Japanese" (*wasurerareta Nihonjin*).[1]

And then the dynamic changed abruptly. Philippine president Elpidio Quirino authorized the execution of fourteen Japanese war criminals, and the executions were carried out on a single night, January 19, 1951, that stretched into the early morning of the next day. After a hiatus of over two years, the Philippines had resumed the process of putting Japanese to death for war crimes without fanfare or publicity. Why the government went ahead with this mass execution remains a minor mystery, but it undoubtedly hardened Japanese views of Philippine notions of justice.

This was also the period that marked a transition from legal retribution to political accommodation and eventual resolution of the war crimes issue that had divided the postwar Philippines and Japan. The sentence review process and resulting executions constituted legal steps in obtaining justice for Filipino victims. The pardons and relatively humane treatment for imprisoned Japanese war criminals represented steps away from pure retribution. Taken together, these steps represented a necessary bridge that eventually allowed Filipinos to become reconciled to the prospect of a political solution that would allow all the war criminals still in custody to regain their freedom.

Postsentence Review: Continued Attention to Judicial Process

The same set of rules governing the conduct of the Philippine war crimes trials also stipulated that verdicts and sentences would be subject to postsentence review. Under Executive Order No. 68, no sentence could be carried out without the approval of the army chief of staff, who was given the authority to approve, modify, or overturn sentences but could not increase the penalties imposed at trial. In cases of a death or life sentence, one additional step was required: the president of the Philippines had to confirm the sentence before it could be carried out. Thus, no Japanese war criminal could be put to death without the express authorization of the president. EO 68 further stipulated that the chief of staff was to create a board of review to assist him in carrying out his sentence approval responsibilities; that board was to consist of not more than three officers, none of whom could be on duty with or assigned to the Office of the Judge Advocate General.[2]

The sentence review process was generally as follows: The Office of the Judge Advocate General, whose jurisdiction included the National War Crimes Office, forwarded trial documentation, including trial transcripts, to the board of review. The board, after reviewing the material as well as any relevant letters or petitions, prepared a written report for the chief of staff summarizing the case and providing a recommendation to affirm the verdict, approve or modify the sentence, or overturn the verdict completely. The chief of staff, after reviewing this material, would then issue his decision, which would be implemented through a separate directive. In instances where the chief of staff approved a sentence of death or life in prison, the review board's report and the trial records would be forwarded to the Office of the President, through the secretary of justice, for confirmation of the sentence. If the chief of staff overturned a death or life sentence, that decision did not require presidential confirmation.[3]

The case of Nakanishi Shioji illustrates this process quite well. Nakanishi had been convicted and sentenced to death on August 13, 1948, for the execution of ten unarmed Filipino civilians in the municipality of Antipolo, Rizal Province, in September 1942. On August 25, 1948, the NWCO, through the judge advocate general, submitted the records of the trial to the board of review through the Office of the Chief of Staff. The board concluded that the verdict

Table 3. Results of the review process

	Sentences			
	Death	Life	Term	Not guilty
Trial verdicts[a]	79	31	28	11
After review	73	31	27[b]	18

Sources: Compiled from Japanese War Crime Records, Case Files, NAP; Philippines Versus Various Japanese War Criminals, Case File, 1947–49, SCAP Legal Section, Prosecution Division, UD 1323 and UD 1328, RG 331, NACP; press release 7-6-6, Office of the President of the Philippines, July 6, 1953, decimal 694.9624/7-653, Central Decimal File, 1950–54, RG 59, NACP; "Hikoku, zensenpan o tokusha," *Asahi Shimbun*, June 28, 1953, 1; and "Zenshikeishū (gokyūmei) muki ni migara wa Sugamo ni utsusu," *Asahi Shimbun*, June 28, 1953, 1.

[a] Includes those who pleaded guilty as well as those who proceeded to trial.

[b] Includes two defendants whose original term sentences were further reduced.

and sentence were justified and prepared a report to that effect, together with draft paperwork for the chief of staff's signature. The board chairman routed these documents and the trial transcript back to the Office of the Chief of Staff. The chief of staff agreed with the board's recommendation and approved the sentence on November 28, 1948, but withheld execution of the sentence pending its confirmation by the president of the Philippines. By letter of the same date, the chief of staff forwarded all the case documentation to the president for his consideration and recommended that the president confirm the sentence.[4]

As a result of the review process, seven defendants found guilty at trial (including two given the death penalty) had their verdicts completely overturned; another seven had their sentences reduced. Table 3 compares the trial and post-sentence review outcomes.

Judging from these data and available documentation, the review process was by no means perfunctory.[5] The review boards' reports were detailed and lengthy, with a clear effort made to outline the evidence presented at trial and the rationale used by board members to reach their decisions. Generally speaking, the review boards found little to quarrel with in terms of the trial commissions' procedures or rulings. Instead, board recommendations to sustain or, alternatively, to change a commission's verdicts or sentences arose directly from an assessment of the sufficiency of evidence on which those judgments were based. In other words, review boards did not see themselves as required to defer to commissions on matters of evidence or witness credibility. The boards recognized the challenges involved: in the words of one board, "In estimating the weight of evidence . . . all we can do is note all the facts and circumstances carefully and estimate its absolute and relative weight by the lights of conscience and experience. We have no test of the truth of human testimony except its conformity to our knowledge, observation and experience."[6]

Documentation exists to illuminate eight of the fourteen instances in which commission verdicts were overturned or modified. Predictably, given the criticality of eyewitnesses to the trial verdicts, boards recommended that cases be overturned when they disagreed with the commissions on the credibility of prosecution witnesses. For example, the board concluded that defendant Kobayashi Yusaku (sentenced to life for involvement in the killing of numerous Filipino civilians in Batangas Province in early 1945) was entitled to an acquittal because the sole prosecution witness against him appeared to have changed her testimony from a prior case in which she had also given evidence. As a result, Kobayashi's alibi defense should be credited and his sentence overturned.[7] In a second case, the board recommended that the guilty verdict against defendant Mineo Shisuhiko be set aside because in its view he had not been positively identified by the lone witness who implicated him.[8] In yet a third case, the board likewise threw out the verdicts against both codefendants, concluding that the prosecution had failed to prove its case beyond a reasonable doubt and casting doubt on the credibility of certain prosecution witnesses. In this instance, the board also appears to have been swayed by petitions submitted by Filipinos supporting the good character of Shimizu Hisamitsu, one of the accused.[9] (It likely did not hurt that Shimizu's case was championed by Senator Ramon Torres, who had testified at Shimizu's trial, arranged for petitions on his behalf, and continued to put pressure on Philippine review officials after Shimizu was found guilty.[10])

In one striking case, the review board came remarkably close to accusing commission members of bias. Satō Matazō, an army private, had been accused of participating in the killing of hundreds of Filipino civilians and the burning of some five hundred houses as part of a punitive expedition in Batangas Province in February 1945. Satō had made a "daring escape" from the stockade shortly before his trial began but had been recaptured. The prosecution produced eyewitness testimony to Satō's involvement and made much of his attempt to escape as proof of his guilt. The defense produced witnesses and documents (including Japanese government records) to show that there had been two soldiers named Satō Matazō and that the other Satō had committed the crimes. Without comment, the trial commission found the accused guilty and sentenced him to life in prison.[11]

The review board report of the Satō trial was scathing. The board found that the trial court had "grossly disregarded the evidence presented and superimposed in its stead a finding of their own which finds no basis in the trial record." Had the commission "not been so over-zealous of convicting the accused," it would have taken better notice of the "inherently improbable and inconsistent" testimonies of the prosecution witnesses. The board concluded that the defense evidence of an alibi for the accused was credible and recommended that the accused be found innocent. Over the objections of judge advocate staff, the army chief of staff reversed the guilty verdict.[12]

Board reviews are not available in two other cases in which verdicts were overturned, but a review of the trial transcripts suggests that the decisions likely were again tied to disagreements over the reliability of prosecution eyewitnesses. In a case involving multiple defendants, Hanada Isie had been convicted and sentenced to death on the basis of the testimony of a single eyewitness, a young girl who said she had seen him stab her father before she had run away in fear. Moreover, one of Hanada's codefendants had taken responsibility for this particular incident.[13] Undoubtedly, the review board found the evidence too weak to sustain the original verdict. A second case is more complicated: Nakamura Fumio had been convicted of multiple counts of involvement in the torture and murder of Filipino civilians and had been sentenced to life based on the testimony of several eyewitnesses and the corroboration of others. The defense produced several Filipino witnesses who claimed that the defendant was being confused with another Nakamura, a Kempeitai officer who had committed the atrocities. These witnesses had particularly compelling stories—one had been a guerrilla during the war; others had been members of the Philippine Constabulary and had been accused or convicted of collaboration after the war.[14] In this instance, the review board apparently found the defense witnesses sufficiently credible to cast doubt on the prosecution's case.

Review boards were also willing to reduce sentences when they deemed them too harsh, in the process demonstrating a willingness to weigh precisely the degree of each defendant's culpability. Take, for example, the case of Gotō Shōzō and Fujii Rokujirō. Gotō and Fujii had been convicted of participating, with other members of their unit, in the killing of noncombatant civilians they had commandeered for convoy duty in early 1945 and were sentenced to death and life in prison, respectively. The two had denied involvement in the deaths, claiming they had been elsewhere at the time. The board agreed with the military commission's judgment that Gotō was at the scene of the crime but found no evidence that he had actually participated, "in the sense that with his sword he killed anyone of the 32 Filipinos." The board surmised that at most he had relayed the orders of his superior to those who perpetrated the actual atrocities. The board therefore recommended that Gotō's sentence be reduced to life in prison. In Fujii's case, the key witness against him had testified that Fujii had attempted to shoot and bayonet him but had missed. Having searched the trial record in vain for any other evidence, the board found itself forced to conclude that Fujii at most was guilty of attempted murder and recommended that his sentence be reduced to twenty years in prison.[15] This is a rather remarkable outcome, considering that the review board agreed with the trial commission that the defendants had lied in claiming an alibi and had actually been present at the scene of the killings. In this instance, the review board agreed with the commission that the defendants bore some criminal liability by affirming the guilty verdicts but disagreed with the commission on the extent of that liability.

This attention to detail is mirrored in other cases even when the ultimate outcome remained unchanged. For example, in its review of Koike Kaneyuki's case, the board reversed Koike's conviction on three counts, in part because "the basis for conviction proceeds from a colored, fabricated, and prejudiced testimony." But it upheld the guilty verdict on six other counts, holding that the commission had been correct in rejecting Koike's "self-serving and uncorroborated testimony" in favor of the prosecution witness accounts. Accordingly, the board concluded that the crimes encompassed in these six counts were "sufficiently heinous" to support the trial sentence of death by hanging.[16]

In rare instances, the board of review's findings were not unanimous. For example, in the case of Harada Shimpei et al., the majority upheld both the verdicts and sentences for all four defendants. The men had pleaded guilty; Harada, the commander, and one of his subordinates, Tezuka Toshio, had been sentenced to death, while the other two subordinates had received life sentences. One board member dissented in the matter of Tezuka's death sentence, arguing that if the other two subordinates had received life sentences because of two mitigating factors (guilty pleas and following orders as subordinates), Tezuka logically deserved a life sentence as well. (The other two board members maintained that Tezuka's sentence was justified by the particular brutality he had demonstrated and the large number of his victims.) In a second case, one board member disagreed with his two colleagues who had upheld the original sentence, arguing that the defendant, Satō Sō, should not be held criminally responsible for participating in a fight against guerrillas.[17]

There is also evidence that recommendations of the review boards were not invariably followed. In the case of Kobayashi Yusaku, Yamamoto Tukuzo (Tokuzō), and Kobayashi Masatake, the board of review concluded that the verdicts for all three defendants should be thrown out on the grounds that the case had not been proved against them. As noted above, the verdict against Kobayashi Yusaku was in fact overturned, and he returned home to Japan in 1952. But the sentences of his two codefendants apparently were allowed to stand: they remained incarcerated until the issuance of general pardons granted in 1953 for all remaining inmates.[18] Why no action was taken to overturn these sentences—and who was responsible for the inaction—is unclear.

Conversely, the board of review had recommended (and the chief of staff had agreed) that the death sentence for Saitō Takao should stand. Saitō had been convicted, along with Kita Heiji, of culpability in the deaths of prisoners in Fort Santiago. The case involved a particularly brutal incident in which over four hundred Filipino prisoners suffocated while in detention (see chapter 1). But on February 8, 1952, the president commuted Saitō's sentence to life, contrary to the review board's findings. Because the president pardoned Saitō's fellow defendant, Kita (see below), it may be that Kita's fate in some way influenced the outcome for Saitō as well. Available documentation does not provide any indication of the basis for Quirino's decision or whether it might have been influenced by a recommendation from the secretary of justice.[19]

Certainly in a large number of cases, the review board and the army chief of staff concurred unequivocally in the judgments rendered by the military commissions. For example, Nakano Shizuo had been found guilty and sentenced to death for directing a roundup (zona) of the inhabitants of two towns in Cavite Province, who were tortured and killed by men acting under his orders. The board of review noted that sufficient evidence had been presented at trial to show that the killings had occurred and to prove that Nakano had been present and had actively participated in the zona: "His responsibility in this case is due not merely because of the position he held as second in command . . . but also because of his direct, active and personal participation in the commission of the crimes charged against him." The chief of staff approved the sentence and forwarded it to the president for concurrence.[20]

Finally, available documentation on the review process also suggests that over time it slowed considerably, although this does not necessarily mean that the review itself was more or less thorough. For some of the earliest cases (those for which verdicts were handed down in 1947 or the early part of 1948), the lapsed time between the verdict and a decision by the chief of staff approximated four to six months; one case took only two months. The time period lengthened significantly for later trials—two years, for example, in the cases of Shirota Gintarō and Yamashita Suekichi.[21] Insufficient information exists to estimate accurately the length of time taken by the secretary of justice or the president in cases involving life or death sentences, although anecdotal data suggest that it too slowed markedly.[22]

Pardons: Mercy for the Few

President Quirino could have chosen to allow the judicial review process to unfold and simply abide by its results. But in a certain few instances, he opted to intervene, granting outright pardons to three individuals during the period between the first Philippine trial verdict and the first general pardon (discussed in chapter 5). It is clear from available trial and pardon documentation as well as statements attributed to President Quirino that he felt a sense of personal indebtedness to at least two of these men.

Matsuzaki Hideichi, a Kempeitai officer, had been convicted of ordering his men to torture and kill numerous Filipino prisoners of war. (One of those abused happened to be Fred Ruiz Castro, then a captain in the armed forces who became the judge advocate general after the war ended.) As noted in chapter 3, President Quirino assisted in Matsuzaki's defense, submitting a letter in which he praised Matsuzaki's help to many Filipinos, including Quirino's family, during the war.[23] Quirino clearly felt a sense of obligation to Matsuzaki and issued him a pardon on February 10, 1951—the first Japanese war criminal to receive one. Matsuzaki said later that Quirino had told him that the president's wife and daughter, had they been alive, would have begged him to free Matsuzaki (both had been killed during the fighting that raged in Manila in early 1945). Quirino's biographer also mentioned Matsuzaki by name, noting that he had befriended Quirino during his imprisonment. The press release explaining the pardon went into considerable detail on the reasons for granting it, citing the "representations made by prominent Filipinos to whom he [Matsuzaki] had given favors during the occupation" as well as petitions from some of his victims. Castro, who had reportedly resisted the idea of a pardon, relented after Matsuzaki offered him a personal apology; he also submitted a petition describing Matsuzaki's many "acts of benevolence and kindness" to Filipinos.[24]

Two other Japanese received pardons from Quirino about a year later—Lt. Kita Heiji and Lt. Gen. Kuroda Shigenori. Kita, a member of the Kempeitai, had been charged with allowing his subordinates to mistreat and torture Filipino prisoners at Fort Santiago, leading directly to the deaths of hundreds. Kita's attorney argued that the defendant's superior officers, already tried and convicted by American tribunals, were culpable for the deaths. And a Filipino witness testified at his trial that Kita had intervened on behalf of President Quirino's brother-in-law Hector Syquia, then in custody, allowing visits from his sister

Kita Heiji was convicted of responsibility for the suffocation deaths at Fort Santiago and was later pardoned by Philippine president Quirino (Photo 87, box 1346, UD 1266, RG 331, courtesy of the National Archives at College Park, MD)

(the wife of the president). Kita was convicted and sentenced to seventeen years at hard labor.[25]

In reviewing Kita's sentence, the board of review recommended that it be upheld, and the chief of staff agreed. Since the sentence was less than life, no presidential confirmation was required, which should have led to an order to formally implement the sentence. Yet no such order had been issued as of October 1950, some two years after the board made its report. What role, if any, the president played during this delay is unclear; what is certain is that he issued a pardon to Kita in February 1952. A Japanese newspaper reported that Kita had been pardoned because he had shown kindness to the president during the war.[26]

General Kuroda, sentenced to life in prison for atrocities committed in the Philippines during his tenure as commander of the Fourteenth Army, was frequently characterized as having been a friend to elite Filipinos during the wartime Japanese occupation. During his trial, prominent Filipinos—congressmen, senators, and high-level occupation officials like Jose Vargas and Camilo Osias—testified or provided affidavits on his behalf. Kuroda received a presidential pardon in December 1951; if news reports are to be believed, he spent one of his last days in the Philippines playing golf with Filipinos at an elite country club.[27]

Thus, there is direct and convincing evidence that Quirino felt a sense of obligation to both Matsuzaki and Kita, and he may well have felt a similar obligation to Kuroda for the general's overall actions toward other members of the elite during the war (or might possibly have been importuned by them on Kuroda's behalf). It was Kuroda's own belief that his Filipino friends had interceded with the president to obtain his release. Moreover, Quirino did not just issue pardons to these three men—he went out of his way to meet with them personally before they returned home. These meetings were widely reported in both Philippine and Japanese newspapers. In Kuroda's case, Quirino stressed that he had no love for the Japanese and their actions during the war but was acting out of a sense of duty and Christian forgiveness. One news account also mentioned that Kuroda had converted to Christianity, a possible factor in the president's decision.[28]

In extemporaneous remarks to the International Council of Christian Churches Conference in early December, Quirino gave other indications of his thinking around this time. He mentioned his own personal losses during the war and his understandable antipathy toward Japanese but also his recognition of the need to move beyond those feelings:

> I don't want our children to inherit the hate that had been temporarily engendered in those days of torture, in those dark days before the liberation of the City of Manila. I have been waiting for an opportunity to express our friendship to Japan as well as to the others who had cooperated with her during those bloody times. . . . Not only officially but personally, I want to assure our friends, especially those from Japan, that following the example of the Lord, we cannot afford to nurture for an indefinite period that feeling of hate, that feeling of resentment, that negative spirit towards our neighbors.[29]

Quirino's timing in pardoning these men also warrants some scrutiny, and suggests that political considerations were also at work. Matsuzaki was issued a pardon on February 10, 1951; Kuroda in late December 1951; and Kita on February 8, 1952. Matsuzaki's release came less than a month after several of the war criminals were executed in a single night, an execution that created a furor in Japan (see chapter 5). Kuroda's pardon, according to news reports, was timed to coincide with the Christmas season; Quirino was also quoted as saying that he had planned to free Kuroda sooner but had decided to wait until after the signing of the peace treaty. Both Kuroda and Kita met with Quirino around the time of the arrival of the first Japanese reparations delegation and the attendant publicity both in the Philippines and in Japan. It seems plausible that their release provided Quirino with a means to reinforce to the Japanese delegates, if they needed any reminders, that, magnanimity aside, he had quite a few more bargaining chips still confined in Muntinlupa. To drive the message home, the president had back-to-back meetings with Kuroda and the head of the Japanese delegation on the same morning.[30]

It is also likely not a coincidence that Matsuzaki, Kita, and Kuroda were all officers, and Matsuzaki and Kuroda were high-ranking ones at that. As officers, these men had opportunities to develop personal ties with members of the elite during the war, which gave them an advantage that lower-ranking soldiers did not have. On the occasion of Kuroda's departure, an *Asahi* reporter who had described the general as "oddly popular among Filipinos" suggested to a Filipino newsman that it would have been better if a subordinate instead of a general had been pardoned. After all, when a ship goes down it is the captain who is supposed to stay to the end. But he also noted that some of those remaining in Muntinlupa had been resigned to the unlikelihood of that eventuality.[31]

In addition to the three pardons cited above, Quirino also freed four other Japanese war criminals shortly after their death sentences had been commuted to life as part of the July 1953 general pardon (see chapter 5). All four men released at this time were officers (Capt. Koike Kaneyuke, Maj. Harada Shimpei, Lt. Tsubaki Takao, and Lt. Hamada Yoshio). Only one (Koike) was described as having any direct claim to Quirino's sympathies. Koike had testified during his trial that he had played some part in recommending the eventual release from Fort Santiago of Quirino as well as his brother Antonio. Japanese news accounts reinforced the link, reporting that Quirino had earlier confided to Kita Heiji that Koike had treated him kindly and quoting Koike himself as having saved Quirino from "stern punishment" (*genbatsu*).[32]

Postsentence review documents show that in Koike's case, a pardon had been seriously considered at least a year earlier. On March 3, 1952, some ten months after the chief of staff had approved Koike's death sentence and recommended presidential confirmation, Judge Advocate General Castro sent a rather extraordinary letter to the president. Castro not only forwarded Koike's clemency petition and numerous appeals from his family and friends but took pains to outline several instances of Koike's "acts of benevolence towards Filipinos" during the war and his exemplary behavior since incarcerated. Castro did not explicitly recommend that Quirino pardon Koike, but it was quite clear where his sympathies lay.[33]

Certainly, President Quirino intervened in a very small number of cases. To the extent that he granted pardons to those he knew personally or to whom he felt a particular degree of gratitude, it might be concluded that this represented no more than the classic Filipino sense of indebtedness. But Quirino was assumed by many to hold a deep and personal enmity toward the Japanese, owing to the fact that his wife, three of his children, and his mother-in-law had been killed by the Japanese forces during the last bloody fighting in Manila in early 1945. Indeed, one of the war criminals eventually released recalled long afterward that those in prison in Muntinlupa feared Quirino's election in 1949 precisely because they assumed he would, given the deaths of his family members, have no compunction about signing their death warrants.[34]

The First Executions: Public Fanfare

Elpidio Quirino, notwithstanding the few pardons he issued, was the only Philippine president to confirm the sentences of all those Japanese war criminals put to death in the Philippines who had been found guilty by Philippine military tribunals. The army chief of staff had approved the death sentence for Kudō Chūshirō (the first war criminal tried by a Philippine military commission) and forwarded that decision to Philippine president Manuel Roxas for confirmation in mid-April 1948. But final review by the Office of the President had not been completed at the time of Roxas's death on April 15. Quirino, his vice president, assumed the presidency and confirmed Kudō's death sentence on July 23, 1948, as well as all subsequent death sentences carried out. In 1950 the law officer in the Office of the President confirmed Quirino's unwillingness to delegate this responsibility to his vice president during his trips out of the country.[35]

Three men were put to death in 1948. The first was Kudō, who had been convicted of ordering the torture and killing of civilians in Laguna Province in February 1945. Kudō's trial began in August 1947, and his sentence was handed down on November 6 of that year. He was hanged nine months later, on August 13, 1948. Press coverage was extraordinary. The *Manila Bulletin* published a lengthy and vivid account, the result of a journalistic coup, of his execution. The night before the execution, a *Bulletin* reporter sneaked onto the grounds of the prison with two ex-guerrillas familiar with the facility and watched, hidden from sight, as Kudō went to his death. The reporter's eyewitness account had Kudō bowing toward the East and singing the Japanese anthem, "Kimigayo," before mounting the scaffold.[36]

The execution was discussed at some length by other papers in somewhat the same dramatic fashion. The *Evening Herald* noted the execution of the "former Jap terror" and his burial in a cemetery near the gallows. The *Manila Times* described the circumstances of Kudō's death under a "gray angry sky" and the resulting rain, which relieved "the tense feelings of a dozen people gathered in a desolate spot in Muntinlupa to witness the hanging." Kudō, "a mild-mannered little Jap," appeared resigned to his fate, although he was "pale and perceptibly trembling" as he approached the gallows and proclaimed his innocence. The *Times* then told its readers that Kudō sang the Japanese national anthem; shouted "Banzai Pirippin, banzai Nippon" (Long live the Philippines, long live Japan!); and bowed from the scaffold in the direction of the Imperial Palace in Tokyo before the trap door was sprung. The tone of the *Manila Chronicle* article was somewhat less lurid, but it described the death and subsequent burial on a "green knoll." One of Kudō's fellow prisoners later commented that the Philippine government had deliberately chosen the ill-omened Friday the thirteenth for the hanging as a way to make a public display of the first execution.[37] Another, noting the second anniversary of Kudō's death in a log kept by the prisoners, observed wistfully that "the stance of this man, who went calmly and coolly to his death insisting to the last that he was innocent, made a big impression on the authorities—might it not cause a halt to executions in future?"[38]

A lengthy article in the *Philippines Free Press* in early October 1948 reflected more deeply on the significance of Kudō's claim of innocence. The article noted that "exhaustive studies" of the case by the review board and the president and his advisors had been undertaken before Kudō's sentence had been confirmed. Nonetheless, Kudō, in numerous letters he had written to his family and to President Quirino, had maintained that he was innocent and had been made the scapegoat for another Japanese—whom he named—who was the real guilty party.

> In the light of these letters, the question inevitably comes up—are the statements of a man about to die to be taken at their face value? Does the fact that a man is about to face his creator—or his honorable ancestor—give his last statements a special validity? Incidentally, it might be said that in the case of a number of Japanese war criminals given the death verdict by U.S. Army military commissions in the past, the same vigorous declarations of innocence were uttered in those critical moments before they plunged to their doom. So the question remains—Will a dying Japanese lie?[39]

On November 9, 1948, two more men were hanged: Nakano Shizuo and Teramoto Tukuji (Tokuji). The two men, both army officers, had been found guilty in separate trials of ordering their men to torture and kill Filipino civilians. The Manila press again reported on the executions, although this time apparently none of the papers could offer an eyewitness account. The *Manila Times* provided full coverage, including a picture of Nakano, and noted that the "Beast of Cavite" (Nakano) and the "Terror of the Mountain Province" (Teramoto) were hanged within an hour of each other. According to the *Times*, the two men read the "Buddhist bible" in their last moments and met their deaths composedly. Nakano was reported to have thanked prison officials for their kindness, while Teramoto was said to have shaken hands with Philippine officers at the foot of the gallows. The *Evening News* offered a brief account under the headline "Two Japs Swing at Muntinlupa," while the *Manila Bulletin* and the *Manila Chronicle* also provided short summaries of the executions.[40]

By the end of 1949, Philippine military tribunals had sentenced seventy-nine men to death but had executed only three. Prior to Kudō's execution, American observers had approached the Philippine authorities to discuss the reasons for the "delay" in carrying out death sentences. The American embassy in Manila advised Washington on July 9, 1948, that twenty-seven Japanese had been sentenced to death by Philippine authorities but that none had as yet been executed, "although as much as eight months has elapsed since sentence was pronounced." Another fifty to sixty cases were still pending. Philippine secretary of justice Roman Ozaeta, when questioned, had stressed that delays were due to the Philippine government's painstaking care in reviewing sentences as well as the "pressure of other important state business."[41]

Execution Hiatus: Prison Life While Waiting in Suspense

Following the three executions in 1948, no further deaths occurred for over two years. During that period, those sentenced to death, as well as their comrades given lesser sentences, remained incarcerated in the Philippines. As part of the original agreement governing the transfer of responsibility for the trials to the Philippine government, the US military had agreed to retain custody of prisoners awaiting trial and to assume responsibility for those Japanese convicted and sentenced to life or lesser prison terms. It was envisioned that these men would be repatriated to Japan to serve out their terms in Sugamo Prison in Tokyo. Those receiving the death penalty were to be transferred to the custody of the Philippine government.[42]

It was not until mid-1948, however, that the Philippine government took the necessary steps to accept custody of Japanese war criminals sentenced to death. On May 27, 1948, the chief of the National War Crimes Office, Maj. Eleuterio Fojas, sent a formal request, through the secretary of justice, to President Quirino seeking authority for the transfer of the prisoners. It was "absolutely necessary" to take this step because "there are now more prisoners condemned to death than can be accommodated at the Prisoners of War stockade under the custody of the United States Army." The justice secretary approved the request on behalf of the president, and by June 1 some twenty inmates (including the three executed later that year) had been transferred to New Bilibid Prison.[43]

The transfer of the remaining Japanese prisoners into Philippine custody—both suspects and those sentenced to life or lesser terms—occurred by the end of 1948. Despite the initial arrangement that the US military would retain physical custody of these men, the Philippine government eventually decided to assume responsibility for them. The deciding factor may well have been reports of US consideration of an early peace treaty for Japan. Japanese independence might have led to the resumption of Japanese control over any war criminals incarcerated in Japan and their release, a prospect unwelcome to the Philippines.[44]

In any event, the Japanese prisoners were leery about any change in their status. A copy (unsigned) of a June 18, 1948, petition to MacArthur as Supreme Commander for the Allied Powers noted that the Japanese prisoners were "fortunate enough to remain under the humane treatment of the American government" at the time of the transfer of the trials to Philippine jurisdiction and requested that American custody be allowed to continue. The petitioners were careful to stipulate that they did not fear any deterioration in their treatment should they in fact be transferred to the custody of the Philippine government but for "psychological and sentimental" reasons wished to be held by the American forces to which they had initially surrendered. Their protestations notwithstanding, it seems likely that the Japanese did fear mistreatment at the hands of Filipinos.[45]

The prison chosen to house the Japanese war criminals, New Bilibid Prison, was located about eighteen miles south of Manila near the town of Muntinlupa. Visitors tended to describe it as an imposing white structure in the Spanish style, with the visual impact of a castle perched on a hill. The prison housed not just Japanese but also Filipino prisoners, although the two groups were generally kept separated. The two Filipinos most directly responsible for the oversight of the Japanese (as well as Filipino) prisoners were the director of prisons, Eustaquio Balagtas, and the New Bilibid prison superintendent, Alfredo Bunye, and both gained the respect and trust of the Japanese. Bunye seemed particularly sympathetic, appearing to go out of his way on various occasions to ease conditions for the prisoners.[46]

For the Japanese imprisoned in New Bilibid (often simply referred to as "Muntinlupa"), the period of their incarceration proved difficult but not draconian, to judge from various accounts of the prisoners themselves. It is possible to glean, from these accounts as well as press reports and comments from other observers, some details about their lives in prison. Those sentenced to death were housed on the ground floor of one of the prison buildings in cells accommodating three men each. They wore blue uniforms to distinguish them from the other Japanese, who wore red (although by 1952 two recently released prisoners reported that some had taken to wearing old US army khaki shirts without objection from the prison authorities). The condemned were not assigned work but were allowed to walk around for an hour in the morning and afternoon. To pass the time, some engaged in studying English or Spanish, while others wrote and shared poetry. On rare occasions the men put together entertainments of singing or theatrics.[47]

The men sentenced to life and lesser terms and those awaiting trial lived communally in a large room in another building of the prison (they were later transferred to the same two-story building, or "brigade," that housed the condemned prisoners). They were assigned various tasks during the day, including kitchen duty and the tending of a garden devoted to the growing of Japanese and other vegetables. This was not hard labor—prisoners described the work as not particularly arduous, and some made a point of contrasting their circumstances favorably with what they had heard of the lives of Japanese prisoners incarcerated on Manus Island by the Australian government. After returning home, Kuroda Shigenori commented that the treatment of prisoners was "surprisingly lenient" (*odoroku hodo kandai*). By early 1952 a Japanese news correspondent who visited the prison and met directly with the prisoners reported that they seemed clean and healthy. Their faces and their stories revealed how desperate they were to return home, but they did not complain of their treatment.[48]

Nonetheless, there are some references to incidents and problems, particularly during the first years after the transfer to Philippine custody. These included hints of discord among the Japanese inmates themselves. A June 1949 report by the Japanese Foreign Ministry, commenting on the difficulties in persuading Japanese translators to stay in the Philippines, observed that some of the Japanese in prison in the Philippines were likely "hoodlums" (*buraikan*) or yakuza, Japanese gangsters, which would explain incidents of violence that had been reported. (In fact, one prisoner later admitted to a reporter that he had been a yakuza before the war.) Testimony at the trials constituted another source of tension. In his diary, Mineo Shisuhiko recounted his hatred toward Ichinose Haruo because Ichinose had broken his promise and given damaging testimony at their trial (both men had been sentenced to death; Mineo later reconciled with Ichinose).[49]

Other problems centered on the interactions, however circumscribed, between the Japanese and the larger Filipino prison community. A May 1949 report by Japanese Foreign Ministry officials observed that the treatment given the prisoners had declined from what they had received under American custody, and there had also been incidents of assaults owing to anti-Japanese feeling among lower-level prison officials and Filipino prisoners.[50]

One particular incident in late May 1950 highlighted the Japanese inmates' sense of vulnerability. Several Filipino prisoners staged an escape attempt, in the process seizing weapons from the prison armory. Although the armed outbreak was successfully contained after a few hours, two guards and all the Filipino escapees died. In the wake of this incident, some of the Japanese prisoners crafted a petition to the director of prisons highlighting their concerns. The petition noted the vulnerability of the Japanese inmates should another incident occur and asked for consideration of the transfer of the prisoners back to Japan to serve out their sentences. Prison authorities tightened up security procedures but did not accede to the transfer request.[51]

The prisoners had other complaints. Food seems to have been a source of particular concern. In mid-1951 the Buddhist chaplain described the meals provided to the condemned prisoners as tasteless and unpalatable, improved only by the addition of powdered miso (soybean paste) and shoyu (soy sauce) sent from Japan. The rice contained sand, and the bread had a tendency to make the men sick. One of the prisoners echoed these complaints about the food and added that the soup provided as a food supplement smelled and was undrinkable; the prisoners' health worsened in consequence.[52]

Such complaints even created a bit of a diplomatic flare-up in 1952. Two war criminals whose sentences had been overturned, Kobayashi Yusaku and Nakamura Fumio, on their return to Japan were quoted in the local press as having been "starved" while in New Bilibid prison.[53] The Philippine government (as reported in the *Manila Times*) reacted quickly to the criticism, producing affidavits from high-level prisoners like Lieutenant General Kuroda and Lieutenant General Yokoyama that the prisoners were well treated and certainly not starving. The Japanese Foreign Ministry, alarmed that the reports might have an adverse effect on efforts to obtain the release of other prisoners, issued an aide-mémoire to the Philippine government stating that an investigation had shown that the returnees had made no such comments—the newspapermen had operated on a "misunderstanding." An internal memo provided a more nuanced account: the two men acknowledged in interviews with Foreign Ministry officials that the news accounts had been exaggerated but maintained that the diet for prisoners, although better, could still stand some improvement. Nonetheless, they admitted that, overall, the treatment of the prisoners was good.[54]

US military officials in Tokyo, having received information from Japanese sources quite soon after the transfer that the prisoners were not being properly cared for, asked SCAP Legal Section Manila Branch staff to investigate. On March 1, 1949, the office's executive officer reported back that he had spent considerable time talking with both condemned and term prisoners, who acknowledged they had no major complaints. They appeared neatly dressed and in good physical condition. Nonetheless, they raised concerns about the lack of cigarettes and toothbrushes, sand in their rice, and the hardness of their wooden bunks. Nakamura Kazunori, a Japanese lawyer posted to the Philippines as legal liaison in early 1949 after the return to Japan of the other lawyers, wrote to SCAP Legal Section Tokyo on March 27, 1949, that he had seen the Japanese prisoners, who "were living a comparatively free life under the sympathetic and warm-hearted treatment given by the constituted authorities of the Philippines." Nevertheless, Nakamura urged that more attention be given to providing "comfort goods" such as cigarettes, soy sauce, and tea, as well as reading materials and even a phonograph.[55]

An International Red Cross inspection conducted in August 1949 tended to corroborate the generally favorable reports of Philippine government treatment of Japanese prisoners. The Red Cross representative reported that the prison's housing was good and that hygiene conditions were generally satisfactory. The food was good, and the prisoners' state of health was also good, although medical services did not seem adequate. A majority of the prisoners worked in the machine shop or were employed in carpentry, gardening, or cooking. They had access to a small library, were allowed an hour of outdoor recreation (some playing baseball, others tennis), and saw movies from time to time. The two concerns the investigator raised were the failure to provide the men with an allowance to make small purchases like cigarettes and the lack of artificial teeth for a few men.[56] Overall, the report concluded that "living conditions are good and POW's morale is high and satisfactory."[57]

Another observer, a member of the Ellinwood Church in Manila who conducted a weekly Bible class for Japanese Christian converts at the prison, provided a sketch of the prisoners' lives in 1951. The condemned prisoners, three to a cell, are allotted a bamboo mat, blanket, two blue uniforms, and a cup, bowl, and spoon. Each week they receive a bar of soap and each month a ration of seventy cigarettes; they are permitted to write a letter once a week. The doors to their cells remain open for much of the day, allowing the men to mingle, play games like mahjong, and study languages or mathematics. They are assigned no work except for cleaning the cells. In comparison, the prisoners given life or term sentences live together in a communal room, receive no cigarettes at all, and may write a letter every two weeks. They are assigned to various tasks such as cooking, laundry, or gardening and are able to walk freely within the confines of the prison.[58]

One of the condemned men recounted a typical day spent in captivity. With the sound of the wake-up bugle, he hears the increasing clamor of inmate footsteps and the calls of the guards. A Japanese term/life prisoner delivers the condemned man's breakfast bread, and around 6:00 a.m. he begins to read and meditate. With the changing of the guard at 8:00 a.m., he and the others line up for their walk outside, where they talk together and play sports. On returning, he bathes, then reads a medical book until lunchtime. Then a siesta, more reading, and dinner with his comrades around 5:30 p.m., followed by talking and singing. At 7:00 p.m. it is time to meditate, write in his diary, or read the Bible. By 9:00 p.m. the prison is immersed in deep silence. "I finish my prayers at 10:00 p.m., and then I go to sleep, holding in my heart the desire that, when the morning of eternity comes, I will rise up and be blessed."[59]

The war criminals were able to attend religious services of their choosing. Spiritually, the men were ministered to by both a Buddhist monk and Christian ministers. A Protestant pastor, Dr. Andrew Nelson, conducted weekly services and led a Bible study group; he spoke fluent Japanese, having served for several years as a missionary in Japan before the war.[60] A Catholic nun of the Franciscan Missionaries of Mary visited the prisoners each Saturday for several years, bringing them candy and books and offering religious instruction to those who wished it. One Christian convert recounted that in October 1949 he and sixteen other Japanese were baptized in a special ceremony; a missionary estimated that over 50 percent of the Japanese inmates attended Christian services of one form or another.[61]

The Buddhist chaplain who arrived in November 1949, Kagao Shūnin, was particularly beloved. Kagao, a member of the Kōyasan Tokyo branch temple of the Shingon sect, had been sent as a replacement for a monk who had arrived only months earlier but had become ill. Kagao had wrestled with the decision to volunteer to minister to the men in Muntinlupa, fearful of the anti-Japanese atmosphere in the Philippines and his unfamiliarity with the language and situation there, but ultimately he concluded that he had a duty to go. Kagao lived in the prison (in a small room of his own) and shared the prisoners' food and living conditions. He conducted weekly teachings and often talked with prisoners who gathered in his room. He had been scheduled to leave the Philippines with the closure of the National War Crimes Office in March 1950, but appeals from the Japanese prisoners and the support of prison officials led to the indefinite extension of his stay, despite the fact that he had developed a heart condition.[62]

Waiting Over: A Mass Execution

On the night of January 19, 1951, the uneasy wait for fourteen Japanese condemned war criminals ended abruptly and with no advance warning. As Chaplain Kagao headed to meet the prison superintendent for dinner, Nakamura Hideichi and twelve others of the "Nakamura case," as well as Mihara Kikuichi, were summoned from their cells. Kagao, not finding Superintendent Bunye where he expected, wandered outside and was vaguely surprised to see military jeeps and a soldier waiting there. It was only when he returned to Bunye's office and was asked by Dr. Nelson, the Protestant pastor, "How many are yours?" that he realized what was going on. Eight Buddhists and six Christians were to be executed that night.[63]

Kagao and Nelson followed the Japanese war criminals to a holding room outside the prison not too distant from the actual site of the gallows. There, Director of Prisons Balagtas read the official orders of execution signed by President Quirino; the men were given time to write their wills and then an additional hour to receive spiritual comfort. Some maintained their innocence;

some talked of their families or their comrades and directed the allocation of their belongings. Kagao offered a final teaching and prayers. Superintendent Bunye urged Kagao, because of his heart condition, not to view the executions, but one of the Japanese begged him to go, asking him to view their dead faces, and so Kagao sought and gained permission to witness the deaths. He went with each man as he was summoned, and while riding in the jeep to the gallows he offered what comfort he could. Kagao later recounted that all the men were calm and composed to the end. Mihara, the first to be summoned, called out, "Tennō heika banzai" (Long live His Majesty the emperor). By the time the last man had been executed, it was past 3:00 a.m. on the morning of January 20. The bodies were wrapped in white blankets and taken to a separate section of the prison cemetery to be buried. Kagao returned to the prison and, in his room, broke down in tears.[64]

Shock and dismay reverberated among the remainder of the convicted Japanese prisoners. Some of the men (those sentenced to life or lesser terms) had gathered and waited outside Kagao's door to learn what had happened. The next morning, at the insistent summons of those who waited in the condemned cell block, he went to the cells and held a meeting to describe the events of the preceding night.[65]

Later, Kagao and others commented on how unexpected the executions had been. According to the chaplain, there had been no intimation that executions were imminent. In fact, he noted that influential Filipinos had hinted to him, albeit informally, that sentence commutations were in the offing. When he asked about repatriation, he was told it would be "very soon." Even the growing predictions of a possible peace treaty were read at the time as a welcome sign. These sorts of signals, coupled with the lapse of time since the 1948 executions, appear to have lessened the anxiety among those sentenced to death and allowed them to settle into a routine of prison life while awaiting their hoped-for return to Japan. Another observer commented that they had been lulled by the belief that the Philippines, a Christian nation, was loath to sanction executions.[66]

In letters home, others echoed the lack of any advance warning. Hamada Yoshio, in a letter to his wife dated January 27, 1951, described the early evening of January 19 in some detail. He told of how, after dinner, he had heard that the men of the Nakamura case were to be summoned to a meeting with the prison superintendent, and he and other cellmates speculated that their sentences were to be commuted. When none of the men had returned by morning they feared the worst. Still, it seemed that at least a few of the fourteen had been suspicious—one told his cellmates about the disposition of his things, while another returned quickly to put on new geta, or wooden clogs.[67]

Kagao also wrote of the profound effect the executions had on those still awaiting their own deaths. They wrote their wills and each evening washed and clothed themselves in spare clean clothes in anticipation of the feared summons. The English and Spanish language classes stopped; the men had no heart to write in their diaries. Kagao redoubled his efforts to find foods or other items that would bring them comfort.[68] Nakajima Shōhei, a young student conscript sentenced to death, wrote of his despair at the executions and how his pen shook in his hand as he wrote his will to send to his mother.[69]

Why Then, and Why So Many?

Two central questions surrounding these executions have to do with the numbers executed and the timing of the deaths. What seems reasonably clear from the available documentation of the trials and sentence reviews is that Mihara Kikuichi and the thirteen men of the Nakamura case were, with slight exceptions, the next in line, thus accounting for the large number executed at the same time. The first three men executed, in 1948, were Kudō Chūshirō, Nakano Shizuo, and Teramoto Tukuji (Tokuji), among the earliest sentenced to death. The next to receive the death penalty were Takahashi Sadakichi (sentenced November 10, 1947), Itō Masayasu (January 21, 1948), Ogawa Eitarō (February 10, 1948), Saitō Takao (April 27, 1948), and then Mihara (May 22, 1948) and the Nakamura defendants (May 27, 1948). The sentences of both Takahashi and Saitō were commuted to life in prison. By a strict adherence to the sentencing dates, Itō and Ogawa should have been executed before the fourteen who died on January 19 and 20, 1951. It is possible, therefore, that a deliberate decision was made to execute a large group rather than the two or three (Itō, Ogawa, and Mihara) precisely next in line. More plausible, however, is the likelihood that the timing of the reviews for Itō and Ogawa was simply slower. The unavailability of complete records of the sentence reviews in the Itō, Ogawa, and Nakamura cases makes a conclusive determination impossible.[70]

Why the men were executed in 1951 is even more difficult to determine with certainty. In the single volume of his published memoirs, Quirino made no mention of the executions, let alone why he might have sanctioned them or whether he was simply acting on the recommendations of the board of review, the army chief of staff, and the secretary of justice.[71] And others who might have been aware of the circumstances—for example, Secretary of Justice Jose Bengzon, Director of Prisons Eustaquio Balagtas, or Prison Superintendent Alfredo Bunye—apparently left no published accounts. What, then, might explain the timing of these executions, over two years after the initial three Japanese were put to death?

Perhaps there is no deeper significance to the timing of the executions. Quite possibly, the review machinery had slowed so significantly that it was only in early 1951 that the reviews for the next in line were completed, thus allowing for executions for the first time since November 1948. If true, the documentation that is available indicates that the slowdown at that time occurred within the Department of Justice or the Office of the President, not the army. In the cases of Itō Masayasu and Ogawa Eitarō, for example, the army chief of staff made his decision only a few months after their sentencing; the evidence shows that in the latter case, the matter had been referred to the Office of the President by no later than December 1948.[72] If pressing matters intervened to delay final action by the president on this and other cases for some two years, at a minimum it suggests that execution of the Japanese war criminals was not a high priority.

The delay does suggest that it was not personal animosity on the part of President Quirino that drove the decision to resume executions in 1951. A desire for revenge would hardly have been surprising, given the deaths of his wife and three of his children during the deadly fighting in Manila in early 1945. But Quirino himself, in statements as early as 1948, discounted his own personal feelings when addressing the need for the Philippines to reengage with Japan.[73] Even more telling, if Quirino had been intent on avenging his family, why wait over two years to execute those waiting on death row?

Perhaps Quirino's decision to authorize the execution of fourteen men in a single night was animated not so much by personal animosity as by the politically felt need to respond to public opinion—a sop to the angry mob, as it were. (Indeed, a Japanese businessman had suggested as much back in 1949, when, on the basis of a conversation with the president, he quoted Quirino as feeling forced by the pressures of public opinion to carry out a certain number of executions.[74]) But if this was Quirino's motivation in 1951, it is curious that no effort was made to announce the executions or take public credit for them, let alone fan public indignation over war crimes. Indeed, the secrecy surrounding the latest executions was striking, especially compared with the publicity surrounding all three 1948 executions. Various Manila newspapers—the *Manila Times*, the *Manila Bulletin*, and the *Manila Chronicle*—had made no mention of the executions by early February, and only later did one of them make a passing reference in the context of reports coming out of Japan. An American missionary in Manila commented at the time that the executions were "top secret," with nothing in the newspapers and no information being circulated either in the Philippines or abroad.[75]

If something was going on besides mere bureaucratic process or payback for perceived grudges, what could it have been? Is it possible that the Quirino administration was under some political pressure, domestic or external, to resume executions? If so, it is not credible that the pressure was coming from the Americans. US officials might have been impatient to hurry executions along back in 1948, but three years later the US government was hoping to persuade the Philippines to accept the terms of the draft peace treaty with Japan, including a reparations clause that angered the Philippine government. It is hardly likely that at this juncture US officials would have encouraged a step—more executions—that would have further complicated relations between Japan and the Philippines. Nor does it appear that the Philippines gave any advance warning to the Americans that executions were imminent. After receiving word of the executions, Richard Ely, deputy director of the State Department's Office of Philippine and Southeast Asian Affairs, expressed surprise that the deaths could have been kept so secret. Moreover, Ely rejected any notion of future US government intervention in the fate of the remaining war criminals, and it does not appear that Ambassador John Foster Dulles raised the issue at all in his early February 1951 meeting with Quirino.[76]

But the timing of the executions—late January 1951—does suggest the possibility that the Philippine government may have wanted to send a signal to either the United States or Japan that its views on the peace treaty should be taken seriously. In discussions on a draft treaty during the latter half of 1950, the US government continued to urge members of the Far Eastern Commission to agree to release Japan from any obligation to pay reparations to countries like the Philippines that had suffered from Japanese occupation. The Philippines strongly resisted the idea of relinquishing claims to reparations, and Philippine officials at this time spoke out passionately about the damage done to the Philippines and the need for Japan to provide adequate compensation. Afterward, Kagao himself speculated that anger over the draft treaty had fueled the decision to execute the men—that its terms had incited not just the people but especially the government.[77]

Finally, it is possible that Quirino felt some domestic pressure, but from members of the Filipino elite rather than the general public. Evidence exists that influential Filipinos sought to intervene in the sentence review process and later in the general pardon decision, so it is not unlikely that pressure might have been exerted in the other direction to implement delayed executions.

While some of the elite eventually looked forward to and encouraged resolution of the issue of the war criminals, others might not have been so forgiving.

The increasingly lengthy sentence review process for Japanese found guilty of war crimes occurred within a broader political and economic context. On the one hand, the huge tasks of rebuilding a war-torn country and grappling with an increasingly dangerous domestic insurgency understandably took precedence. What could otherwise appear as a reluctance to execute most of the Japanese waiting on death row might then have resulted from an understandable preoccupation with other priorities as well as an attention to the niceties of judicial process. In the interim, the war criminals remained, along with their comrades given lesser sentences, incarcerated in a Philippine prison. Philippine sensibilities required that the prisoners receive comparatively humane treatment as well as the benefit of a painstaking postsentence review process.

On the other hand, by 1950 members of the elite and ordinary Filipinos alike had united in opposition to the notion that Japan might not be held accountable for wartime damage. Growing resentment over the failure to win full support for the Philippine government's reparations demands might have been enough to outweigh any reservations, if they existed, about completing sentence reviews or resuming executions. The decision to execute fourteen men could simply have been the culmination of a bureaucratic process that prevailed in the absence of any incentives to halt it. Whether President Quirino signed the men's death warrants as a result of active pressure, the power of his own convictions, or the passive outcome of a commitment to judicial process, the result was the same: a mass execution that echoed powerfully in Japan whether he intended it to or not. The irony is that, had the Philippines placed more emphasis on a speedy process, and (as the Americans did) executed most of the convicted within months of their sentencing, the outcry in Japan would have been less sustained, and, conceivably, far fewer Japanese would have been roused to complain of perceived Philippine injustice.

The January executions validated and reinforced two competing and diverging views of the meaning of the trials and their outcomes. For Filipinos, the careful review process that preceded the deaths was consistent with the Philippines' continued commitment to due process and the rule of law. And the care of the convicted in Muntinlupa was also evidence of the Philippines' adherence to standards of humane incarceration. For Japanese, the inescapable conclusion was that Filipinos privileged process over fair outcomes—and had, indeed, embraced outright miscarriages of justice. That the review process did result in changed outcomes for some could not mitigate the outcome for the Nakamura defendants—and perhaps even reinforced the notion that the military commissions were capable of prejudiced judgments.

The fact remains, the postsentence review process represented a serious and conscientious effort by the Philippine government to ensure that the justice system lived up to its responsibilities to weigh the evidence impartially and fairly. The review panel's failure, if such it was, to exonerate certain of the Nakamura defendants does not change the fact that it served as an important corrective mechanism in other cases.

5

From Retribution to Resolution

The Journey from Executions to Pardons

Philippine trials of Japanese war crimes suspects had ended by the close of 1949. Of the 138 men convicted of one or more of the charges against them, more than three-quarters were sentenced to death or to life in prison (79 received death sentences). Yet a mere four years later, all but seventeen had been repatriated and released. The contrast with American notions of justice for crimes committed in the Philippines is striking: of the more than ninety Japanese sentenced to death by US tribunals, sixty-nine were executed.[1] Others found guilty by the Americans and sentenced to lesser penalties remained incarcerated for longer periods in Tokyo's Sugamo Prison, with the last few only regaining their freedom in 1957 or 1958.[2]

The path to the pardon and release of the war criminals proved a delicate one as Filipino and Japanese officials sought to balance domestic economic and political realities. The process was helped along by the interventions of private citizens in both countries. In the end, the Philippines made a pragmatic choice to eliminate a roadblock to the renewal of bilateral ties, apparently without any concrete assurances of Japanese reciprocity in the continuing reparations negotiations.

Immediate Aftermath: Initial Responses to the 1951 Executions

Word of the execution of fourteen Japanese on January 19–20, 1951, reached the Japanese public in early February, when brief news accounts noted the deaths and provided the names of those executed. The news itself appears to have arrived first in a letter from Buddhist chaplain Kagao Shūnin, in which he related the circumstances and described the executions. Kagao had been cautioned by Philippine prison authorities not to discuss the executions, but he chose to ignore the warning in the interests of informing the Japanese government and the families of the dead.[3]

The bereaved families were no less shocked than the chaplain and the inmates in Muntinlupa that executions had been carried out after a delay of more than two years. Word had filtered back to family members that repatriation of those held in the Philippines was an increasing possibility; certainly, there had been no counterindications of possible executions. Kagao himself acknowledged that he had unintentionally misled the families in his letters home—the clouds had gathered unseen. Immediately after word of the deaths reached them, representatives of the families approached Philippine government officials in Tokyo with a petition for President Quirino to halt further executions.[4]

Their fears apparently were well founded. In mid-February Kagao learned from a Filipino inmate at the prison (a former collaborator) that more graves had already been dug. Some ten excavations awaited the remains of the next to die, with executions to begin again in the very near future. Kagao reacted immediately, sending a telegram back to Japan to alert the authorities and asking for petitions and appeals to be sent to the Philippine government. A second report of several more graves, coming on the heels of the first, caused Kagao to renew his appeals for help to forestall any more deaths and resulted in a second flurry of messages and requests to halt further executions. Meanwhile, those in Muntinlupa who knew about the freshly dug graves (the chaplain and a few of the term/life prisoners) hoped to keep the news secret from those awaiting execution.[5]

The remainder of 1951 saw an increase in Japan of informal efforts to persuade the Philippine government to abandon any thought of further executions and to consider repatriating the remaining war criminals. The mass execution proved to be a turning point—it galvanized public sentiment in a population that had been seen as indifferent to the fate of the "forgotten" Japanese in Muntinlupa. This was the beginning of mass petition drives; eventually, appeals signed by millions were directed to the Japanese and Philippine governments. As early as February 6, 1951, a Manila newspaper reported that clemency petitions continued to pour into Malacañan (the presidential palace), not just from Japanese but also from Americans and Filipinos.[6]

Various news accounts suggested that the appeals were having an effect. In February, in the wake of the first outcries in Japan over the reported executions and the arrival of the first petitions, Malacañan spokesmen emphasized President Quirino's intention to review personally the documents related to each case and his plan to give "due consideration" to petitions for sentence commutations. The president had been receiving and would continue to receive recommendations from the secretary of justice. A second positive signal came with the presidential pardon of Matsuzaki Hideichi the same month.[7] (Nonetheless, the press release announcing Matsuzaki's pardon made clear that this was not a harbinger of any blanket pardons for all.[8])

Japanese Government Efforts: Progress and Setbacks

Japanese government efforts to aid the war criminals and work for their eventual release were generally characterized by cautious determination and a reliance on indirect or informal approaches during the occupation years. Illustrative of these efforts were approaches the Japanese Foreign Ministry made to various individuals with ties to the Philippines. A Foreign Ministry representative met with businessman Imamura Eikichi in 1949; Imamura, who had lived in the Philippines for thirty years before the war and was acquainted with President Quirino and other influential Filipinos, was viewed as a useful contact for future dealings with the Philippines. Likewise, officials also approached Murata Shōzō, former ambassador to the Philippines, asking him to form a group to work for the improvement of Philippines-Japan relations. He agreed to do so, although it was not until 1951 that the Firippin Yū no Kai (Friends of the Philippines Society) was formally inaugurated with Murata as president and Imamura as director.[9]

After Japan regained its independence in April 1952, efforts to gain the release of the war criminals—or at least commutation of their sentences—intensified and employed official as well as less formal means. The two countries had not yet reestablished formal diplomatic relations, so official government-to-government contacts were facilitated through offices maintained in each country that served in lieu of embassies. In Japan the Philippines had already set up, during the US occupation, a diplomatic mission accredited to SCAP, and it was this office that assumed the liaison function after April 1952. Japan in turn had established an office in Manila by October 1952 in accordance with an agreement reached with Philippine government officials in September. Japan's office was to have the same diplomatic status and privileges as the Philippine government's mission in Tokyo.[10]

The Japanese government used these official channels to submit periodic appeals to the Philippine government seeking the return of the war criminals. The first, presented just prior to independence, asked for repatriation of the prisoners on humanitarian grounds, noting the many appeals from their families and promising to pay the expenses of their return. A second communication, in

November 1952, again sought clemency and repatriation of war crimes prisoners in the Philippines, reiterating an appeal made verbally in August to members of the Philippine mission in Japan.[11] The government also continued to seek out other intermediaries; aware of the power of appeals to Christian sensibilities, overtures for help were made to the Vatican and representatives of the pope.[12]

But the Japanese government remained highly sensitive to the potential for a backlash from Filipinos if it was perceived as pushing too openly for the release of the war criminals. Thus the head of the Japanese mission in Manila stressed that Japan's official role in obtaining Philippine permission to send food and other "comfort" items to the prisoners should be kept quiet. Likewise, a Foreign Ministry official cautioned against any signals that petition drives in support of prisoner releases were being directed by the government; such petitions should be sent directly to the Philippines rather than through official channels.[13]

The flurry of correspondence and contacts between Japanese and Philippine officials between 1952 and the first half of 1953 clearly indicates the urgency that the Japanese government attached to the return of the war criminals. This is hardly surprising, given the increasing domestic pressure to get the men home. The Philippine position, at least as conveyed through the Japanese diplomatic correspondence, appears more ambivalent; whether that was due to a real reluctance to agree to the release of the war criminals or represented a negotiating posture is hard to say.

In any event, the Japanese government interpreted the signals it received in early 1952 as positive—in private conversations, various Filipinos offered assurances that executions had been halted. One Japanese emissary recounted that he had heard from President Quirino himself that executions had been postponed pending further review. Quirino reportedly added that more prisoners might be pardoned in future, notwithstanding their "grave crimes," and that he hoped to return the war criminals to Japan "as soon as possible."[14]

By mid-1952 Japanese government representatives were making cautiously optimistic statements in public. In May Foreign Minister Okazaki Katsuo was able to state that he believed the war criminals in the Philippines would be spared their lives, although he later observed that the Philippine government (as well as the Australian government) might continue to detain the war criminals out of consideration for public sentiment and domestic politics. In June the deputy foreign minister told a Diet committee that he believed no more death sentences would be carried out; a subsequent ministry clarification confirmed that although the government had received no promises, there had been various indications that President Quirino would not impose the sentences. In July a Diet member visiting the Philippines said that Quirino had told her he was not contemplating taking the lives of the condemned, although their return home was far from imminent. Finally, in December 1952 Wajima Eiji, chief of the Foreign Ministry Asian Affairs Bureau, visiting Manila on the occasion of the funeral of Ambassador Jose Melencio (who had served as chief of the Philippine mission in Tokyo), was told by Joaquin Elizalde, Philippine secretary of foreign affairs, that it was possible that all but a very few could be repatriated even before ratification of the peace treaty.[15]

Subsequent leaks to the press in Japan on the possibility that the Philippines would agree to repatriation alarmed Japanese mission chief Nakagawa Toru, given the sensitivity of the whole issue: "It is true that the attitude of the Philippine government on this matter continues to improve. But the hostility toward Japan among the general population remains quite strong, and it is not impossible that, depending on circumstances, the opposition party would use the war criminals matter as a political issue."[16] Accordingly, Nakagawa urged the Foreign Ministry to take steps to avoid any further publicity that might be reported in the Philippines, given the Philippine government's expectation that the whole matter would be handled with particular care. Still, Nakagawa argued for renewed confidential approaches to Elizalde to ensure the return of all, not just most of, the war criminals. With Foreign Ministry concurrence, Nakagawa subsequently met with Elizalde twice in January 1953.[17]

Those conversations indicated that the Philippines was still not ready to accede to the Japanese government's pleas to return all the war criminals in Philippine custody but was contemplating the release of the majority. At one point, Elizalde, while assuring Nakagawa that he wanted to help, stated that some "political problems" (*seijiteki mondai*) had delayed the timing of any release. When asked directly, he also stated that even with a general release, some five to eight men might be left behind. Nakagawa surmised that it could have been the intervention of influential Filipinos that "complicated" the return of these few.[18]

The remaining months until the June general pardon announcement continued to follow a pattern: reports by Nakagawa of evidence of progress coupled with anxieties about the potential for failure. Thus in February Nakagawa suggested the advantages that might obtain from a personal message from Japanese leaders to President Quirino, but in March he delayed delivery of the resulting message from Prime Minister Yoshida Shigeru to Quirino in order to avoid giving the appearance of pressuring the president. June produced more disquieting news: Nakagawa reported learning from Elizalde that Quirino might release only a few men rather than the great majority, as hoped. Contrary to the president's expectations, ratification of the peace treaty had been postponed again, and that news, coupled with the political risks of granting amnesty in an election year, had resulted in a more cautious stance. Still, the Japanese mission in the Philippines and the Foreign Ministry continued to press for the release of more men, and in mid-June the Foreign Ministry expressed the hope, based in part on confidential information from the Philippine mission in Tokyo, that the great majority, if not all, would be freed.[19]

Reparations Negotiations: A Complicating Factor

The Japanese government's delicate diplomacy on behalf of the war criminals took place amid the ongoing, if intermittent, negotiations between the governments of Japan and the Philippines on the amount and kind of reparations Japan should pay for war damage. Reparations, far more than the fate of the war criminals, loomed large in the public discourse between the two countries in the years immediately prior to and after the signing of the peace treaty in San Francisco in September 1951.

The United States had begun as early as 1947 to consider the terms of a treaty with Japan. With growing concerns over the threat posed by the Soviet Union (and faced with the fall of China to the communists in 1949), policymakers increasingly embraced the need to strengthen Japan economically and politically to more firmly ally it with the United States. The resulting advocacy of a nonpunitive peace alarmed Philippine officials, who were particularly exercised over the Americans' push for the Allies to waive reparations from Japan as part of the peace terms. Largely as a result of the strong resistance of the Philippine government, the final treaty did incorporate language on reparations, albeit not nearly as strong as that government would have liked.[20]

Article 14 of the treaty acknowledged that Japan should pay reparations but further recognized that Japan's resources were not then sufficient to pay full compensation while sustaining a viable economy. "Therefore, Japan will promptly enter into negotiations with Allied Powers so desiring, whose present territories were occupied by Japanese forces and damaged by Japan, with a view to assisting to compensate those countries for the cost of repairing the damage done, by making available the services of the Japanese people in production, salvaging and other work for the Allied Powers in question."[21]

The Philippines did so desire. In accordance with the terms of Article 14, Japanese representatives met with their Philippine counterparts in Manila in early 1952 to discuss reparations, even before the Philippine Senate took up ratification of the treaty itself. At that time, Philippine negotiators articulated the Philippines' demands: Japan should recognize the Philippines' claim of $8 billion; the Japanese government should settle this claim within ten to fifteen years; and the Japanese government should pay interim reparations even before the conclusion of a reparations agreement or the Philippines' ratification of the peace treaty. In response, the Japanese delegation noted Japan's moral obligation to pay reparations but maintained that the sum demanded was far beyond the ability of Japan to pay; that no commitment on an amount could be made before considering other claimants; and finally that Japan was under no legal obligation to pay reparations until the Philippines had ratified the peace treaty. The Japanese delegation left for home without making any commitment on reparations.[22]

Later that year, the Philippine Senate refused to ratify the treaty, largely out of dissatisfaction with Article 14. The Quirino administration continued to push for treaty ratification; Under Secretary of Foreign Affairs Felino Neri argued in October that failure to act would not result, as some argued, in a better deal on reparations. But the opposition Nacionalista Party, bolstered by Senate gains in the 1951 elections, was able to block ratification.[23]

By December, shortly before resumption of discussions with Wajima, Elizalde expressed the hope that members of the opposition had become more amenable to compromise. Nonetheless, the Philippines and Japan continued to disagree on the amount and kind of reparations Japan should provide. The Philippines embraced a more liberal interpretation of reparations that envisioned cash and in-kind payments; Japan insisted on a strict interpretation of Article 14 that meant Japan should provide only services within its capacity to pay. As a consequence, the reparations negotiations remained at an impasse (except for an interim agreement on vessel salvage concluded in March 1953) throughout the period that the Japanese government was seeking return of the war criminals.[24]

Acknowledgment of any concrete linkage between payment of reparations and repatriation of the war criminals was a delicate business. Neither side wanted to officially embrace such a crude formulation. However, these two issues remained the single most compelling outstanding problems between the two countries. It was impossible to ignore the fact that each side had something the other wanted: the Philippines the maximum in reparations, and Japan the return of the men imprisoned in Muntinlupa. As a consequence, Japanese observers remained wary that the Philippines would see the war criminals as bargaining chips and would seek to use them as leverage to gain greater concessions. At a minimum, public pressure in the Philippines to force Japan to pay a suitably large amount of reparations was seen as an impediment to the release of the men in Muntinlupa.

In 1952 an *Asahi Shimbun* reporter summarized popular Filipino beliefs about this linkage based on what he had learned from talking with Filipinos of various occupations—politicians, teachers, lawyers, and newspapermen. The consensus that emerged, he reported, was that while there would likely be no more executions, it would be a "minus" for the government to make such a promise officially. These Filipinos believed that "the fate [of the war criminals] hangs on whether or not the Philippines ratifies the peace treaty with Japan. And whether the Philippines ratifies the peace treaty hangs on whether Japan will pay reparations sufficient to satisfy Filipinos or whether Japan shows some sort of sincerity [*sei-i*]. If Japan doesn't show sincerity, ratification will be protracted, and if feelings toward Japan grow increasingly worse, it is impossible to predict what will occur."[25]

The reporter concluded that even though the Philippines could not survive economically without Japan, the US government wanted the Philippines to quickly ratify the treaty, and the Quirino administration was pushing for ratification, these incentives might not outweigh the increasing popular animosity toward Japan that was at the root of the demand for an enormous sum in reparations: "Japan cannot agree to pay that amount of reparations. And so the Philippines will not ratify the treaty. So long as they do not ratify the treaty, the war criminals cannot return home."[26] The US political adviser in Tokyo also remarked on the speculation that the two issues were linked in a September 1951 cable to Washington recommending that some efforts be taken to influence the Philippine government not to execute any more of the war criminals: "It is believed that the silence of the Philippine government with respect to its intentions may have as its reason a desire to keep the ultimate fate of the war criminals as a latent bargaining point in future negotiations with Japan on reparations or other peace settlement issues."[27]

Still, the issue of an explicit quid pro quo remained sensitive. A *Manila Times* editorial explained why in early 1953:

> There is absolutely no connection between the war criminals now expiating their crimes, after having been submitted to due process of law, and the obligation of Japan to make good the destruction and pillage committed by her forces here. A war criminal found guilty of having committed atrocities, and sentenced in lawful form, must pay the price exacted by the sentence, whether or not his government arranges to pay for the damage and destruction committed here in the name of the Japanese government of the time. The Philippine government is not in the ransom business, and cannot be a party to an agreement that would set at naught the verdict and sentence of a duly constituted court of law.[28]

The same sentiment was echoed in a *Nippon Times* editorial of the same day that professed "great shock" at the idea of exchanging the war criminals for Japanese concessions on reparations. Both editorials appear to have been responding to a report from unnamed opposition Nacionalista Party sources that the party would support releasing the prisoners if Japan offered a satisfactory solution to the reparations issue. But Nacionalista Senator Camilo Osias, visiting Tokyo to discuss reparations, was quick to discount the charge that the Philippines would use the war criminals to gain greater reparations. Even so, Osias was rumored to be the source of the original report.[29]

Likewise, around the same time Elizalde was at pains to stress to Japanese officials that a presidential decision on repatriation of the war criminals was entirely separate from questions of reparations or treaty ratification. The decision should be viewed as a humanitarian act grounded in a spirit of Christianity. However, Elizalde was less circumspect in private; in proposing cabinet consideration of a recent Japanese government request for clemency, he noted that "it might be to our government's financial benefit if the Japanese war criminals still in the Philippines not convicted of very serious crimes could be pardoned and repatriated to Japan." Whether he meant that better reparations terms could be extracted or merely that the Philippines could save on prisoner costs is unclear. Regardless, Elizalde was not proposing return of all the men.[30]

The prisoners themselves had varying perspectives on the issue of reparations and its implications for their eventual return home. Some of the men said they feared that Japanese negotiators might give too much away in an effort to gain the prisoners' release. Rumors that the reparations talks might prove successful, leading to ratification of the peace treaty and the repatriation of the prisoners, were greeted with a mix of joy and misgivings. It was still possible, some feared, that repatriation of those sentenced to term and life sentences would be accompanied by the swift execution of the remainder sentenced to death.[31] At the same time, Chaplain Kagao fretted that even the successful resolution of the reparations issue and the subsequent signing of the peace treaty would not necessarily result in the repatriation of any of the war criminals. After all, Australia had ratified the treaty, but the release of those incarcerated on Manus Island was still only a hope.[32]

The Prisoner Release Movement: Mounting Pressure

In Japan, efforts to gain the release or at least the repatriation of those war criminals convicted and still held overseas gained momentum, especially after Japan regained its independence in April 1952. These efforts took the form of

Diet hearings, public demonstrations, and petition drives. The plight of the war criminals incarcerated in the Philippines became a particular focus, especially given the increasing publicity devoted to their cause. Of the various people who committed themselves to the Philippine prisoner release movement, three Japanese in particular arguably had the greatest impact. These men—a Buddhist monk, a lower-level government bureaucrat, and a newspaperman—approached their cause from very different backgrounds but were united in their efforts to get as many of the war criminals as possible safely home. Their combined efforts amounted to a calculated strategy to win over public opinion and channel it to pressure Philippine and Japanese officials alike to act.

Chaplain Kagao, of course, has already been mentioned for his efforts to minister to the war criminals in Muntinlupa. But his efforts went far beyond the spiritual in his relentless campaign to gain their release. After the January 1951 executions Kagao wrote to various Japanese government officials, including the prime minister, to urge them to greater action and appealed to Diet members for help. At the same time, he wrote directly to General MacArthur. He maintained contact with the Japanese government representatives eventually stationed in the Philippines and also met with the head of the Japanese reparations delegation when it arrived in Manila in early 1952 to convey personally his views on how the talks might affect the war criminals. In mid-1951 Kagao guided five Diet members around the prison, the first such delegation to visit. Since they were en route to a conference in Rome, he importuned them to ask the pope to intercede on behalf of the war criminals.[33]

Kagao also cultivated members of the Filipino elite and sought their help and advice. After the executions, he met with Philippine senators Camilo Osias and Felisberto Verano in Manila to obtain assurances about the fate of the remaining prisoners and also talked with a *Manila Chronicle* reporter. He met personally with President Quirino on at least one occasion and continued to greet what became an increasing stream of visitors, both Filipino and Japanese, to the prison by late 1952 and early 1953. He also shrewdly capitalized on the advantages of wider publicity in Japan over the fate of those in Muntinlupa: he authored a number of articles that appeared in Japanese periodicals that were clearly intended to garner sympathy and support for those incarcerated.[34]

Kagao has also been credited with the idea that sparked one of the more romantic explanations for President Quirino's eventual decision to grant amnesty. Kagao reportedly suggested to two of the war criminals, Shirota Gintarō and Itō Masayasu, that they write a song that "everyone can sing." The resulting collaboration (Shirota wrote the lyrics and Itō the music) was sent back to Japan, where it was recorded by a well-known singer and became a hit. The song, "Ah, the

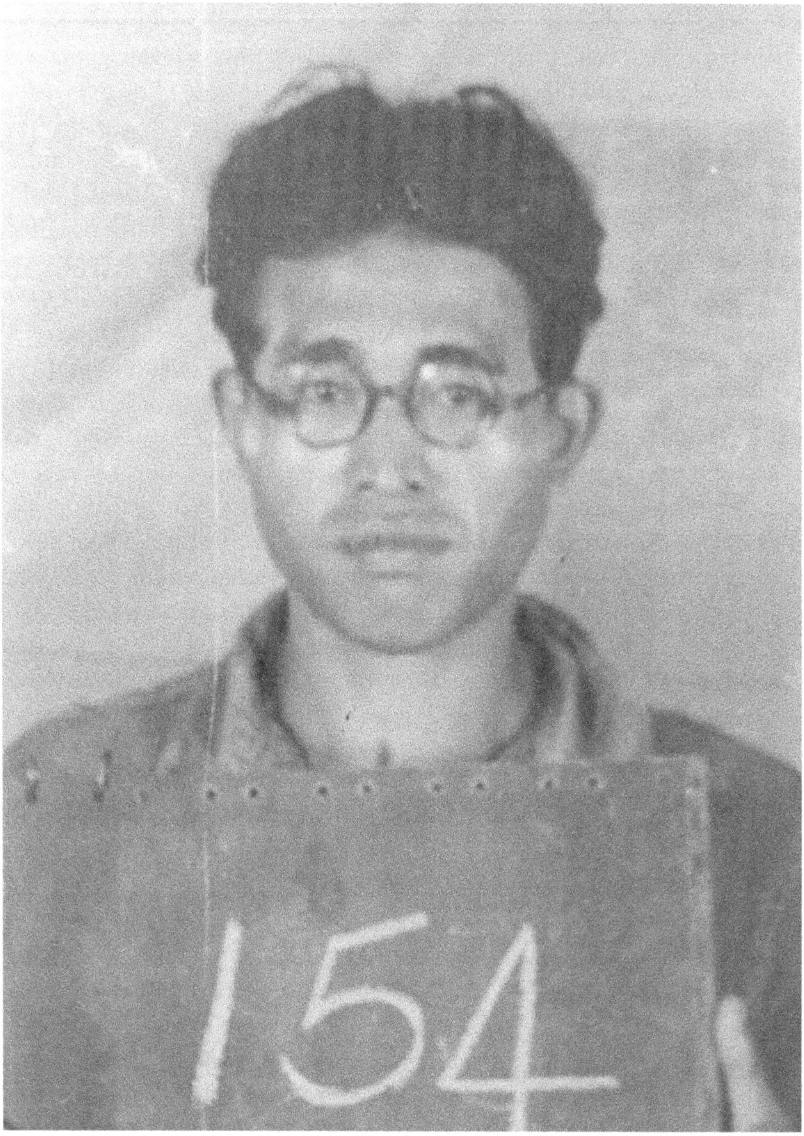

Shirota Gintarō, convicted and sentenced to death, helped write the song "Ah, the Night Is Deep in Muntinlupa" during his incarceration (Photo 154, box 1346, UD 1266, RG 331, courtesy of the National Archives at College Park, MD)

Night Is Deep in Muntinlupa" ("Aa, Montenrupa no yo wa fukete"), not only helped to further publicize the sad fate of men in prison so far from home but also was said to have personally influenced Quirino. As the story goes, Kagao presented a music box with the song to the president, who, upon hearing it, was so moved by the haunting melody that his heart softened and he made up his mind to release the war criminals.[35] (This music box story has acquired the force of legend in Japan but apparently not in the Philippines. In 1999 President Quirino's daughter was quoted by *Kyodo News* as having never heard of the music box and its reported effect on her father; she found it a "fascinating story."[36])

One of Kagao's main correspondents back in Japan was Ueki Shinkichi, the Japanese official in the Demobilization Bureau (an agency of the Ministry of Health and Welfare) who had been given responsibility for monitoring the status of the war criminals in Muntinlupa. While the trials were going on, Ueki laboriously compiled lists of those awaiting trial or convicted and in 1949 organized what eventually became Montenkai (Muntinlupa Society), whose members, both family members and friends, championed the cause of the war criminals. A newsletter, *Monten*, published under the auspices of the society, became an important vehicle for conveying news about the war criminals, and Ueki kept in regular contact with Kagao in order to report their circumstances.[37]

For Ueki, the fate of the war criminals became a crusade, and he increasingly focused on ways to publicize their circumstances and thereby gain them greater sympathy among the Japanese public. It was Ueki who leaked the full account of the January 1951 executions to a *Mainichi* reporter.[38] The resulting story raised the specter of innocent men being put to death and the prospect of more deaths to come. Ueki reasoned that unless the Japanese public could be roused to action, further executions were inevitable. With criticism of war criminals becoming generally less strident and with the emergence of discussions in the Diet about a prisoner release movement, increased publicity about the men in Muntinlupa might turn the tide in their favor. Through Montenkai and its newsletter, Ueki and Kagao were able increasingly to publish communications about and from the men in Muntinlupa.[39]

Ueki was aided and abetted in his efforts to achieve the widest possible publicity and sympathy for the war criminals by the increasing access of newsmen to the Philippines. It was Japanese newspaper reporters who provided the Japanese public with some of the first descriptions of the postwar Philippines and, in particular, the feelings of Filipinos with respect to the Japanese. The Philippine government, which had barred Japanese from entering the country since the end of the war, had by 1950 loosened the restrictions just enough to allow layovers not to exceed twenty-four hours, and at least one enterprising newsman took advantage of that fact to spend his limited time in Manila talking with Americans, Chinese, and others to gain whatever appreciation he could of the Philippine scene.[40]

In late January 1952 a group of reporters was allowed to accompany the Japanese government delegation that had been invited to Manila to pursue provisional talks on reparations, and the result was a flood of stories and articles about the reporters' experiences. As more opportunities for travel presented themselves, the coverage continued steadily, culminating in an outpouring of stories about the return of Japanese war criminals in mid-1953.[41]

Tsuji Yutaka was one of these reporters. Writing as a special correspondent for *Asahi Shimbun*, Tsuji seems to have been remarkably committed to talking with Filipinos of all social and economic strata and asking about their wartime experiences and feelings toward Japan, even at some risk. In one of his early reports, Tsuji noted that he and other reporters had been advised that the Philippine government could not guarantee their safety, and he had been warned not to venture out alone. He did so anyway and reported hostile glances and shouts of "thief" but nothing worse. He did decide, however, to take the precaution of sometimes responding to Tagalog speakers in Cantonese to avoid being taken for a Japanese.[42] (One of Tsuji's competitors, a representative of the *Mainichi Shimbun*, also tried to convey the feelings of animosity that pervaded Manila. Aware of the dangers, on his travels around the city he was accompanied by a plainclothesman assigned by the Manila police.[43])

In his newspaper articles and in a full-length book he edited that was published in 1952, Tsuji wrote frankly and explicitly about Filipino hatred and what had caused it, at times graphically describing the torture and casual brutality inflicted by Japanese troops. In one moving segment of his book, he described how often Filipinos used the term "atrocities" in talking about the Japanese occupation and how, when he asked them what they meant, they turned shocked faces to him, unable to believe his claims of ignorance. A Filipino newsman to whom he posed his question, after asking, "You mean you really don't know?" showed him the marks of his torture by members of the Japanese Kempeitai in Fort Santiago. He offered to take Tsuji to Fort Santiago to show him, and Tsuji accepted. Tsuji's account of that visit and the descriptions his guide gave him of tortures like the water treatment and being hung in chains provided a vivid and unflinching picture for his readers of what had happened during the war.[44]

Still, Tsuji also introduced the idea that Filipinos, at least some of them, had begun to distinguish between the Japanese military and individual Japanese—or perhaps this was the message that Tsuji himself believed and wanted to convey. During his first postwar visit to Manila, he told of encounters with Filipinos and their willingness, at some point, to move past the war:

> In actuality, those who began with forced smiles to speak, once the conversation had progressed a little ways, said, "Let us speak frankly," and then spoke of the atrocities of the Japanese military during the war. I had to just listen in silence. I was not a newspaper reporter [then]; I was a Japanese. Once they had poured out their hearts, they suddenly dropped the tone of their voices an octave and smiled, saying, "However, this is past for everyone. I personally don't think that I have any more hatred for the Japanese." And from this point the real conversations begin. Filipinos are a good people.[45]

Tsuji's many articles and writings undoubtedly contributed to the mounting public pressure, evidenced by the increasing flood of petitions and appeals to the Philippine authorities, to bring the men home. Kagao himself commented that the news accounts and broadcasts by Tsuji and others contributed substantially to heightening awareness among Japanese to the fate of their countrymen in Muntinlupa. Ordinary citizens who learned about the men's plight felt encouraged to help in whatever way they could. In addition to signing petitions, individuals like Dr. Imai faithfully wrote letters and sent "comfort articles" to the men. Miss Yamamoto, a student who had visited the war criminals in Muntinlupa as a member of the Japan-Philippines Student Conference, pleaded for their release. An artist made a sketch of family members to send to one of the condemned prisoners. Three young people showed up at Ueki's office bringing books they wanted to send to the prisoners.[46]

These Japanese efforts on behalf of the war criminals were further aided by an oddly assorted group of supporters from among the Filipino elite whose motives may have varied but who united around the notion of resolving the war criminals issue. Senator Felisberto Verano, a member of the opposition Nacionalista Party, figured prominently among them. According to Japanese diplomats, Verano had experienced an epiphany of sorts during a 1951 visit to Japan. The senator, a former guerrilla leader and staunch member of the "anti-Japan" faction in Philippine postwar politics, met with various Japanese during his visit and at the end of his trip vowed to return home to work for friendly relations between the Philippines and Japan: "I have realized the difference between the Japanese of my imagining and real Japanese."[47]

When he returned to the Philippines, Verano made good on his promises. He visited Muntinlupa often. More than once, he appealed directly to President Quirino on behalf of the prisoners. Japanese observers were convinced of

Verano's sincerity and frequently commented on his commitment to gain the release of the war criminals and to work for better relations between Japan and the Philippines. (Sincerity aside, it was also rumored that Verano hoped to profit from establishing business ventures with Japanese industrialists.)[48]

Two other Philippine politicians—both prominent collaborators during the war—embraced the cause of the Japanese war criminals. Congressman Pio Duran, well known for his pro-Japanese sympathies before, during, and after the war, made periodic visits to meet with the prisoners in Muntinlupa; on a visit to Japan in 1952 he met with their families and promised his help. Senator Camilo Osias and his wife also supported efforts to release the prisoners. Osias's Nacionalista Party had successfully blocked ratification of the Japanese peace treaty in the Senate, but he had served in the Laurel government during the later part of the war and maintained cordial relations with many Japanese. In any event, Osias made it clear where his sympathies lay. During a visit to Japan he and his wife met with the families of the prisoners, and in one noteworthy exchange, he was quoted in the Japanese press as having made an "apology" (*owabi*) to the families because their men still had not been allowed to come home.[49]

Osias was just as forthright back in Manila. In February 1952 he suggested to Philippine government leaders that newspapers should avoid use of the pejorative "Jap" and also advocated the early repatriation of the war criminals both as a gesture of goodwill and to save the expense of housing them. Osias and his wife made periodic visits to Muntinlupa to meet with the war criminals and the chaplain.[50] Whatever his motives, Osias apparently feared no retribution, political or otherwise, from championing the cause of the war criminals.

One obvious potential supporter of fostering good relations between the Philippines and Japan, former president Jose Laurel, appears to have remained more in the background, although some Japanese remained convinced of his sympathies. Japanese businessman Imamura Eikichi (the former long-term resident of the Philippines) told the Japanese Foreign Ministry back in 1949 that Laurel had said that if he won the upcoming presidential election he would suspend executions indefinitely and look for an opportune time to release all the prisoners. A *Mainichi* reporter who interviewed him in mid-1951 reported that Laurel had claimed to be working for the repatriation of the Japanese and had expressed disappointment in the failure, thus far, to achieve that goal.[51] Still, given the ongoing enmity between Laurel and Quirino, stemming from their bitter fight in the 1949 presidential election, it seems unlikely that Laurel was in a position to influence the president directly.

Members of the Christian community also championed the cause of the prisoners. Dr. Andrew Nelson, the Seventh-day Adventist pastor and president of Union College who was present along with Kagao at the January 1951 executions, made his own appeals to members of the Philippine government. According to Kagao, Nelson led the Christian movement in the Philippines in support of amnesty for the war criminals. These Christian groups and committees presented numerous petitions to the Philippine government, visited President Quirino to appeal to him personally, and also worked to gain the sympathy of the Filipino people.[52]

Success: Going Home

On June 27, 1953, sooner than expected, the Philippine government officially announced that it intended to repatriate all Japanese war criminals still incarcerated in the Philippines. The men serving life or term sentences would be granted their freedom immediately; those sentenced to death would have their sentences commuted to life. President Quirino's amnesty proclamation, effective July 4, meant that 106 war criminals would be allowed to return home. It also meant pardons for some three hundred Filipino collaborators still in prison.[53]

Official statements from Malacañan stressed Quirino's humanitarian motives, his desire for the early restoration of normal relations between the Philippines and Japan, and his hope that the Japanese people might yet be friends.[54] According to Japanese mission chief Nakagawa, the statement issued by the Office of the President expressed Quirino's hope that the gesture would lead to progress in resolving outstanding issues between Japan and the Philippines, particularly reparations, and would be a basis for the restoration of formal relations between the two countries. Foreign Affairs Under Secretary Neri privately reiterated this formulation to Nakagawa two days later; he noted that while Quirino had been motivated by Christian and humanitarian principles, it was hoped that the pardons would have a desirable impact on solving pending questions, particularly reparations.[55]

Clearly, at this point Philippine officials were willing to signal that they expected to see some reciprocal gesture on Japan's part. A *Manila Times* editorial delicately conveyed similar sentiments soon after the pardon announcement: while the Philippine government likely had some thought of reparations in mind, the major motive was to demonstrate good faith in the pursuit of better relations; Japan should respond with an equal demonstration, with adequate proof, of Japanese good faith. Japanese Prime Minister Yoshida's statement to the Diet on June 29 that Japan was prepared to consider reparations in forms other than services was widely interpreted as just such a gesture. However,

Yoshida's statement was followed quickly by a "clarification" from the Foreign Ministry that essentially denied any substantive change in Japanese policy.[56]

President Quirino's decision triggered a series of subsequent steps and arrangements required to implement the pardon decree. The Philippine government made it clear that some conditions applied. The Japanese government must accept the judgments of the Philippine war crimes tribunals. Those term and life prisoners granted their freedom would have to promise never to return to the Philippines. Those whose death sentences had been commuted to life in prison would be required to serve out their sentences in a Japanese prison. Any decision to grant clemency, reduce sentences, or parole such prisoners would require the agreement of the Philippine government as well as the recommendation of the Japanese government. (Although the Philippine government had not ratified the San Francisco Peace Treaty, these stipulations paralleled the language in the treaty that spelled out the disposition of war criminals in Japanese custody after Japan regained its independence.) Moreover, the costs of repatriation and imprisonment were to be borne by the Japanese government. The Japanese government accepted all these conditions.[57]

On the afternoon of July 15, the Japanese ship the *Hakusan Maru* left Manila bound for Yokohama, Japan. It carried a total of 111 Japanese leaving the Philippines: 106 war criminals sentenced by Philippine military tribunals; 2 Japanese who, having taken Philippine citizenship at the end of the war, were tried and convicted by civilian courts; 2 Japanese stragglers who had recently surrendered; and the chaplain. The voyagers also included Ueki, who had been permitted to join the official group traveling to the Philippines to escort the men home. Japanese reporters ultimately were not allowed to make the trip, likely to the satisfaction of Nakagawa, who had feared that some of the returnees might make derogatory comments to the press about the fairness of their trials and sentences, with consequences for Japan-Philippines relations.[58]

The ship bore not just the living but also the ashes of the dead. Soon after the amnesty decision had been announced, the Japanese government had petitioned for the return of the remains of the seventeen men previously executed and buried in the prison cemetery. Even before the formal request was made, a Manila paper editorialized on the appeal:

> This is a request that should be granted before it is even asked. . . . The men in whose memory this is asked have wiped out their obligations. By their lights, they did their duty as long as the breath of life was in them. So their people revere their memory, and want, their mortal remains to rest in their homeland. No man of soul and of conscience—qualities in which this Christian nation is

rich—will fail to understand this desire. No government animated by the spirit of such a people will fail to respond to this desire.[59]

The Philippine government did approve the request at a cabinet meeting on July 7 but apparently not without some reservations. In reporting that the appeal had been granted, Nakagawa also noted that he had learned confidentially of fears that the remains of the executed might be given some sort of military honors or treated as "heroes." To allay these concerns, Nakagawa took it upon himself to assure Neri that the remains would be treated as general war dead and given no special honors. The bodies of the dead were exhumed and cremated, and the ashes accompanied the returnees on their voyage home.[60]

In a revealing coda, the Japanese government sought but failed to obtain the ashes of the men tried and executed by the Americans in the Philippines. The remains of Yamashita, Homma, and sixty-five others had been buried in numbered graves in the Philippines, but in 1948 the US army issued orders that any remains in US custody be secretly exhumed, cremated, and disposed of at sea. The action was precipitated by the impending relinquishment of responsibility for maintaining cemeteries not just in the Philippines but also in Japan and the concurrent fear that if Japan acquired access to the remains, it might lead to unwanted glorification of war criminals. The orders were apparently carried out by the end of 1949; a subsequent investigation at the behest of the State Department found no trace of the bodies.[61]

The *Hakusan Maru* arrived in Yokohama on the night of July 21, 1953, and the men disembarked the next morning. Thousands of people thronged the harbor to greet the ship and welcome the men home. The newspapers had been filled with stories of the men's impending return and moving accounts of their families awaiting them. The news reports of their arrival combined the joys of homecoming with solemn descriptions of the men descending the gangplank carrying the ashes of their dead comrades and the departure to prison of those now under life sentence.[62]

Pardons for those headed to prison were in fact not long delayed. The Japanese officials who had gone to Muntinlupa in June to tell the men they would be going home also predicted that those whose sentences had been commuted to life would regain their freedom quite soon. They were right. On December 28, 1953, as virtually his last act before leaving office, President Quirino issued pardons for the remaining fifty-two war criminals incarcerated in Sugamo Prison in Tokyo.[63]

Still, this final action was not without some additional drama. In November the Quirino administration had signaled that Quirino would pardon those remaining in Sugamo if Tokyo would formally request amnesty. At the repeated urging of the Japanese mission in Manila, the Japanese government finally did so on December 11. The Japanese recommendation for clemency rested on several grounds, including the prisoners' commitment to rehabilitation and cordial relations between Japan and the Philippines, the hardships of their families, their good records while in Sugamo, and the sufficiency of their suffering; it did not mention the crimes for which pardons were being sought.[64]

By the time the request arrived, however, prospects for release of the remaining war criminals appeared to have dimmed for reasons explicitly tied to dissatisfaction with the reparations negotiations. In early December Ohno Katsumi, who had replaced Nakagawa as Japanese mission chief in Manila, presented a proposal that Philippine negotiators viewed as reneging on an earlier verbal commitment from Foreign Minister Okazaki. On December 10, Neri, now acting secretary of foreign affairs, went public with his objections while also voicing his belief that the reparations issue had to be resolved before any pardons for war criminals could be considered. The *Mainichi Shimbun* commented that this represented the first time that the Philippine government had formally linked the issues of reparations and the war criminals.[65]

Neri conveyed his concerns directly to Ohno on December 12. According to Ohno, Neri mentioned the atmosphere produced by Japan's "extremely unsatisfactory response" on reparations, making it difficult to persist with release of the remaining war criminals. In response, Ohno cautioned that any attempt by the Philippine government to link the war criminals with reparations could result in an adverse public response in Japan and urged that the two issues be kept separate.[66]

The agenda for the Quirino administration's last cabinet meeting in late December indicates that Neri planned to maintain his opposition. In forwarding the Japanese government's request for clemency for discussion at the meeting, Neri observed that "it may not be timely or advisable at this particular time to consider the recommendation of the Japanese Government favorably because it may distract or divert the attention of the Philippine Government from the reparations question and because a grant of clemency coming so soon after the receipt of the [latest] Japanese reparations offer may be misinterpreted in Japan even in the slightest degree as an indication of lack of strong opinion in the Philippines on the inadequacy of the Japanese reparations offer."[67]

Worried that the objections of the Department of Foreign Affairs were causing Quirino to vacillate on amnesty, Ohno met again with Neri on December 22, prior to the cabinet meeting. Ohno pleaded for Neri's support. According to Ohno, after a long pause Neri agreed to reconsider and urge Quirino to release the remaining prisoners, citing the receipt of a letter from Prime Minister Yoshida. Ohno continued to monitor developments and finally was able to report that Neri had telephoned the news that the president had signed the pardon documents.[68]

Consequences and Implications

President Quirino issued pardons to the war criminals in Muntinlupa during an election year. Quirino's Liberal Party and the opposition Nacionalista Party had sparred for two years over ratification of the peace treaty with Japan, and reparations was one of several issues raised during the hotly contested 1953 presidential campaign. The power of the reparations issue to move the electorate had been clearly demonstrated in the 1951 senatorial elections—all the Nacionalista candidates, who ran on a platform of satisfactory reparations as a condition of treaty ratification, won.[69]

Nonetheless, it is not at all clear that the July 1953 pardons—as distinct from the reparations negotiations—had any material effect on the outcome at the polls. For one thing, although some Nacionalista senators, notably, Claro Recto, reportedly opposed the pardons, Congressman Duran and Senator Osias had for some time been actively working to gain the release of the war criminals, and the evidence suggests that the most prominent Nacionalista politician, Jose Laurel, was also sympathetic. To further complicate matters, Osias, in one of those maneuvers characteristic of Philippine politics, had made common cause with the Liberals to gain the Senate presidency in April 1953 (only temporarily, as it turned out). He was attacked by his Nacionalista colleagues and retaliated by backing Quirino in the upcoming election.[70]

Japanese diplomats occasionally expressed the fear that Quirino would not be willing to jeopardize his reelection by sending the Japanese war criminals home. If political calculations did figure in Quirino's decision (which would hardly be surprising), he obviously concluded that whatever risk existed was manageable. That was the interpretation of one Manila newspaper editorialist, who commented that the president would not have been likely to do anything in the midst of a campaign that would cost him votes—he would not have dared "risk national displeasure" by freeing the war criminals—hence the logical conclusion that Filipinos would not be too exercised over the decision.[71] Of course, Quirino did lose the election, but as a result of turmoil within the Liberal Party and the success of the Nacionalistas in persuading Quirino's defense secretary, Ramon Magsaysay, to bolt the Liberals to run under their party banner. Thus it was Magsaysay who assumed the presidency in 1954.

The political fallout, when it did come, occurred after the election and in the context of a more general attack on Quirino's use of his pardon power. With the Nacionalistas in control of the presidency and the Senate, the Senate designated a blue-ribbon committee to conduct an investigation in early 1954. The pardons for the Japanese prisoners were included in the general indictment, but the resulting report focused more on Quirino's pardoning of other prisoners. The committee concluded that the previous administration was guilty of "carelessly and lavishly" bestowing pardons on the undeserving. In its summation of the Japanese pardons, the committee focused on the December pardons, which had been granted despite the opposition of then Acting Secretary Neri. The report concluded that the pardons for all the Japanese war criminals "were granted without regard to the merits of each particular case and under circumstances impressing upon them the nature and character of amnesty which under the Constitution could not have been granted without Congressional sanction."[72]

The decision to release the Japanese war criminals was the culmination of a process begun with the execution of the fourteen Japanese war criminals in January 1951—a turning point in the way the Philippines and Japan perceived and pursued the war crimes issue. In Japan the public, moved by the increasing publicity generated by Kagao Shūnin, Ueki Shinkichi, and Tsuji Yutaka, exerted pressure to save those still imprisoned, and the Japanese government, responding to that pressure, used both official and private channels to try to gain the war criminals' release. In the Philippines President Quirino, perhaps surprised at the furor created by the executions, eventually offered private assurances that there would be no more executions and by 1952 was reportedly considering ways to free some if not all of the war criminals.

The issue of reparations, however, proved a barrier to the resolution of the issue of what to do about the war criminals, whether the two sides chose to publicly acknowledge it or not. As pressures mounted in the Philippines to obtain the maximum compensation for the damages and suffering experienced during the war, efforts intensified in Japan to bring the war criminals home. In the end, the Philippine government elected, for pragmatic reasons, to agree to the repatriation of all the Japanese in mid-1953, with half pardoned at that time and the remainder gaining their freedom by the end of the year. Clearly, public opinion mattered, perhaps more so in Japan than in the Philippines. The ability of men like Kagao, Ueki, and Tsuji to convince ordinary Japanese to sign millions of petitions and appeals ensured that the Japanese government would continue to press for the men's release. Arguably, the volume of petitions that flooded Malacañan also persuaded the Quirino administration of their importance as bargaining chips, if nothing else.

In the Philippines, observers at the time suggested that members of the elite in both major political parties had the ability and wherewithal to look past the war years to the economic and political advantages of reengaging with Japan, and it was these individuals who consequently drove the decisions on pardons and amnesty. Men like Osias and Duran, to say nothing of Laurel and other postwar survivors of collaboration charges, took a direct interest and played an active role in working to gain the release of Japanese convicted of war crimes and incarcerated in the Philippines. Others, by their stance in the ongoing reparations negotiations, had a concrete influence on the timing of the war criminals' release. It is members of the Filipino elite, then, who are key to understanding the otherwise surprisingly rapid release of the Japanese war criminals just four years after the last trial ended. The government may have been sensitive to the risks of reinvigorating public anger—hence the secrecy attached to the mass execution in January 1951—but influential Filipinos appeared willing to intervene on behalf of individual Japanese prisoners, notwithstanding the potential for public dissatisfaction. Quirino himself seems to have believed that Filipinos would understand the sense of obligation as well as Christian charity that prompted his actions. More striking, as a symbol of elite inattention to public sensibilities, it is hard to beat the image of the newly released former Lieutenant General Kuroda playing golf with Filipinos at a well-known country club over a year before the general pardons were announced.

In 1956 the Philippine and Japanese governments reached final agreement on the reparations to be paid by Japan for the damages the Philippines suffered during the Pacific War. The resolution of this issue paved the way for Philippine ratification of the San Francisco Peace Treaty, and finally Japan and the Philippines were no longer formally at war. The terms of the reparations agreement were a far cry from the Philippines' original demand of $8 billion: Japan agreed to pay the Philippine government a total of $550 million in capital goods and services over a twenty-year period, and it was further agreed that during that same period Japanese private firms would extend commercial loans totaling $250 million.[73]

It seems reasonable to conclude that the Philippine government's decision to allow the return of the war criminals to Japan in mid-1953 was not based on any explicit assurances on the conclusion of a satisfactory reparations agreement, if only because it took an additional three years of hard bargaining before agreement was reached. That is not to deny that the men's release may have contributed, in some measure, to an improved atmosphere in the bilateral negotiations or that Filipinos hoped Japanese would reciprocate with concessions or that tangible benefits may have accrued to some. Nonetheless, President Quirino's amnesty proclamation did not lead to any immediate breakthrough in the normalization of Philippines-Japan relations. It would require a series of steps over time that led to incremental gains in the softening of Filipino attitudes toward Japanese.[74]

The decision to pardon the overwhelming majority of men found guilty of atrocities could not disguise the fact that Japanese and Filipinos had come to very different conclusions about the meaning and validity of the judicial proceedings that had condemned many of the war criminals to death or lengthy prison terms. Both sides might have been able to reach some level of agreement about or acknowledgment of the extent of atrocities inflicted by the Japanese military on Filipino civilians. But the issue of individual culpability remained unreconciled.

6

Constructing Narratives and Assessing Impact

By the mid-1950s the war crimes issue had been removed as a formal barrier between the Philippines and Japan. The last incarcerated war criminals had been freed, on President Elpidio Quirino's authorization, at the end of 1953. The two countries had also succeeded in negotiating an end to the reparations issue; an agreement was signed in 1956, opening the way to the formal resumption of full diplomatic relations.

These outcomes could scarcely have been imagined in 1945; the depth of hatred felt by Filipinos for Japan and all things Japanese was palpable. One congressman drafted a bill titled "An Act Providing for the Execration of Japan and the Japanese," which would make it unlawful to learn or speak Japanese, to own anything Japanese, or "to utter or write any praise, defense, justification or extenuation for Japan or things Japanese or for any Japanese individual."[1] Others continued to embrace the notion that it would take decades for Japan to rid itself of militarism and be worthy to rejoin the world community.[2] Long after his repatriation, one of the convicted war criminals recalled the terror he and others felt when the truck in which they were being transported to a POW camp was pelted with rocks by Filipinos shouting, "Kill! Kill!"[3]

How, then, was the release of the war criminals made possible? The straightforward answer is that economic calculations, as well as the geopolitical realities of the Cold War, made some sort of rapprochement desirable and that it was members of the Filipino elite who had a keen appreciation of those realities. But that does not fully explain the (relatively) passive acceptance of Filipinos, nor does it tell the whole story of the role of those Japanese who worked to propel the Philippine government to grant pardons to so many. Even as the two

Filipinos on Cebu jeering Japanese POWs being transported to camps at the end of the war (Photo SC-392658, courtesy of the National Archives at College Park, MD)

governments moved toward a resolution of their differences, individuals in both countries found opportunities to shape public opinion about the war criminals and what should happen to them. In Japan this meant the metamorphosis of victimizers into victims. In the Philippines it meant emphasizing the high moral ground and the virtue of forgiveness. The constructed narratives that emerged allowed ordinary Filipinos to acquiesce in the pardons as an act of a Christian, civilized nation; at the same time, these narratives encouraged Japanese to see the convicted criminals as innocent in fact or at least by virtue of circumstances beyond their control.

In both cases, the focus deliberately shifted *away* from the actual trials and what individuals had done (or not done) and *toward* a more generalized perception of all the convicted as a monolithic group either all innocent (in Japanese eyes) or all guilty but pardonable (in Filipino eyes). As a result, both sides could sidestep their very real differences over the specific outcomes of the trials. Questions of individual guilt or innocence became moot—Filipinos could remain satisfied with a judicial system that allowed for just retribution while taking the high road in sanctioning pardons for those found guilty. Japanese could proffer genuine expressions of gratitude while intimating a generalized acceptance of collective responsibility for the commission of atrocities in the Philippines (yet absolving these particular war criminals of individual responsibility).

To be sure, the aforementioned economic and geopolitical realities—the Philippines' need for reconstruction assistance and American pressure on both countries to resolve their differences in a Cold War world—represented strong inducements. And these constructed narratives could only go so far in reconciling Filipinos who had been directly affected by the actions of Japanese during the war or Japanese who felt themselves unfairly blamed for the actions of others. But these narratives nonetheless mattered: they gave agency to citizens as part of the decision-making calculus, and they supplanted the specifics of the trials with constructed versions that provided one of the foundations for the subsequent formal reconciliation between the two countries.

Contemporaneous Perspectives on the Trials: Process versus Justice

It should come as no surprise that Filipinos and Japanese at the time held very different perceptions about the conduct of the war crimes trials in the Philippines and the fairness of the proceedings. Two quotes succinctly capture this difference of opinion:

> Japan . . . will certainly be interested to know that we have done fairly by her war criminals, guilty of atrocities against our people.[4]

> A young officer of twenty-seven years of age was put into the empty cell next to mine. He was sentenced to be hanged owing to the usual false testimonies of thirteen Filipinos.[5]

The first comment was offered by Fred Ruiz Castro, the Philippines' judge advocate general, who had jurisdiction over the National War Crimes Office that had been established to prosecute war crimes cases; Castro, it will be remembered, had been tortured by the Japanese during the war. The second quote comes from a letter written by Fujii Hajime, who was executed in April 1947. Fujii had been tried by the Americans, but his views about Filipinos' testimony were commonly voiced by other prisoners facing trial in Philippine courtrooms.

Philippine and Japanese perceptions of the trials were, perhaps unavoidably, grounded in the differing emphases accorded due process versus outcomes. For Filipinos, the trials represented a broader test of the Philippines' legitimacy as a newly sovereign state. Early press reaction to the Philippine government's assumption of responsibility for war crimes trials combined pride with some nervousness. The *Manila Bulletin* observed on July 31, 1947, that "recurrently it falls to the lot of the Philippines as one of the world's newest republics to break with precedent and do something that has never been done before," but it also worried that "as a test of national fairness it will not be easy to pass." The *Manila Tribune* on July 30, 1947, editorialized that the fears of some people that the army would be unable to administer "true justice" was an unfair prejudgment of the army's abilities. Still, the army should bear in mind that "all the world will watch the event with interest." By November 1947 the US Embassy in Manila was reporting that the local press had commented favorably on the conduct of the trials to date, with the orderly process of the trials reflecting favorably on the Philippines.[6]

For Filipinos associated with the trials—judges, prosecutors, and defense attorneys—the proceedings constituted a means to affirm the Philippines' commitment to justice and a way of demonstrating Filipino adherence to the norms of behavior befiting a civilized country. In some of the early trials, commission members were at pains to emphasize the appropriateness of the proceedings. For example, in both the Takahashi and Kudō trials, in which commissions sentenced each defendant to death, the commissions praised the efforts of both prosecutors and defense counsel, noting in the former trial that their fairness and mutual cooperation reflected "credit to themselves and the governments to which they belong." In its explanation of the verdict in the Takahashi case, the commission went even further, noting that it had not focused on the nationality of the accused so as to ensure that "posterity and the world at large will not find occasion to brand the Filipinos as a bunch of uncivilized, rancorous sadists seeking blood to quench their thirst for the sake of cheap revenge."[7] In the trial of Itō Saburō, the prosecutor reacted angrily to the notion that Filipinos were motivated by revenge, as had been suggested by one of the witnesses: "It may be that some people still are resentful but here we are giving [the Japanese] a fair trial and that we are teaching them the tenets of democracy and we are showing to the whole world that we are not harboring anything against the Japanese. I feel insulted as a Filipino that another Filipino should say that the Filipinos are still resentful against the Japanese."[8]

In some sense, it became almost a source of national pride that Filipinos' behavior would contrast so obviously with that of the Japanese during the war. A *Liberty News* editorialist who commented on the behavior of the Japanese defense attorneys in 1947 suggested that they deserved to be given the same treatment the Japanese had accorded their Filipino victims during the war, but "our superiority to Jap methods and ways forbids us to descend so low."[9] The *Philippines Free Press* printed "Letter to Madame Tojo" in December 1948. In it the writer said that his family sympathized with Mrs. Tōjō on the impending execution of her husband (wartime prime minister Tōjō Hideki had recently been sentenced to death by the International Military Tribunal for the Far East in Tokyo) but contrasted the fair trial received by Tōjō (and, by inference, the fairness of the trials conducted by the Philippine government) with the treatment meted out to Filipinos by the Japanese army. The author's brothers and thousands of others had been killed without trial.[10] In an earlier commentary, a writer speculated that a Japanese about to be executed must have been bemused at the trouble the Americans and Filipinos went to in assuring a fair trial: had Japan won the war, there would have been no such "degenerate democratic processes."[11]

The Japanese popular reaction to the trials during this period (1947–49) is more difficult to discern. Japanese newspapers, operating under US occupation censorship and limited by newsprint shortages and the inability to send correspondents overseas in the early postwar years, at most reported the bare facts of verdicts as gleaned from wire reports. Nonetheless, the overall impression began to be formed that the trials, however well structured in procedural terms, still represented demonstrations of Filipinos' undifferentiated hatred toward Japanese, a hatred that resulted in unfair verdicts and sentences. In letters to their families, Japanese defendants not infrequently protested their innocence. For example, Owari Saburō, writing to his wife while in detention awaiting indictment, urged her to believe that he was not to blame for any incidents for which he might be charged. "I know of many people who died on the gallows because of the false testimonies against them. . . . And in fact, practically all of the real perpetrators of the crimes have now gone home while those unlucky but honest persons who have a stronger sense of justice are left behind, made to shoulder and to die for the responsibility of others."[12] Given the probable timing of this missive, Owari was likely discussing the outcomes of the American trials, but he was articulating a widely held perception that held true for the Philippine trials as well.

Some Japanese observers noted that an emphasis on process could not avoid miscarriages of justice. Some concluded that the judicial process was flawed—fatally—through its inability to distinguish truth from lies. Filipino witnesses, blinded by hatred, had corrupted the process to serve their thirst for revenge. Filipino prosecutors, perhaps driven by similar motives, coached witnesses to gain convictions.[13]

Former general and convicted war criminal Kuroda Shigenori, soon after receiving a pardon, wrote that the trials followed regular procedures so in that regard could be considered "normal and fair." Moreover, postsentence review was carried out extremely carefully. Still, "I think it is very difficult for the military of the victors to try these matters. It is not a lie that there were actual war crimes. But there is some doubt as to whether those who were charged with these crimes did them or not."[14] Mineo Shisuhiko, a former naval lieutenant commander who was convicted and sentenced to death in early 1949, fretted that some more lenient sentences given to a few others might convey the mistaken impression that the trials were actually fair and reinforce to Filipinos that justice had been served.[15]

It was Owari Saburō, in another letter home, who provided one of the more comprehensive indictments of the Philippine trials from the Japanese defendants' point of view. In an undated letter to his brother written while he was awaiting trial, Owari complained that Filipino prosecutors were "generally held to be vindictive against any Japanese whether innocent or guilty" and charged that the specific prosecutor in charge of his case was biased because he had once been head of the barrio where the alleged incident took place. Even though there were exceptions, the American trials had been fair, but ever since the Philippine government had assumed jurisdiction "not a single trial has been conducted fairly and impartially by a Filipino military commission." Prosecutors coached witnesses to testify in support of the charges, and the commissions would usually "give credit to whatever false testimonies the prosecution witnesses made." Owari lamented the fact that it would be impossible for any subsequent reviewer of the trial proceedings to discern, let alone prove, that justice had not been served: "Even if [the] time came for Japan to raise questions regarding the absence of justice in the war crimes trials, these records are so made that the government of the Philippines would be able to justify fully its stand."[16]

It is possible that correspondence as critical as Owari's did not reach the intended recipients owing to screening by Philippine or US occupation authorities. Nonetheless, enough information was filtering through to allow Japanese observers to form their own views of the trials. In a report prepared at the behest of the prime minister in May 1949, the Japanese Foreign Ministry commented on the increasing concern of the war criminals' families and members of the public with respect to the treatment given the war criminals in the Philippines. These concerns, the report noted, stemmed in part from doubts about the fairness of the trials, specifically from criticisms that the verdicts had been rendered without sufficient evidence, that prosecutors had engaged in a "frame-up" in the submission of testimony, and that as a result harsh sentences had been levied on the basis of lies or mistaken identifications. The report concluded that these outcomes were not surprising, given the extremely rampant anti-Japanese sentiment among Filipinos.[17]

The case of Nakamura Hideichi and his twelve codefendants, all of whom were convicted and sentenced to death, seemed to offer concrete proof, if any was needed, that the Philippines had no commitment to justice. One of the defendants, Abe Sueo, offered perhaps the bitterest denunciation of the trials. He charged that the Philippines was determined not just to stigmatize any Japanese as a war criminal but also to publicize to the world the barbarity of the Japanese military. Filipino witnesses lied; collaborators aided the prosecution to protect themselves; one prosecutor sanctioned perjured testimony despite the existence of evidence to the contrary. The trials, in short, were about revenge, not justice, and constituted a form of judicial murder.[18]

One of the original Japanese defense attorneys who had since returned to Japan and helped with the gathering of affidavits for the accused was shocked by the verdict and was described by a colleague as "resentful that the true facts of the Nakamura case were not properly assessed."[19] The Japanese Foreign Ministry took the view that the case had been a "frame-up" and further noted that petitions and appeals to Philippine authorities to rectify the injustice had been unsuccessful.[20]

Many Japanese defendants remained convinced that no amount of procedural safeguards could prevent shocking miscarriages of justice. It was not just the Nakamura case—other defendants such as Kudō Chūshirō had been found guilty and sentenced to death despite the presentation of alibis. Satō Sō later castigated the lead Filipino prosecutor, Capt. Nicanor Maronilla-Seva, as "wicked" (*akuratsu*) and a "devil" (*akuma*) who would do anything to win cases. Satō observed that the trials were simply political revenge disguised as "justice."[21]

Context: The Broader Early Postwar Climate of Opinion in the Philippines

The outcomes in the war crimes trials apparently did little immediately to dissipate the anger felt by Filipinos. During and after the trials and the first executions, observers both in and outside the Philippines continued to comment on the depth of Filipinos' hatred toward Japan and the Japanese. The experience of one of the few witnesses who did manage to arrive from Japan to testify at an early trial is telling: he complained that upon his arrival he was immediately thrown into a cell for condemned prisoners and only released some hours later.[22] Reports of any dealings between the two countries tended to trigger angry reactions among ordinary Filipinos. It was as if any provocation reminded the general population of wartime abuses and could incite popular anger.

One such provocation occurred with the emergence of proposals for increased trade between the Philippines and Japan. As early as 1947 the Philippine government had quietly agreed to a resumption of some commerce with Japan under the direct control and supervision of the US occupation authorities. But the May 1948 arrival of a SCAP delegation to discuss expanding bilateral trade triggered widespread and heated debate. It did not help that the head of the mission, Maj. Gen. Daniel Noce, chief of the Civil Affairs Department of the army, made statements that suggested to Filipino audiences that the United States hoped to enlist the Philippines in the rehabilitation of Japan. One editorialist commented with disdain about US "officialdom," "concerned with wet-nursing the Japs back to Bushido." In the end, after much public comment and debate, the Quirino administration announced its intent to continue limited trade with Japan. Quirino himself in public remarks distinguished between his own continued personal enmity toward Japan and his belief that the Philippines needed to move beyond the war years and focus on encouraging Philippine prosperity.[23]

As suggested by the above controversy, many Filipinos continued to greet the very idea of resuming any sort of contact with revulsion. In March 1947, just when the Philippine government had agreed to take over control of the war crimes trials, the *Philippines Free Press* summarized the responses it had received from readers on the question of whether the Philippine government should reestablish trade with Japan. Of the sixty-eight readers who responded, forty-eight denounced the proposal with "varying degrees of bitterness," eighteen favored it, and two offered noncommittal reactions. "The refrain of those who oppose the resumption of trade relations with Japan shows little variation. The horrors of the Japanese occupation are fresh and vivid in their memories. Their reaction is emotional. To most the very thought of holding out a hand to the Japanese in friendship is abhorrent."[24]

A second informal poll revealed similar findings. A *Free Press* reporter who interviewed seventy-five people in La Union from "all walks of life" reported that seventy of those queried voted no on resuming trade with Japan. He noted that only three voted yes wholeheartedly, and they were "professionals." Those who voted no were the most emphatic, giving what the reporter characterized as "sentimental" reasons but some also citing fear of trade giving rise to a powerful Japan ready to wage another war against the Philippines.[25]

Other sources of reader opinion confirmed the depth of feeling among Filipinos. A September 1948 letter printed in the Cebu *La Prensa* newspaper was signed "Gaston" and was directed to General MacArthur: "I only want to remind you of one thing. The Japanese are not human. They are the worst savages that the world has ever produced. . . . Now you want to flood us with Japanese products. No, by God! . . . WE DON'T WANT ANYTHING JAPANESE IN THE PHILIPPINES! . . . The Japanese are not human beings. Let them live like beasts in the forests."[26] Another letter to the same newspaper opined that President Quirino knew very well that most Filipinos had no desire to trade with "ex-murderers" but was bowing to pressure from the Americans: "Only the Filipino traitors and those who make money with Japanese products are the ones who ask that these relations be resumed."[27]

It was not just among ordinary citizens that anger remained palpable. Jorge Bocobo, who had served as a justice of the Philippine Supreme Court during the war years and for a time faced collaboration charges after the war ended, expressed his continued hatred for Japan. In his speeches and articles, Bocobo castigated Japan as untrustworthy and undeserving of independence for another fifty years; he spoke bitterly of the cold-blooded slaughters by Japanese "outlaws" during the war. For Bocobo, Japan remained a "barbaric and cruel empire."[28] But Bocobo notwithstanding, there remained those who believed that the Filipino elite did not necessarily harbor the same degree of animosity. A Japanese businessman commented in 1950 that he perceived no ill will toward Japan on the part of "upper-class" Filipinos, but such sentiments still existed among the lower and middle classes. The US chargé d'affaires in Manila also distinguished between the "average" Filipino and "Filipinos at a higher level": some of them were rabidly anti-Japanese, while others were more realistic or practical.[29]

One telling anecdote illustrates this gap between the elite and the general public, which did not necessarily incline to the pragmatic approach championed by the former with any deep sense of forgiveness or reconciliation. In 1951, during a visit to Japan, Philippine senator Felisberto Verano gave a speech in which he commented on the ways in which Japan could demonstrate the sincerity of its desire to improve relations with the Philippines. Start small, he urged, with meaningful gestures that could warm the hearts of Filipinos. Little girls in his country loved dolls—why not send some to children who otherwise would have a poor Christmas? With the informal encouragement of President

Quirino, hundreds of dolls were produced and sent to the Philippines, where they ended up gathering dust in Malacañan. A group of Filipinas widowed in the war objected to the dolls' distribution because they brought back bitter memories.[30]

Even as overall public opinion, as expressed in news accounts and letters, remained bitter, a thread of forgiveness also began to emerge, however slight and tentative. The informal *Philippines Free Press* reader poll cited above concluded that the responses favoring trade with Japan had been motivated by a "Christian spirit of forgiveness." Two letters printed in the same newspaper offered a concrete sense of the journey some were making from hatred to tentative reconciliation. In the first, written in April 1946, Rafael Bautista describes the prewar friendship he and his wife had with their neighbors Mr. and Mrs. Nakashima. But the war made them hate all Japanese, including the Nakashimas, and now that the war is over he hopes they never meet again, because he is not sure whether he would choose to renew the friendship or hold to his feelings of enmity. In 1951 Bautista wrote again. He recounted that he had received a letter from Mr. Nakashima "full of old time friendship and apology"; after reading it, his "heart was literally melted—the old scar of anti-Japanese feeling seemed to have disappeared."[31]

Another reader wrote that despite Japanese brutality against members of his own family (including some burned alive), "I still regard the Japanese as my Oriental brothers. . . . Men must live together, or die separately." In 1947 the paper described, in sympathetic tones, the case of two "Japanese waifs" who had been taken in by a Filipino family. A second article profiled a brave Japanese woman who had lived in the Philippines for many years and was "universally loved and respected" for her courage in helping Filipinos during the war.[32] In mid-1948, at the height of controversy over the trade issue, another Filipino wrote that "the Philippines as a Christian nation should show true brotherhood and good neighborliness. . . . The loss of my three children during the war and the sufferings I have experienced have given me reason to hate Japan and everything Japanese. But as the bitterness of these memories has been mellowed by the passing of time, I have thought that the only way of disentangling myself from the deadly clutches of hate and revenge, is to reconcile myself to the consoling Christian ideology, which is, forgiveness."[33]

A Sunday news magazine article published in late 1950 conveys both the depth of the continued hatred toward the war criminals confined in Muntinlupa and the ability of some Filipinos to reach out to them. The author, having actually been granted interviews with some of the men, sees them as now "docile" but once having been among the "hordes of squat, yellow men who held sway over the life and death of 19 million Filipinos." Although there are those who maintain their innocence, many write letters to the prison authorities apologizing for Japan's behavior during the war. They keep their cells and barracks clean, "yet the familiar Jap stink permeates them." But the article goes on to note that these Japanese are not without friends among Filipinos, who pay visits and provide money for cigarettes and toothpaste.[34]

This was the uneasy state of opinion toward Japan that existed in the early 1950s as press accounts seesawed between broad condemnation of Japan and the Japanese people and individual stories of forgiveness. It was also the context in which the last executions had been carried out in January 1951. But the Philippine government, faced with an opportunity to remind its citizens of Japanese wartime brutality, seems deliberately not to have chosen to do so. This perhaps represents an initial hint of the governing elite's intent to shape a narrative that would ultimately allow acceptance of pardons for the war criminals in Muntinlupa and the reestablishment of relations with Japan.

Climate of Opinion in Japan: Constructing a Narrative

The return in 1953 of all the Japanese war criminals still imprisoned in Muntinlupa represented the culmination of efforts to present these men in a light very different from the one that had existed in the months following the end of the war. The pictures of the crowds that met the arriving *Hakusan Maru* in July and the outpouring of news stories chronicling the joy of their families vividly convey the shift in Japanese public sentiment toward the men who had been convicted of atrocities and incarcerated in the Philippines. They had been transformed, over the course of less than ten years, from criminals awaiting punishment to innocent victims of the war. Even the diplomatic correspondence began to capture the nature of the change, occasionally referring to the inmates as "war convicts" (*sensō jukeisha*) instead of the more usual "war criminals" (*senpan*).[35]

The very earliest postwar news accounts of Japanese brutality in the Philippines had shocked and disturbed ordinary Japanese, who responded with a combination of revulsion and disbelief. The evidence about atrocities introduced during the Tokyo trial provided additional proof for those willing to believe it. Commenting on the Tokyo trial verdicts, editorialists in certain Japanese newspapers were troubled by the apparent sympathy of some for the defendants; it would be better if Japanese remembered the Filipinos and Chinese who suffered severe oppression and "barbarous acts" at the hands of the Japanese military.[36]

The Japanese facing trial or already convicted of crimes in the Philippines were well aware of the likely sentiment back home. One wrote, characteristically, that his countrymen who judged them as shameless had no idea of the real facts. Other observers talked about children being taunted for the crimes of their fathers and wives seeking to divorce husbands in prison. The prisoners and their families believed that, at best, the wider Japanese public was indifferent to their fate.[37] And so the families concentrated during this period on trying to ameliorate conditions for their men and to persuade the Philippine authorities to commute the sentences of those sentenced to death. As the verdicts were announced, the private pleadings of families and friends that their loved ones be spared reflected an overriding disbelief that the men they knew could have been capable of such acts of brutality.

During and immediately after the conclusion of the trials, there was scant coverage in the major Japanese newspapers of legal decisions affecting the war criminals; at most, there were brief factual references. For example, the *Asahi Shimbun* noted without comment that Kudō Chūshirō and Tsuneoka Noboru had been sentenced to death.[38] Among other things, censorship rules imposed by the US occupation authorities would have constrained any direct criticism of the proceedings. One exception occurred in early 1950, when the *Asahi* published an account of the claims of innocence of two men sentenced to death. Itō Katsumi, maintaining that the real killer in his case had died during the war, nonetheless pleaded guilty in order to allow his fellow soldiers being held in the Philippines to return home. Without elaboration, the article also stated that there was evidence to prove that another defendant, Saitō Tasuke, was innocent.[39]

With the January 1951 executions of fourteen of the war criminals, the tide began to turn. That summer, Buddhist chaplain Kagao wrote of the lives of the men in prison and their feelings of despair in the wake of the January executions, which he described in some detail. But he also wrote rather extensively of the sentiments of Filipinos toward Japan and their tendency, in conversations of any length, to bring up atrocities committed by Japanese during the war. He told of how he still encountered animosity when shopping and sometimes heard derogatory Japanese words like *dorobō* (thief)—perhaps, he speculated, the only words ordinary Filipinos knew from their wartime contacts with soldiers. Still, Kagao's primary concern remained the fate of the war criminals—he fretted that unmet Filipino demands for reparations and fears of Japanese rearmament would result in renewed anger directed toward the Japanese still in prison.[40]

A Japanese Diet member as early as May 1951 evoked the narrative that would be seized upon and cultivated by those seeking the return of the prisoners in Muntinlupa. Kora Tomiko, a wife and mother of three children, sent a letter to a Philippine publication begging Filipinos to ask President Quirino for amnesty for the war criminals in Muntinlupa. She starts out by noting that it was "very sad" that Filipinos had not yet realized how sorry the Japanese people were for the atrocities committed during the war. She blamed the "black hearted militarists" in Japan who were really responsible, not those who were simply following orders. What is really striking, however, is how in the course of her short letter she moves from a recognition that "most" of the war criminals had committed killings, but only on the orders of their superiors, to "some" of the war criminals being guilty, to the generalization that all of those sentenced to death (the sixty men remaining on death row) were innocent. The implication that the trials resulted in unfair verdicts is less explicit but conveyed clearly: the Philippine tribunals may have "done their best," but cases would be overturned if only the president would allow rehearings.[41] (In the wake of expressed Filipino outrage at her comments, Mrs. Kora later retrenched on her position, writing, "About those who have received the death sentence, we have no complaint, but only beg the sympathy and religious mercy of your people."[42])

This was the structure on which three men in particular—Chaplain Kagao Shūnin, Demobilization Bureau bureaucrat Ueki Shinkichi, and newspaperman Tsuji Yutaka—began to construct their narrative of innocent men incarcerated far away and being made to pay for the sins of others. In taking up the cause of the war criminals as part of the prisoner release movement (discussed in chapter 5), they did much to reinforce the victim narrative the public began increasingly to embrace. They did not entirely abandon references to conditions in the Philippines and the rationale for Philippine anger, but these were increasingly coupled with or shifted to ever more sympathetic portraits of the men and their lives in prison. With the return of Japanese sovereignty and the increasing focus on the reparations negotiations, attention shifted away from the war itself and focused more on the plight of the war criminals and their families at home in Japan.

Sympathetic portraits were among the first to emerge as the Japanese public began to have access to direct accounts of those incarcerated in Muntinlupa. Ueki convinced the *Mainichi Shimbun* to publish an account by Nakajima Shōhei (who had been sentenced to death), which generated reader support in the form of letters to the paper and to the families. Nakajima wrote of his shock at the January 1951 executions and his own efforts to face his impending death; the newspaper's introduction to Nakajima's story emphasized the pathos and nobility of the young student conscript: "While each day and night he greets a life that has no tomorrow, he prays for the rebuilding of Japan and thinks of his mother. Perhaps in this we will remember anew that there are young victims [*giseisha*] of war."[43]

Ueki also approached the editor of *Bungei Shunjū*, a popular monthly magazine, and persuaded him to publish Fujita Takefumi's moving account of his visit to the graves of his comrades on the occasion of the Japanese Obon festival. Fujita and five other term/life prisoners, together with Chaplain Kagao, were granted permission to visit the graves of their fellow Japanese on a day traditional for paying respects to the dead. In the company of a single armed guard, the men made their way to the cemetery, where they tended the graves and watched as the chaplain buried a lock of hair sent by the wife of one of the executed men. Fujita commented that the graves were marked not by names but only by numbers, evoking feelings of loneliness mixed with resentment. As they walked back to the prison, they passed the gallows, and Fujita reflected on the feelings of his comrades who had gone to their deaths innocent, saying that if it had been him, he could not have suppressed his bitterness. The article noted briefly that Fujita, a former member of the Kempeitai, was serving a life sentence but did not add that he had been convicted of allowing his men to torture and kill Filipino civilians.[44]

After he was allowed to visit Muntinlupa, newsman Tsuji provided his own prisoner profiles, which emphasized the poignancy of their fates rather than the crimes they had been charged with committing. When Tsuji first met Fujimoto Takao on a visit to Muntinlupa, Fujimoto was tending a dog, a lizard, and a mouse. As Tsuji describes it, Fujimoto lovingly cared for these creatures; the mouse, which he named after his daughter Takako, figured in a sentimental poem he composed. Fujimoto recounted that, having been sentenced to death, he could not bear to kill anything, so other prisoners brought him the dead cockroaches he fed the lizard. When Tsuji saw Fujimoto again right before the paroled prisoners left for home, he was without his pets—he had set them free. In Tsuji's eyes, Fujimoto's story was a morality tale. Fujimoto, a yakuza, or gangster, before the war, was filled with resignation at receiving a death sentence, but thoughts of his family waiting for him and the tending of his pets brought him solace. What Tsuji never told his readers was that Fujimoto was convicted and sentenced to death for the rape, torture, and killing of Filipino civilians or that Fujimoto initially sought to plead guilty to some of the charges.[45]

Tsuji also offered the narrative of Benjamin Sugimoto, the son of a Japanese father and Filipina mother who had been born and had lived his whole life in the Philippines; he had never seen his father's homeland. His father had immigrated to the Philippines to work as a laborer on the construction of the Benguet road, and his parents had "lived together in harmony and happiness for fifty years in Baguio." The youngest of seven children, Sugimoto was only seventeen when the Japanese military arrived and he was ordered to serve as an interpreter.[46] Tsuji did not mention that Sugimoto had pleaded guilty to torturing and mistreating several Filipino civilians and killing another. (At his trial, Sugimoto testified that he had committed these acts on the orders of a superior officer and because he feared retribution if he did not obey; he was sentenced to life in prison.)[47]

All of this was surely calculated to remind Japanese readers of their countrymen far away and to convey the sense of their suffering without dwelling on the reasons for their incarceration. Undoubtedly, Tsuji and Ueki exercised care in the men they chose to showcase the plight of the prisoners in Muntinlupa. Nakajima and Fujita, profiled in newspaper accounts in 1951, were lower-ranking officers—a second lieutenant and a captain, respectively. Fujimoto, the animal lover, was a superior private, while Sugimoto was a young civilian interpreter. Clearly, highlighting the experiences of prisoners like Lieutenant General Yokoyama and Rear Admiral Furuse, both of whom had been sentenced to death and also remained incarcerated in Muntinlupa, would have been impolitic—such high-ranking officers presumably could not be expected to garner the same sympathy back home as the others. Indeed, there might still be cause to blame them for Japan's fate or at least the fate of their subordinates—they were better left unmentioned.

Tsuji appreciated—as did Kagao and Ueki—that sympathetic portraits of individual prisoners, although helpful, would not be enough. They understood that a prisoner release movement powerful enough to move politicians required men worthy of being saved—they *had* to be innocent. And so the effort to portray the prisoners sympathetically became coupled with increasingly explicit avowals of innocence or at least a refusal to entertain squarely questions of their individual guilt. Tsuji provided concrete instances where he argued that individuals had been wrongly convicted. In the case of "Y.H.," for example, the accused was sentenced to death for involvement in an incident in Batangas even though he was in Baguio at the time—a clear case of mistaken identity. Three others ("X, Y, and Z") were unfairly blamed for incidents simply because they were members of the units responsible, even though they themselves had nothing to do with the charges. Tsuji expressed the view, quite commonly found in Japanese accounts of the trials, that Filipino witnesses would point at any Japanese to avenge the deaths of their loved ones.[48]

Tsuji does ask some of those sentenced to death about the atrocities they were charged with committing ("You now say that you are innocent, but how the hell did such a stupid thing happen?"), but he appears to accept their denials at face value. And he clearly becomes an advocate for their innocence. He quotes one Filipino who claimed that the Japanese in Muntinlupa were directly and specifically guilty of atrocities, but then Tsuji explicitly rejects this view. Based on what he was able to learn and speaking as a Japanese, he concludes that those imprisoned were not the perpetrators (*kagaisha*) of the acts of the Japanese military but rather victims (*higaisha*). By Tsuji's calculations, Japan sent about 400,000 men to the Philippines during the war; some 70,000 to 80,000 survived; and of these about 350 were tried as war criminals. Given the verdicts in these trials, it would appear that fewer than 200 men had assumed responsibility for the acts of 400,000. Would it not be better, Tsuji asks, if responsibility for the acts of the 400,000 rested with those, the Japanese people, who sent them?[49]

Writings about the Nakamura case further illustrate this effort to elide questions of individual guilt. Accounts of the executions of these men in January 1951 almost without exception focus on the belief that half were completely innocent, having been nowhere near the location where the crimes occurred. These contemporaneous narratives emphasize the unfairness of the trial and its tragic consequences. The inescapable inference—that the others were in fact guilty—is ignored or at best glossed over. Chaplain Kagao, in a letter to Japan's minister of health and welfare, decried the executions of those who had been "falsely incriminated in the eyes of everyone."[50] Satō Sō, writing in an issue of *Monten* commemorating the men who were executed, mourned their deaths and lamented that they had lost forever the opportunity to persuade their countrymen of their innocence. He looked forward to the day when they would gain the heartfelt sympathy of their fellow Japanese. It was only much later that Satō, in his memoir dealing with his own trial and sentence, hinted that some had refused to take responsibility for the atrocities in the hopes of avoiding punishment, even at the risk of dooming others who were innocent.[51]

Two compilations during this period gave direct voice to the men in Muntinlupa and tended to reinforce the dual messages of injustice and pathos. *Seiki no isho* (Testaments of the century), published in 1953, gathered the letters and last statements of Japanese who had been executed not just in the Philippines but throughout Asia. It included communications from those executed in January 1951: a statement from Abe Sueo on the unfairness of the trials; the last words of Kaneda Sadao and Suzuki Mitsutada maintaining their innocence as they headed to the scaffold; and letters from many of the others.[52]

Nokosareta hitobito: Hitō senpan shikeishū no shuki (Those left behind: Memoirs of the war criminals sentenced to death in the Philippines), published a year earlier, offered even more extensive writings and essays by those condemned to death in the Philippines and awaiting execution. Okamoto Torao, the book's editor, sought to remind the Japanese people that even though Japan had regained its independence and could look to the future, those who remained behind in a foreign prison should not be forgotten. A brief foreword offered the opinion that whether these men had committed crimes was not the issue—it was their countrymen as a whole who should assume responsibility and work for their return. The first letters, written by Hamada Yoshio, were prefaced by an introduction that stressed his innocence—he was a victim of a case of completely mistaken identity. Letters sent by Teshima Hiroshi and Kobayashi Masataka protested their innocence; others wrote to their families about their lives in prison and their thoughts of those waiting for them at home.[53]

Among these predictable letters and diary entries, however, was a rather remarkable essay by Satō Ichirō. Included in the latter half of the volume, Satō's essay summarized the reasons why he had decided to plead guilty to charges that he had ordered and participated in a massacre of Filipino civilians. Satō argued that he had a duty to protect his subordinates, especially since his superior officer had so signally failed to take on the responsibility himself. He also maintained that he had no choice—that a failure to follow the orders of his superiors meant death. But he also did not shrink from what had happened, questioning why so many, even children, had to be killed. The editor's introduction to Satō's piece acknowledged that Satō had been charged with a terrible (*susamajii*) atrocity but stressed how manfully he took responsibility and the respect he had earned for trying to have the initial orders countermanded and for seeking to protect his men.[54]

Satō's essay suggests that the increasingly dominant narrative of innocence continued to coexist with a second narrative that recognized the atrocities but sought to situate them in a sympathetic context. Former Japanese ambassador to the Philippines Murata Shōzō, reflecting on the reasons for postwar Filipino animosity, stressed the factors that made Japanese wartime behavior explicable or inevitable, if nonetheless regrettable. Murata focused on the period immediately before the end of the war, when Japanese troops, harried by the Americans, committed unforgivable acts. But Murata concluded that the soldiers, faced with death and enormous deprivations, acted no differently from how any other men would act if placed in similar circumstances. Because innocent people were killed, Murata argued that some reparations should be paid. Former Lt. Gen. Kuroda Shigenori, who had been granted a pardon and had returned home in 1952, also tried to frame what had happened in the Philippines in a broader context. It was true that Japanese military commanders had failed to exercise effective discipline over their troops, but the increasing guerrilla activity and the return of the Americans had created an atmosphere of despair that led to acts of destruction and killing.[55]

The families of the convicted embraced a similar logic. In a petition presented to the Japanese representatives on their way to the San Francisco Peace

Conference in September 1951, family representatives argued that reports of atrocities committed by the Japanese military were one-sided and distorted. The incidents that had occurred were the result of the increasingly severe guerrilla attacks in the later stages of the war. The environment made the accurate identification of war crimes suspects extremely difficult, and the subsequent trials were unfair—local witnesses burned with revenge against anyone who was Japanese, and the defendants had no one on their side. Hence those individual Japanese convicted of war crimes were really innocent.[56]

What such commentaries did was to provide a broader contextual framework in which to situate the stories of individual war criminals. This in turn allowed for the construction of a tiered and interwoven narrative of innocence. Individuals like the men of the Nakamura case and the others still incarcerated in Muntinlupa were not guilty—they had been convicted of the crimes of others and allowed to assume responsibility for the sins of all Japanese. But any challenges to that hypothesis—and men like Kagao, Ueki, and Tsuji worked hard to prevent such challenges—could be met by explanations of what happened in the Philippines that mitigated the entire issue of individualized guilt. The conviction that a miscarriage of justice had occurred—that some innocent men had been executed—came to be conflated with the notion that all the men sentenced to death were innocent and all those incarcerated in Muntinlupa had been made to suffer for the acts of others. The cumulative effect of these writings at the very least served to publicize the existence of Japanese soldiers in prison in the Philippines and to marshal support for their release. The mounting volume of petitions signed by ordinary Japanese seeking commutation of their sentences and repatriation back to Japan is testimony to the increasing sympathy with which their countrymen viewed their circumstances.

Historian John Dower has written about the kind of "willful forgetting" that ordinary Japanese engaged in, a pattern that appears entirely consistent with the efforts of Kagao, Tsuji, and Ueki to focus public attention on the men in Muntinlupa rather than their crimes. War criminals came to be rehabilitated in the public consciousness: "Defendants who had been convicted and sentenced to imprisonment became openly regarded as victims rather than victimizers. . . . Those who had been executed, often in far-away lands, were resurrected through their own parting words. One remembered the criminals, while forgetting their crimes."[57] Indeed, it is quite striking how comfortable some commentators became in applying the word "victim" to describe those convicted of war crimes and incarcerated in the Philippines.

Dower argues that several factors contributed to this transition in perception. After the war ended, the soldiers who made it back home and their waiting families faced years of deprivation and hardship: "In this milieu, the plight of Japan's Asian victims, even when acknowledged, seemed remote and abstract." Geopolitical considerations contributed still further to mitigating the development of any deeper sense of Japanese responsibility for the war or its victims, as US Cold War policy dictated a focus on close ties with Japan.[58]

The voices of the Japanese war criminals incarcerated in Muntinlupa came through clearly at a time when the direct voices of Filipino victims of atrocities did not. This was true by virtue of what Japanese commentators stressed in the early 1950s, but it was also true earlier during the actual conduct of the trials in the Philippines. The testimony of survivors was not widely publicized, nor did the Tokyo trial of Japan's leaders provide a forum for Filipino witnesses directly to share their stories. The key witnesses during the Philippines phase of the Tokyo trial were Americans, who testified principally to their experiences as POWs and internees. The sufferings of Filipinos were presented in written summaries of affidavits or through excerpts from the Yamashita and Homma trials.[59]

Philippine Response: A Counternarrative

In the early 1950s observers of the Philippine scene tended to see a softening in overall attitudes toward Japan. The war criminals' release in July 1953 prompted a Manila newspaper editor to comment that there was now a "slow lifting of the curtain of active hatred residual in the Philippines. It will not bear pushing too hard, or hurrying too much."[60] Willard Hanna, a member of the American Universities Field Staff, wrote in 1955 that he sensed a changed mood: "The bitter hatred of Japan and the determination to exact the last possible sen in expiation for the savageries of the wartime years are beginning to die down."[61] It was also somewhat helpful that the Japanese response to the pardon news had included some recognition of what the Philippines had suffered as well as effusive expressions of gratitude for the Philippine government's "magnanimous" "act of grace," which reflected the "generous and fair spirit" of the Filipino people.[62]

Filipinos had already exacted a measure of retribution: their own government had put 155 Japanese on trial for war crimes, convicted 138, and ultimately put 17 to death. And the simple act of assuming responsibility for the trials offered a basis for the incorporation of a grander narrative combining civilized behavior and Christian forgiveness. President Roxas, in issuing an announcement to the press about the transfer of responsibility back in 1947, noted, "It is only fitting and proper that our government exercise the prerogative of trying and punishing those guilty of war crimes against our people. In conducting these trials, we are taking our place with other nations of the world that have seen fit to bring the guilty to justice and to perpetuate on record, through fair and reasonable trials, the story of what happened to the innocent when the enemy ran berserk all over the world."[63] His statement provides a remarkably cogent articulation of Philippine motivations: to be viewed as a legitimate member of the international community; to be seen as capable of conducting fair trials; and to document the brutality of the Japanese occupation.

As the Philippine government contemplated release of the war criminals in the early 1950s, this nationalist narrative with its echoes of the Philippines as a civilized country meshed well with a narrative that stressed the virtues of Christian forgiveness. The Quirino administration sought to couch the pardons in moral and humanitarian terms (as well as expressions of the anticipated better relations to come), presumably in the belief that this was the best way to gain popular acceptance.[64] If the trials could be seen as an expression of the Philippines' commitment to the highest norms of justice, so too could the pardons be viewed as evidence of Filipinos' magnanimity.

Perhaps as proof of the success of this message, the pardoning of the war criminals in 1953 did not appear to meet with widespread condemnation for reasons that commentators attributed to the passage of time and a pragmatic assessment of available options. Editorials in the Manila press suggested variously that the Philippines had acted wisely; that Filipinos must focus on hard work rather than efforts to cash in on wartime suffering; and that clemency would free the Philippines from war memories and allow Filipinos to look to the future. The Philippines had taken the high road—and Japan should be under no apprehension that the pardons represented an attempt to buy cash reparations or parlay a humanitarian act into financial advantage.[65]

David Steinberg, in a different context, has suggested another possible interpretation of Filipino reaction to the pardons. In his thoughtful examination of how the Philippines addressed the issue of wartime collaboration, he argues that Filipinos' willingness to abandon retribution for collaborators can be explained by the wartime trauma that left many exhausted: "The death and destruction of the last months of the war so stunned the country that the nation was comatose. . . . Feelings still ran high, but most people were left numb with their personal grief, and vengeance would not restore life. In such chaos, the society very humanly recoiled from hate and closed ranks as the only hope for beginning life again. The horrors of war were repressed as too grim to remember, and the busy tasks of reconstruction served as a welcome sponge, absorbing energy and attention."[66]

Such feelings might also help to explain the apparent indifference among Filipinos to the ultimate fate of the war criminals. A *Mainichi Shimbun* reporter on hand to cover the pardons commented that he felt no sense of anti-Japanese feeling among Filipinos. His taxi driver told him that his two brothers had been killed by Japanese forces and his sister had been "slaughtered" (*gyakusatsu*) by members of the Kempeitai at Fort Santiago. For a while he burned with hatred, but now he felt absolutely nothing. Indeed, according to the reporter, the driver believed that in order for the Philippines to prosper it needed to reengage with Japan.[67]

Others echoed this more pragmatic rationale. A Japanese observer, an editor of *Kyōdō News* service, suggested that the pardons had been driven by economic considerations. Saitō Masami argued that Filipino business interests as well as government officials had brought pressure to bear on the president in order to remove a barrier to increased trade and economic opportunities. Perhaps President Quirino, a Catholic, was motivated by humanitarian concerns, but he could do nothing without supporters, and they desired improved relations with Japan in their own interests. With such motivations, the attitudes of the Filipino elite toward Japan were increasingly favorable. Not so those of ordinary Filipinos, who, with the passage of time, were simply moving away from hatred to indifference. Saitō counted it as progress that Filipinos around Manila were no longer inclined to hit or kill Japanese on sight.[68] The belief (or perhaps hope) that the elite were more receptive to a rapprochement with Japan was not uncommon; for example, the president of *Nippon Times* was reported as seeing a "subtle" shift in attitudes among merchants and the intelligentsia as early as 1952, in contrast to the remainder of the general population.[69]

Regardless of the motivations for the pardons—Christian charity, a pragmatic desire to move beyond the war, economic incentives, or even the suggestion that influential individuals sought to reap personal gain—Filipinos generally retained an underlying belief in the legitimacy of the judicial proceedings that had convicted and sentenced Japanese for war crimes.[70] They were by no means disposed to discard the validity of the trials or ignore the realities of atrocities committed by the Japanese. As noted passionately by one commentator, the Japanese in Muntinlupa were "all criminals, every one of them, perhaps the most cold-blooded and hardened bunch the country has behind bars."[71] A *Manila Times* editorial emphasized that the war criminals given amnesty had been "duly tried according to law," and the act of pardoning them was not "merely a casual gesture, but a civilized one that can come only from a civilized neighbor who forgives so that bygones may not be repeated."[72]

This belief in the Philippines' adherence to fair trial proceedings was reflected in the impassioned response to Diet member Kora's letter. Readers challenged both her facts and her logic:

> If Mrs. Kora had been here when [the Japanese] were slaughtering the innocent people, young and old, she would have seen how overly-anxious they were in carrying out the inhuman orders they had received from their superiors. The lives of these "innocent" officials are not enough to pay for the lives of the thousands of innocent men, women and children killed by them. . . . What does Mrs. Kora mean by her appeal for a rehearing in behalf of the Jap war criminals? . . . They were tried fairly before an unbiased tribunal and were even represented and defended by attorneys. Were their Filipino victims given any hearing at all before they were massacred?[73]

Yet the passage of time had caused a reconsideration by some. In a remarkable letter directed to President Quirino, the mayor, parish priest, and many others of the town of Hinundayan, Leyte, expressed gratitude that the president had set such a fine example of forgiving one's enemies: "[The] freeing of the Japanese soldiers will enhance before the eyes of the people of the Far East still living in the darkness of idolatry, our Christian civilization." But the writers went much further, conveying their belief that one of the Japanese war criminals, Mori Kenkichi, had been wrongly convicted and sentenced to death as a consequence of the "blind hatred" that existed at the time. Mori had been kind to the townspeople; accordingly, the writers appealed to Quirino to pardon him rather than simply commute his sentence to life.[74]

It must also be noted that a narrative of Christian forgiveness could only be pushed so far, as an incident in 1957 illustrates quite well. In February, after the long-awaited resolution of the reparations negotiations, a Japanese goodwill mission headed by a member of the upper house of the Japanese Diet arrived in the Philippines. To the embarrassment of the Japanese government, the Manila press discovered that the party included the notorious Capt. Yanase Shoichi, the "tiger of Fort Santiago." Yanase had escaped prosecution for war crimes by helping the Americans build cases against other defendants; his superiors and subordinates were not so lucky.[75] Amid the resulting protests and outcries over his return to the Philippines, it was revealed that he had been warmly received by Senate president Eulogio Rodriguez, who credited Yanase with saving the life of one of his sons. The group quickly left for home. Back in Tokyo, Yanase explained that Senator Rodriguez had personally invited him, with assurances that "he would not experience any unpleasantness in the Philippines." A *Manila Times* columnist asked why Japan expected the Philippines to welcome, as a goodwill ambassador, a "dreaded torture artist."[76]

Trials and the Path to "Reconciliation"

The war criminals had been pardoned and repatriated to Japan, but this did not in any sense represent agreement between Japan and the Philippines on the conduct or meaning of the trials. Even as the incentives to release the men prevailed, the underlying positions of the two countries toward the issue of the war criminals and their guilt remained fundamentally unreconciled. Filipinos did not accept a Japanese-sponsored narrative of the innocence of those who had been incarcerated in Muntinlupa. Japanese could not accept Filipino views on their guilt. Members of the Japanese public came to accept the assurances of the men and their families that they were innocent—that they had been victims either because of their absolute innocence or, at worst, because of the circumstances in which they found themselves. In the Philippines, the issue of innocence did not matter—or, rather, it was not an issue that engendered much concern. Filipinos, emphasizing the due process of the proceedings that led to guilty verdicts and the painstaking nature of sentence reviews, were content with the verdicts that had resulted from their military courts.

The pragmatic decision of the Philippine government to pardon the war criminals, and the effusive expressions of thanks by Japanese government officials and private individuals, obscured these differing perceptions among Japanese and Filipinos. Although Filipino commentators were quick to object to any challenges to the legitimacy of Philippine justice, the two governments chose not to contest (let alone resolve) the differing narratives of the trials that had been constructed. Japanese, by focusing on the magnanimity and Christian charity displayed by the Philippine government, and Filipinos, by taking credit for a civilized and moral choice, could find a shared ground that avoided any hard scrutiny or resolution of the specifics of guilt or innocence.

If Japanese and Filipinos could not agree on individual culpability for war crimes and indeed persisted in constructing conflicting narratives about the trials, what ramifications did this have for the broader issues of reengagement and reconciliation? Even if, as some have argued, war crimes trials cannot be envisioned as a direct means to move toward reconciliation, how might the trials have affected, for better or worse, the normalization of relations between Japan and the Philippines? It is tempting to argue that the trials had, ultimately, very little direct impact on the subsequent course of Philippines-Japan relations and certainly were of far less consequence than economic or broader geopolitical considerations. But the way in which the issue of the war criminals was resolved, as much as the trials themselves, arguably had an impact on the climate in which the Philippines and Japan pursued greater interactions at both state and societal levels.

One legitimate argument is that the very act of holding the trials operated as a necessary (whether or not sufficient) condition for the steps that followed: the pardons granted the war criminals, the conclusion of a reparations agreement, the restoration of diplomatic relations, and the resumption of trade and other exchanges. Of course, this need not have involved trials conducted by the Philippine government—the trials initially convened by US military commissions could have continued with Philippine support. But the visible demonstration that Japanese were in fact being made to face their victims in a Philippine court of law—and that at least some paid the ultimate price—contributed to an atmosphere in which the Filipino elite could pursue a postwar relationship with Japan with the acquiescence, if not the wholehearted support, of ordinary Filipinos.

Moreover, disagreements over the trials themselves need not have prevented a more general ability to move toward a shared understanding of the war and what happened in the Philippines. Susan Dwyer has articulated steps in a process toward reconciliation that rests on this concept. She argues that this process embodies "the core notion . . . of bringing apparently incompatible descriptions of events into narrative equilibrium." The stages in the process involve a simple articulation of the circumstances, followed by an appreciation of a range of interpretations of the events in question: "Finally, parties to the reconciliation attempt to choose from this range of interpretations some subset that allows them each to accommodate the disruptive event into their ongoing narratives. *It is not required that all parties settle on a single interpretation, only that they are mutually tolerant of a limited set of interpretations*" (emphasis added).[77]

Without belaboring the point too much, a sense of *collective* Japanese responsibility might have served as a vehicle to begin to bridge the differences between Filipino and Japanese perceptions of justice for war crimes. By focusing less on the guilt of specific individuals and more on generalized expressions of responsibility (or, indeed, remorse), the possibilities for achieving "mutual tolerance" for a limited set of interpretations about the war conceivably increased. Some of those most directly concerned with the fate of the war criminals in Muntinlupa had already begun, by mid-1952, to accept the notion of collective responsibility. The participants in a Radio Tokyo broadcast of the "Sunday

Club" on May 25, 1952 (including newsman Tsuji Yutaka and pardoned war criminal Kita Heiji), voiced the belief that Japan, and the Japanese people, should shoulder the burden for the "national crimes" (*kokuminteki na zai*) perpetrated in the Philippines.[78]

Even so, the ability to move beyond the differing narratives about the war crimes trials and, more broadly, to avoid the recriminations that have unsettled Japan's relations with its East Asian neighbors has arguably depended in large measure on the attitudes of Filipinos. Nakano Satoshi has argued that, some decades after the war, Filipinos have been willing to accept general expressions of apology from Japanese mourners, essentially avoiding a "collision of memories" about specific horrors (and perpetrators). This pattern that Nakano describes—Japanese visitors willing to offer general apologies but only rarely being able to "admit their own, their lost loved one's, or their lost comrade's wrongdoings"—finds a clear link back to the postwar resistance to the idea of the individual guilt of those incarcerated in Muntinlupa.[79]

Conclusion

At war's end the Philippines, like other Allied governments, had to grapple with the ways and means of trying Japanese accused of war crimes. The Philippine government chose to use military commissions for this purpose, adopting and adapting the rules employed by the Americans to hold Japanese individuals accountable for atrocities committed against Filipino citizens. In accepting responsibility for trying war crimes suspects, Philippine president Manuel Roxas articulated the basic purpose of the trials: to conduct "fair and reasonable" proceedings and then punish the guilty. At the same time, he conveyed two additional goals: to document the brutalities suffered by Filipinos at the hands of the Japanese and to contrast Japan's lawless behavior with the Philippines' commitment to international (read: civilized) standards of justice.

Having assumed responsibility for the trials in 1947, the Philippine government put much effort into ensuring that they proceeded in a manner that would be seen to be obedient to the rule of law and sensitive to the legal rights of the accused. Circumstances necessitated some compromises, notably in the matter of legal representation for Japanese defendants and their access to witnesses for their defense, but those responsible for the trials hoped and intended that the conduct of the trials would reflect well on the Philippines. Yet, perhaps inevitably, Japanese differed from Filipinos in their conclusions about the fairness of the trials. The heavy percentage of guilty verdicts and the numbers of death sentences, coupled with what appeared to be outright miscarriages of justice (specifically, the Nakamura case verdicts), only reinforced the belief that anti-Japanese sentiment in the Philippines was too strong to allow for disinterested justice.

This dilemma of how the victors can possibly bring the losers to justice in fair and just proceedings is not unique to the Philippine trials, nor are questions of how best to accomplish that goal. Gary Jonathan Bass, for one, has argued that an "impartial international tribunal," while not devoid of risk, represents a better choice than the alternatives: national trials or vengeance. David Crocker is more sanguine, noting that the rule of law "is capable of more or less institutional embodiment," with the possibility of developing sufficient safeguards to protect defendants in national jurisdictions.[1] Others who are more focused on the need for postconflict resolution and eventual reconciliation shift the discussion away from trials to alternate postconflict mechanisms, such as the truth commissions established in South Africa and the courts in Rwanda.[2] But each of these choices is situational, depending on the nature of the conflict, the needs of the victims, and, of course, practical constraints on a state's ability and commitment to finding and bringing perpetrators to account.

The Philippine trials posed a number of challenges, ranging from the difficulties in collecting evidence and obtaining witnesses to the dilemmas represented by the convening of proceedings in the aftermath of a harsh and destructive occupation. The judges were members of the Philippine military; verdicts and sentences were reviewed by Filipino officers; the Philippine National Defense Forces chief of staff approved verdicts and sentences; and Philippine president Elpidio Quirino ruled on sentences of life imprisonment and death. These men could hardly have escaped direct exposure to Japanese conduct during the three years of enemy occupation. (Indeed, the chief of staff was a survivor of the Bataan Death March, and the president had survived incarceration and suffered the deaths of several family members at the hands of Japanese snipers.)

A central question is, then, did the Philippine trials tilt toward the inherent bias implied by Bass's criticism of national trials, or did they successfully embody the safeguards suggested by Crocker? Bass and others have posited the fundamental safeguards/criteria employed to ensure the essential fairness of war crimes trials: basic standards of due process (rights of defendants to retain counsel, to present evidence, and to cross-examine witnesses), the possibility of acquittal, appropriate standards of evidence, and proportionality of punishment. The distinction between trials conducted by those "steeped in Western domestic legal traditions" and Soviet-style show trials should be manifest.[3]

By these standards, the Philippine government–led trials measure up rather well. The regulations governing the conduct of the trials (closely patterned after the American regulations) stipulated that each defendant was entitled to see, in advance, a copy of the charges and specifications against him; to be represented by counsel; and to testify on his own behalf, present evidence in his defense, and cross-examine witnesses. Trial transcripts indicate that procedural requirements were adhered to with some rigor. Defendants acknowledged receiving notice of the charges against them, and all were represented by counsel who (after resolution of the issue of Japanese versus Filipino defense counsel) were generally viewed as competent and who mounted vigorous defenses for their clients. The vast majority of the defendants were able to face their accusers. All defendants were afforded the opportunity to testify, and many did so. Philippine trials did not foreclose the possibility of acquittal: eleven defendants were found not guilty at trial, and fourteen others had their sentences overturned or reduced during the painstaking sentence review process that followed. Viewed in comparative terms, Philippine military tribunals do not appear to have levied disproportionately harsh sentences; the percentage of defendants given death sentences (and certainly the percentage actually executed) was not out of line with the penalties levied by other governments. Finally, the trials were open to the public and received ongoing scrutiny by an active press.

The existence of various safeguards—due process, proportional punishments, the potential for not-guilty verdicts, and sentence review—has led some observers to conclude that the trials in Asia (at least those conducted in accordance with Western legal standards) served the interests of justice reasonably well. Individual problem cases were not viewed as destructive of the general proposition that the trials were fair. Emblematic of that assessment is Ricardo T. Jose's characterization of the Philippine trials: "There were failures along the way, but many of the trials were indeed handled responsibly."[4] Moreover, the Philippine trials measure up well when compared with counterpart trials by other Allied countries in Asia.

Certainly, the Philippine government made a conscientious effort to establish a system and procedures that afforded defendants due process, notwithstanding the compromises made regarding legal representation and admissible evidence. And judgments about the overall fairness of trials in the Philippines must take into account the rigor with which trial verdicts and sentences were scrutinized by a separate panel of reviewers. Still, did a process that could be considered a good-faith effort under the circumstances have resulted in miscarriages of justice? It seems likely that it did in some few instances. The plain truth is that there was merit in both prosecution and defense criticisms: some Japanese defendants did lie to protect themselves and their colleagues and did collude on their testimony; some prosecution witnesses did lie or at best mistakenly identified the wrong Japanese as the perpetrators. The conclusion that, on the whole, the trials were conducted creditably does not negate the likelihood that some few verdicts were rendered in error, not least because of the commissions' reliance on then established legal precedents privileging eyewitness testimony over defendants' claims of alibi.

There is also the matter of feasible alternatives. The Philippine trials dealt, for the most part, with those accused of directly ordering or committing atrocities rather than those charged with broader command responsibility or leadership. These were defendants who had no serious prospects of facing any sort of international tribunal. Neither of the two alternatives on opposite sides of the spectrum for dealing with such suspects—vengeance in the form of summary execution or repatriation without accountability—represented acceptable outcomes. Given the commitment to bring to trial those charged with the actual commission of atrocities, and faced with the impracticality (and lack of political will) to convene any sort of international proceedings, let alone contemplate turning over prosecutions to the Japanese government, the path chosen (national trials) proved the most feasible in the context of the times and the resources available. To be sure, the resulting trials were trials by the victors, but to borrow a phrase from Bass, what mattered was *which* victor and *which* justice.[5]

Nonetheless, it is important not to be too complacent in assessing the trial outcomes in the Philippines and elsewhere in Asia, especially as regards the "generally fair with some exceptions" rubric (with its implied notion that good intentions mitigate bad outcomes) and the corollary argument that the trials should not be judged by contemporary standards. In the Philippines case, this means that, yes, the trials stand up well to both comparative assessments with other World War II proceedings and the standards then in place. But it also means that they offer up some cautionary observations about the key attributes of fair trials, particularly the importance of competent defense counsel, judges whose impartiality is manifest, and the soundness of judgments about the legal liability of individual defendants.

Beyond questions of fairness or legitimacy, the trials in the Philippines raise important questions about the broader utility and impact of such trials. In theory at least, trials place responsibility where it belongs—on individuals—and by so doing prevent the condemnation of whole societies for the actions of individual members. This in turn, it is argued, could ease future efforts at reconciliation.[6] Paradoxically, however, one can make the argument in the case of the Philippines that Japanese and Filipinos could more readily agree—within certain limitations—on *collective* Japanese responsibility for atrocities even as they disagreed over who was *individually* criminally responsible. Compare, for example, the views of two survivors decades later, the first a former Japanese war criminal and the second a Filipino:

> For no particular reason, I was tried as a war criminal. . . . But when I think about the 600 Chinese and many Filipinos killed [in San Pablo], I can understand

> [Filipinos'] anger. Even though I did not kill their compatriots my fellow Japanese killed those innocent people.[7]

> It is irrelevant to complain to the Filipinos and judges [about the trials' unfairness]. All Japanese officers and soldiers and Makapili, who collaborated [with the] Japanese Army, were guilty. . . . View things this way and you will see that those who are complaining forget the fact that all of them are guilty.[8]

In the case of the Philippine trials, a somewhat ambiguous embrace of collective responsibility was viewed at the time as a means to obtain the release of those still imprisoned and facing the ultimate punishment. That is, the *collectivization* of responsibility would mitigate against the guilt of the convicted and could be used to persuade Japanese to petition for their release and Filipinos to be receptive to those appeals. In the words of newsman and commentator Tsuji Yutaka, better to hold accountable the Japanese people who had sent soldiers to the Philippines rather than the few convicted war criminals who had shouldered the whole burden of how the war was waged there. Still, once the war criminals had been safely repatriated, the narrative constructed about the trials helped to solidify the conviction in Japan that victors' justice had triumphed over "real" justice and that those convicted of atrocities were more deserving of pity than opprobrium. In hindsight, the initial willingness to assume some sort of collective responsibility takes on a more tactical guise focused on an immediate objective—release of the war criminals—rather than a sustained conviction about war responsibility. For those Japanese made accountable for war crimes, the sense remained that the trial system imposed by the victors simply failed to appreciate the nature of the war and the circumstances that led to the abuses that occurred.

From a Philippine vantage point, the trials had important uses that were entwined with but reached beyond the outcomes in specific trials. A singular focus on how fair the Philippine trials were in comparative or even absolute terms tends to obscure these broader considerations. Arguably, the conduct of the trials—particularly, the very act of taking responsibility for them—helped to validate the status of a newly independent (and former colony) as equal to the task. Once the legal proceedings had been concluded, moreover, the Philippine government could lay claim to treating Japanese prisoners comparatively humanely and agreeing to their relatively rapid repatriation. Filipinos, in short, could claim the moral high ground: they had treated Japanese with far more consideration and mercy than Japanese had shown Filipinos during the war, and they had proven more forgiving (or perhaps more pragmatic) than the Americans in agreeing to a general amnesty by the end of 1953.

It was on this foundation that members of the Filipino elite constructed—with a certain amount of Japanese assistance—a narrative of Christian forgiveness that ultimately allowed for the pardoning of the war criminals and paved the way for the resumption of a bilateral relationship with Japan. Nonetheless, it remains striking that Filipinos so quickly managed to look beyond the wartime brutality sufficiently to enable the Philippine government to proceed on the tandem fronts of release of the war criminals and negotiation of reparations for war damage. Historian Nakano Satoshi has argued that the Philippines and Japan have since embarked on a journey characterized by a pattern of "apology and forgiveness" that has allowed the past to recede.[9] If so, the seeds of that journey can be traced to the handling of the trials and the pardoning of the convicted.

Epilogue

The men who returned from Muntinlupa had forged bonds that, for many, lasted until their deaths. It was the Muntinlupa Society that provided a concrete locus for their efforts to maintain those ties. The group had grown to nearly a thousand members by the time the last of the war criminals had been released in 1953. Its purpose fulfilled, it reconstituted itself as a much smaller group of returnees, their families, and a few supporters.[1]

A central avowed purpose of the society was to keep alive the memory of the seventeen who had been executed—who had been sacrificed so that the others might live. To that end, members of the society convened a meeting each month in Tokyo for a "day of remembrance" in recognition of the night in January 1951 when fourteen of their number had gone to their deaths. Those who could attended faithfully. In 1979, for example, these monthly meetings attracted as many as twenty members; Yamamoto Tokuzō and Masuda Masukazu rarely missed a meeting that year.[2]

The society also held periodic general conventions for the entire membership. The second general meeting was held in Tokyo to mark the tenth anniversary of the men's return from Muntinlupa. On the thirtieth anniversary, the society published a commemorative history that included diary entries from their time in Muntinlupa as well as a detailed chronology of the society's postwar meetings and activities.[3]

Members of the Muntinlupa Society welcomed visits from Filipinos who had supported the prisoner release movement. The group hosted a party for the visiting former president Quirino, and at its third general convention, in 1966, the group honored prison superintendent Alfredo Bunye and his wife. Chaplain Kagao and former prisoners, including Mineo Shisuhiko, Onoyama Masaichi, and Ichinose Haruo, warmly greeted the couple at Haneda airport on their arrival. On Bunye's death in April 1971, members of the society took up a collection for his wife to pay for his grave marker.[4]

Over time, some members of the society also found ways to communicate publicly about their experiences in the Philippines. In 1966 Mineo Shisuhiko published a memoir—essentially his diary entries for the period of his trial and incarceration (he had written a page at a time and had them sent to his wife through intermediaries). Mineo, who had been sentenced to death, returned to Japan in 1953 after his sentence had been finally overturned by the sentence review panel. He and his family, traumatized by his experience, kept silent until he came across the diary years later where he had hidden it away. And it was then, realizing how his experiences as a death row inmate had transformed his life, that he decided to publish it.[5] Satō Sō, who had been sentenced to life in prison, wrote his own account in 1981. For Satō, the trials had been about revenge. Japanese soldiers caught up in the desperate struggle at the end of the war were made to pay the price for the increasing number of incidents caused by the nurturing of anti-Japanese guerrilla movements. It became impossible to distinguish between the guerrillas and the civilians, and it was not difficult to imagine that soldiers who had lost their emotional balance and were surrounded by guerrillas would commit war crimes. In writing this account, Satō hoped to educate the many in his country who had no real understanding of what had happened.[6]

The ranks of the returnees had thinned to eighty by 1983, the thirtieth anniversary of their release from Muntinlupa. The generals were among the first to leave the scene. Rear Adm. Furuse Takasue died in 1960, Lt. Gen. Yokoyama Shizuo and Maj. Gen. Kawaguchi Kiyotake in 1961, and Lt. Gen. Kuroda Shigenori and Maj. Gen. Masuoka Kensichi in 1964.[7] Among the last were Shirota Gintarō and Itō Masayasu, the composers of "Ah, the Night Is Deep in Muntinlupa." Both lived to see the twenty-first century; Shirota passed away in 2006 at the age of ninety-two, and Itō died in 2009 at age eighty-six. Their obituaries highlighted their roles in writing the famous song.[8]

It was Kagao Shūnin's death in 1977 at the age of seventy-six that sparked the greatest outpouring of sorrow. After his return from Muntinlupa, Kagao had received letters of commendation from the ministers of justice, foreign affairs, and welfare in recognition of his services to the prisoners in Muntinlupa. He became one of the leaders of the Kōyasan Tokyo Branch Temple and continued his advocacy on behalf of the war criminals. In 1956 he visited temple affiliates in Honolulu and Los Angeles and also met with representatives of the U.S. State Department to appeal for clemency for the remaining war criminals incarcerated in Sugamo Prison. In August 1953, just after his return from the

Philippines, he published his memoirs, *Montenrupa ni inoru* (Living in Muntinlupa), in August 1953, and he and Ueki Shinkichi both participated in various documentaries. His obituary remembered him as the "father of Muntinlupa" and paid tribute to his dedicated efforts to see the men home safely.[9]

Tsuji Yutaka continued his career as a newsman. Famous both for his championship of the war criminals and his unsuccessful efforts in 1952 to coax straggler Onoda Hiroo from his hiding place on Lubang Island, Tsuji went on to serve in various capacities for the Asahi Shimbun Company. He died of pneumonia in 2008 at the age of eighty-nine. Former war criminal Nakamata Tomisaburō, in his reflections on his own career as a news correspondent, reminisced about Tsuji's arrival at Muntinlupa and the hope he brought to them all. (Nakamata, one of the student conscripts who had been condemned to death, had gone on to a varied career as a journalist, working in Vietnam and China. He managed to return to the Philippines in 1965.)[10]

Ueki Shinkichi continued to manage the affairs of the society but was able to relax his single-minded focus on the fates of the war criminals once they had been repatriated. He married and in 1954 accepted a transfer to the Japan Defense Agency. Retired after a long career in government, he turned eighty-six in September 2007, still healthy and the custodian of the issues of the *Monten* newsletters and aging clippings of the prisoner release effort mounted so long ago.[11]

Notes

Introduction

1. Arai Emiko, "Montenrupa no atsui kaze," *Shio* 475 (September 1998): 253.

2. Ibid., 248–55.

3. Nakano Satoshi, "The Politics of Mourning," in *Philippines-Japan Relations*, ed. Ikehata Setsuho and Lydia N. Yu-Jose (Manila: Ateneo de Manila University Press, 2003), 356–59.

4. Arai, "Montenrupa no atsui kaze," 255; Itō Masayasu et al., eds., *Monten: Kikoku 30 shūnen tokushūgo* (Tokyo: Montenrupa no Kai, 1983), 157–62.

5. Transcript, 192–217, and prosecution exhibit 6, case no. 23, *Philippines v. Teramoto Tukuji* (as in transcript; name characters suggest it should be Tokuji), box 1692, UD 1323, Records of Allied Operational and Occupation Headquarters, World War II, RG 331, NACP.

6. Hayashi Hirofumi, *BC-kyū senpan saiban* (Tokyo: Iwanami Shoten, 2005), 12, 19, 200–214. For references to the general characterization of these trials as unfair, see Madoka Futamura, *War Crimes Tribunals and Transitional Justice: The Tokyo Trial and the Nuremburg Legacy* (London: Routledge Taylor & Francis Group, 2008), 75–76; and Utsumi Aiko, "Changing Japanese Views of the Allied Occupation of Japan and the War Crimes Trials," *Journal of the Australian War Memorial* 30 (April 1997), www.awm.gov.au/journal/j30/utsumi.htm.

7. Historians have explored the emergence of a Japanese victim narrative whereby, as John Dower observes, "one remembered the criminals, while forgetting their crimes." John Dower, *Embracing Defeat: Japan in the Wake of World War II* (New York: W. W. Norton, 1999), 513.

8. Ishida Jintarō, *The Remains of War: Apology and Forgiveness—the Testimonies of the Japanese Imperial Army and Its Filipino Victims* (Quezon City: Megabooks Company, 2001).

9. The full text of the Potsdam Declaration is available at http://www.ndl.go.jp/constitution/e/etc/c06.html.

10. Two of the original twenty-eight defendants died during the trial, while another defendant was deemed insane.

11. The trial of Class A war criminals has continued to receive critical attention and analysis, particularly among Japanese scholars. The landmark English-language study was Richard H. Minear, *Victors' Justice: The Tokyo War Crimes Trial* (Princeton, NJ:

Princeton University Press, 1971). More recently, scholars have explored the legal and procedural aspects of the trial in admirable detail, given needed focus to the conventional war crimes aspect of the trial, and provided a thoughtful survey of Japanese perspectives. See in particular Neil Boister and Robert Cryer, *The Tokyo International Military Tribunal: A Reappraisal* (Oxford: Oxford University Press, 2008); Yuma Totani, *The Tokyo War Crimes Trial: The Pursuit of Justice in the Wake of World War II* (Cambridge, MA: Harvard University Asia Center, 2008); and Futamura, *War Crimes Tribunals.*

12. A less official interpretation also existed wherein officers with responsibility for atrocities would be charged with Class B crimes, whereas soldiers who actually committed the atrocities would face Class C crimes charges. See Sandra Wilson, Robert Cribb, Beatrice Trefalt, and Dean Aszkielowicz, *Japanese War Criminals: The Politics of Justice after the Second World War* (New York: Columbia University Press, 2017), 7.

13. These figures do not include trials conducted by the People's Republic of China and the Soviet Union. See Wilson et al., *Japanese War Criminals*, 77–78, 93, 97, for data cited here and an explanation of sources.

14. Early studies include Philip R. Piccigallo, *The Japanese on Trial: Allied War Crimes Operations in the East, 1945–1951* (Austin: University of Texas Press, 1979); and R. John Pritchard, "Historical Experience of British War Crimes Courts in the Far East, 1946–1948," *International Relations* 6, no. 1 (1978): 311–26. Japanese scholars, by comparison, have given more sustained attention to these trials. Hayashi Hirofumi and Iwakawa Takashi, among others, have produced numerous studies on which to base our understanding of the trials. Hayashi's *BC-kyū senpan saiban*, for example, offers a systematic review of the trials conducted by various Allied countries. These examinations have been coupled with efforts to delve more deeply into the national trials, for example, explorations of the British trials in the Far East and the US trials in Yokohama. See also Hayashi Hirofumi, *Senpan saiban no kenkyū: Senpan saiban seisaku no keisei kara Tōkyō saiban, BC-kyū saiban made* (Tokyo: Shohan Bensei Shuppan, 2010); Hayashi, *Sabakareta sensō hanzai: Igirisu no tai-Nichi senpan saiban* (Tokyo: Iwanami Shoten, 1998); Iwakura Takashi, *Kōto no tsuchi to narutomo: BC-kyū senpan saiban* (Tokyo: Kōdansha, 1995); and Yokoyama Bengoshikai, *Hōtei no seijōki: BC-kyū senpan Yokohama no kiroku* (Tokyo: Nihon Hyōronsha, 2004).

15. For a discussion of the Yamashita trial and the doctrine of command responsibility, see David Cohen, "Beyond Nuremburg: Individual Responsibility for War Crimes," in *Human Rights in Political Transitions: Gettysburg to Bosnia*, ed. Carla Hesse and Robert Post (New York: Zone Books, 1999); Allan A. Ryan, *Yamashita's Ghost: War Crimes, MacArthur's Justice, and Command Accountability* (Lawrence: University Press of Kansas, 2012); and Yuma Totani, *Justice in Asia and the Pacific Region, 1945–1952: Allied War Crimes Prosecutions* (New York: Cambridge University Press, 2015), 33–46.

16. See Suzannah Linton, ed., *Hong Kong's War Crimes Trials* (Oxford: Oxford University Press, 2013); Barak Kushner, *Men to Devils and Devils to Men: Japanese War Crimes and Chinese Justice* (Cambridge, MA: Harvard University Press, 2016); Georgina Fitzpatrick, Timothy L. H. McCormack, and Narrelle Morris, eds., *Australia's War*

Crimes Trials 1945–51 (Leiden: Brill Nijhoff, 2016); Dean Aszkielowicz, *The Australian Pursuit of Japanese War Criminals, 1943–1957: From Foe to Friend* (Hong Kong: Hong Kong University Press, 2017); Lisette Schouten, "Colonial Justice in the Netherlands Indies War Crimes Trials," in *Trials for International Crimes in Asia*, ed. Kirsten Sellars (New York: Cambridge University Press, 2016), 75–99; Totani, *Justice in Asia*; Wilson et al., *Japanese War Criminals*; and "Special Feature: After the Trials—Repatriation and Release of Japanese War Criminals, 1946–1958," *Japanese Studies* 31, no. 2 (September 2011): 141–228.

17. Alexander Zahar, "Trial Procedure at the British Military Courts, Hong Kong, 1946–1948," in Linton, *Hong Kong's War Crimes Trials*, 13–69; Fitzpatrick, McCormack, and Morris, *Australia's War Crime Trials.*

18. See, for example, Narrelle Morris and Tim McCormack, "Were the Australian Trials Fair?," in Fitzpatrick, McCormack, and Morris, *Australia's War Crimes Trials*, 805–9; and Zahar, "Trial Procedure," 41–45.

19. Pritchard, "Historical Experience," 320.

20. Morris and McCormack, "Were the Australian Trials Fair?," 789–809.

21. Zahar, "Trial Procedure," 65–69.

22. Wilson et al., *Japanese War Criminals*, 10–11.

23. Kushner, *Men to Devils.*

24. Wilson et al., *Japanese War Criminals*, 4–6.

25. Filipino historian Ricardo T. Jose has provided an overview of the trials, but the only comprehensive treatment remains that of Japanese scholar Nagai Hitoshi. Neither of these works delves into the trial transcripts or thoroughly examines the actual conduct of all the trials and the legal and practical issues involved. See Ricardo Trota Jose, "The Philippine War Crimes Trials, 1947–1949," *Social Science Information* 33, no. 1 (January–June 2005): 33–34; and Nagai Hitoshi, *Firipin BC-kyū senpan saiban* (Tokyo: Kōdansha, 2013).

26. Jose P. Bengzon, *The Philippine Judicial System* (Manila: G. Rangel and Sons, 1968), 11–20; Enrique M. Fernando, *The American Constitutional Influence in Asia: Its Impact on the Philippine Legal System* (Manila: Supreme Court, 1976), 100–101; Joseph Ralston Hayden, *The Philippines: A Study in National Development* (New York: Macmillan Company, 1950), 240–42.

27. Theodore Friend, *The Blue-Eyed Enemy: Japan against the West in Java and Luzon, 1942–1945* (Princeton, NJ: Princeton University Press, 1988), 85–89. As another example, Jose Yulo, wartime chief justice of the Philippine Supreme Court, reminisced fondly about the legal training he had received during his employment with an American law firm in Manila and his acquisition of the "fundamentals of corporate practice" from American lawyers. See Alfred W. McCoy, "'Politics by Other Means': World War II in the Western Visayas, Philippines," in *Southeast Asia under Japanese Occupation*, ed. Alfred W. McCoy (New Haven, CT: Yale University Southeast Asia Studies, 1980), 161.

28. Early steps included the Philippine Bill of 1902, which authorized the creation of a Philippine national assembly with elected Filipino members that shared legislative

functions with the commission, and the 1916 Jones Act, which explicitly promised independence, albeit with no set time table, and provided for the establishment of an elected, completely Filipino, bicameral legislature to replace the hybrid assembly/commission arrangement.

29. Teodoro Agoncillo, *A Short History of the Philippines* (New York: Mentor Books, 1969), 192–94; Bengzon, *Philippine Judicial System*, 26–27; Fortunato Gupit Jr. and Daniel T. Martinez, *A Guide to Philippine Legal Materials: A Text on Philippine Legal Bibliography, Philippine Legal History, Philippine Legal System, Legal Philosophy, Methods of Legal Research* (Manila: Rex Book Store, 1993), 52–53.

30. In their struggle against the Spanish, revolutionary leaders like Emilio Aguinaldo and Artemio Ricarte had sought weapons and ammunition from the Japanese government, and some individual Japanese rallied to the revolutionary cause. See Ikehata Setsuho, *The Japanese Military Administration in the Philippines and the Tragedy of General Artemio Ricarte*, trans. Elpidio R. Sta. Romana (Singapore: National University of Singapore, 1991), 3, 27; and Elpidio R. Sta. Romana and Ricardo T. Jose, "'Never Imagine Yourself to Be Otherwise . . .': Filipino Images of Japan over the Centuries," *Asian Studies* (Quezon City) 29 (1991): 65–94.

31. Serafin D. Quiason, "The Japanese Community in Manila: 1898–1941," *Philippine Historical Review* 3 (1970): 191; Motoe Terami-Wada, "The Manila Japanese (1888–1942)," *Bulletin of the American Historical Collection* 17, no. 1 (January–March 1989): 84–85; Yoshikawa Yōko, "Jose M. Tagawa and the Japanese Commercial Sector in Manila, 1898–1920," *Philippine Studies* 43, no. 2 (1995): 182–85; Grant K. Goodman, "The Japanese Occupation of the Philippines: Commonwealth Sustained," *Philippine Studies* 36 (1988): 106; Lydia N. Yu-Jose, "World War II and the Japanese in the Prewar Philippines," *Journal of Southeast Asian Studies* 27, no. 1 (March 1996): 69–70.

32. For a discussion of the wartime role of Japanese residents in Davao, see Shinzo Hayase, "The Japanese Residents of 'Dabao-kuo,'" in *The Philippines under Japan: Occupation Policy and Reaction*, ed. Ikehata Setsuho and Ricardo Trota Jose (Manila: Ateneo de Manila University Press, 1999), 247–87.

33. Lydia Yu-Jose, *Japan Views the Philippines, 1900–1944* (Manila: Ateneo de Manila University Press, 1992), 84–90, 136–40; Yu-Jose, "Philippine, American, and Japanese Relations as Seen through the Issue of Neutralization," in Ikehata and Yu-Jose, *Philippines-Japan Relations*, 63–69.

34. Ricardo Trota Jose, "The Philippines: From Occupation and Japanese 'Independence' to Independence," in *1945 in Europe and Asia: Reconsidering the End of World War II and the Change of the World Order*, ed. Gerhard Krebs and Christian Oberländer (Munich: Iudicium, 1997), 272.

35. Grant K. Goodman, "The Japanese Occupation of the Philippines: Successful Collaboration of Invading and Indigenous Power Elites," *Journal of International Studies* (Sophia University) 5, no. 2 (December 1982): 36.

36. The Sakdal Party was founded by Ramos as a peasant organization that championed the interests of the poor against politicians and landlords; the party advocated

immediate independence as opposed to a commonwealth period, and the May 1935 uprising was intended to disrupt the plebiscite on the commonwealth constitution. After the revolt was ended, the Japanese government agreed to Ramos's extradition, and he returned to serve a jail sentence in the Philippines. See Agoncillo, *A Short History*, 196–97; David Joel Steinberg, *Philippine Collaboration in World War II* (Ann Arbor: University of Michigan Press, 1967), 24; and Hayden, *The Philippines*, 382–400.

37. Ikehata, Japanese Military Administration, 2–4, 9–10, 12–14; Pio Duran, *Philippine Independence and the Far Eastern Question* (Manila: Community Publishers Inc., 1935), 119–64; Theodore Friend, *Between Two Empires: The Ordeal of the Philippines, 1929–1946* (New Haven, CT: Yale University Press, 1965), 37.

38. Kanegae Seitarō, *The Path to Friendship: A Tale of a Japanese Immigrant in the Philippines*, trans. Shimamura Kaoru and Mizuno Teruyoshi (Tokyo: Keiso Shobo Publishing Company, 1987), 136–39; Friend, *Between Two Empires*, 37; Grant K. Goodman, "Consistency Is the Hobgoblin: Manuel L. Quezon and Japan, 1899–1934," *Journal of Southeast Asian Studies* 14, no. 1 (1983): 79–81.

39. Ronald H. Spector, *Eagle against the Sun: The American War with Japan* (New York: Vintage Books, 1985), 68–69.

40. Ibid., 106–19, 134–39.

41. Steinberg, *Philippine Collaboration*, 34–37; Bernardita Churchill, "The Japanese-Sponsored National Assembly & Post Liberation Congress, 1943–1946," in *The Philippine Senate*, ed. Remigio Agpalo et al. (Manila: Dick Baldovino Enterprises, 1997), 106; Rommel C. Banlaoi and Clarita R. Carlos, *Political Parties in the Philippines: From 1900 to the Present* (Makati City, Philippines: Konrad Adenauer Foundation, 1996), 94.

42. Nakano Satoshi, "Appeasement and Coercion," in Ikehata and Jose, *The Philippines under Japan*, 23; Friend, *Between Two Empires*, 232–41; Jose M. Veloso, "Collaboration as a National Issue: A Grave Government Problem," *Lawyers' Journal* 10, no. 4 (December 31, 1945): 170.

43. Spector, *Eagle against the Sun*, 417–28, 511–31; Ryan, *Yamashita's Ghost*, 41–49.

44. Of the twenty-four members of the Senate elected in 1941, thirteen attended the legislative session, nine others were under detention as suspected collaborators, and two had died. Of the ninety-eight representatives, seventy participated, seventeen others were under detention, and eleven had died. See Churchill, "Japanese-Sponsored National Assembly," 115–16.

45. Roxas, an early supporter of Manuel Quezon who became Speaker of the House in the 1920s, was one of those elected to the new Senate in 1941. At the outbreak of war he served as a liaison officer between MacArthur and Quezon; arrested by the Japanese in Mindanao, he escaped execution and went on to hold an economic post in the Laurel government while resisting greater involvement. See Steinberg, *Philippine Collaboration*, 42, 73–74, 107, 118.

46. A. V. H. Hartendorp, *History of Industry and Trade of the Philippines* (Manila: American Chamber of Commerce of the Philippines, Inc., 1958), 209–13, 225–27; Churchill, "Japanese-Sponsored National Assembly," 117.

47. Agoncillo, *A Short History*, 255; Bobby M. Tuazon, ed., *Oligarchic Politics: Elections and the Party-List System in the Philippines* (Quezon City: CenPEG Books, 2007), 13.

48. US president Harry Truman, receiving complaints from various sources that the Philippine government was not acting with sufficient dispatch in dealing with collaborators, had instructed the US attorney general to conduct an investigation but chose not to accept the resulting recommendation that the United States directly intervene in treason cases. Consequently, he left it up to the Filipinos themselves to determine what actions would be taken against suspect collaborators. See Grant K. Goodman, "President Harry S. Truman and the Problem of Philippine 'Collaborators,'" *Pilipinas* 28 (Spring 1997): 131–36.

49. Bengzon, *Philippine Judicial System*, 33–37.

50. US Embassy Manila cable no. 600, February 28, 1947, decimal 804.41, folder 804.411 Collaboration, Manila Embassy Security Segregated Classified General Records, 1946–52, box 7, entry 3101, Foreign Service Posts of the Department of State, RG 84, NACP; Steinberg, *Philippine Collaboration*, 128–39, 146, 159–63; Manuel A. Roxas, *Speeches, Messages, and Other Pronouncements of President Manuel Roxas* (Manila: Bureau of Print, 1947), 606–7.

51. "Freed Jap POWs, PI Collaborators Listed," *Evening News* (Manila), July 4, 1953, 5.

52. See, for example, Secretary of State to US Embassy Manila, telegram no. 1482, December 7, 1949, US Embassy Manila to US Political Adviser, Tokyo, Japan, telegram no. 2772, December 8, 1949, and US Embassy Manila to Secretary of State, telegram no. 2814, December 13, 1949, decimal 510.1, folder "Int'l Trade," Manila Embassy Security Segregated Classified General Records, 1946–52, box 18, entry 3101, RG 84, NACP.

Chapter 1. War Crimes during the Occupation

1. This chapter relies on information drawn from both the US and Philippine government trials, whereas subsequent chapters focus on the Philippine government trials. Citations to specific trials use *United States v. (defendant)* and *Philippines v. (defendant)*, respectively.

2. In addition to simulated drowning, the Japanese also employed other creative approaches subsumed under the description "water cure," including the use of hoses jammed down prisoners' throats to pump water into the stomach and the application of forced pressure against the abdomen. See, for example, transcript, 82, case no. 2, *Philippines v. Fujisaki Saburō*, box 1728, UD 1328, transcript, 197–98, case no. 11, *Philippines v. Morishita Tsuneo*, box 1689, UD 1323, and transcript, 21, case no. 58, *Philippines v. Koike Kaneyuki*, box 1704, UD 1323, RG 331, NACP.

3. See, for example, transcript, 9–24, 71–83, case no. 1, *Philippines v. Fujita Takefumi*, box 1728, UD 1328, transcript, 75–88, case no. 2, *Philippines v. Fujisaki Saburō*, box 1728, UD 1328, transcript, 19–30, case no. 21, *Philippines v. Miyamoto Shimao* et al., box 1692, UD 1323, transcript, 192–201, case no. 23, *Philippines v. Teramoto Tukuji [Tokuji]*,

box 1692, UD 1323, and transcript, 9–31, case no. 25, *Philippines v. Itō Masayasu*, box 1693, UD 1323, RG 331, NACP.

4. See Totani, *Justice in Asia*, 21–55, for a discussion of these trials.

5. During the American colonial era a Philippine constabulary had been organized that generally functioned as a police organization; in early 1942, during the Japanese occupation, a successor constabulary was established and charged with domestic policing and counterinsurgency activities, although the Japanese military was reluctant to arm it and shouldered the main burden of dealing with the guerrillas. But increasing resistance as the war progressed led the Japanese army to consider greater reliance on the constabulary, even though its willingness to support the Japanese efforts was suspect. With the landing of American forces in the fall of 1944, many in the constabulary deserted. See Steinberg, *Philippine Collaboration*, 57–58, 94–95; and Konrad Lawson, "Wartime Atrocities and the Politics of Treason in the Ruins of the Japanese Empire, 1936–1953" (Ph.D. diss., Harvard University, 2012), 179–85.

6. For a detailed account of the Japanese invasion, see Lewis Morton, *The Fall of the Philippines* (Washington, DC: Office of the Chief of Military History, United States Army, 1996), 92–157.

7. Totani, *Justice in Asia*, 25–27.

8. Specification 13k, *United States v. Homma Masaharu*, box 1671, UD 1322, RG 331, NACP. Other sources place the actual casualties lower. See, for example, Wilson et al., *Japanese War Criminals*, 14.

9. Transcript, 1972–73, *United States v. Homma Masaharu*, box 1671, UD 1322, RG 331, NACP.

10. Ibid., 1980–83.

11. Ibid., 1993–2008.

12. Ibid., 2439–97, 3029–128.

13. Ibid., 1284–96.

14. Specifications, case docket no. 230, *United States v. Tsuneyoshi Yoshio*, box 1607, UD 1321, RG 331, NACP.

15. Ibid., transcript, 27–50, 153–56.

16. Ibid., 351–405, 518–32, 539. Tsuneyoshi had the distinction of facing charges in both US and Philippine courtrooms and was sentenced to life in prison in both trials. He served his sentence in the Philippines and was released as a result of the general pardon granted by Philippine president Quirino in 1953. The US authorities only belatedly realized that he had likely not been transferred to Sugamo Prison in Japan to serve out the US sentence but apparently did not take steps to reincarcerate him. See Conrad Snow to FE, memo, December 14, 1953, decimal 694.0026/12-1453, Central Decimal File, 1950–54, box 3022, Records of the Department of State, RG 59, NACP.

17. Specifications, *United States v. Kou Shiyoku*, box 1559, UD 1321, RG 331, NACP.

18. Transcript, 65–81, 114–24, 129–30, *United States v. Kou Shiyoku*, box 1559, UD 1321, RG 331, NACP.

19. Transcript, 1097, 1156–64, 1189–324, 1380–99, 1417–33, *United States v. Kou Shiyoku*, box 1560, UD 1321, RG 331, NACP.

20. Morton, *Fall of the Philippines*, 236–37.

21. Transcript, 48–63, *United States v. Ohta Seiichi*, box 1554, UD 1321, RG 331, NACP.

22. Ibid., 59.

23. Ibid., 84–85.

24. Transcript, 118–48, *United States v. Nagahama Akira*, box 1579, UD 1321, RG 331, NACP.

25. Transcript, 47–63, *United States v. Toyonaga Tsunao*, box 1557, UD 1321, and transcript, 12–25, *Philippines v. Kita Heiji* et al., case no. 8, box 1688, UD 1323, RG 331, NACP.

26. Transcript, 48–304, 411–25, 479, *United States v. Ohta Seiichi*, box 1554, and transcript, 907–8, 927, *United States v. Nagahama Akira*, box 1579, UD 1321, RG 331, NACP.

27. In March 1945 the Military Intelligence Section, General Staff, General Headquarters Southwest Pacific Area, compiled the results of studies of guerrilla movements on islands throughout the Philippines, including Luzon, Leyte, Cebu, Panay, and Negros: "Guerrilla Resistance Movements in the Philippines," March 31, 1945, document L-458, War Crimes Division, Law Library Files, box 84, entry A1 135, Records of the Office of the Judge Advocate General, RG 153, NACP. For the perspective of a former guerrilla fighter, see also Robert Lapham and Bernard Norling, *Lapham's Raiders: Guerrillas in the Philippines, 1942–1945* (Lexington: University Press of Kentucky, 1996).

28. Lapham and Norland, *Lapham's Raiders*, 209.

29. Transcript, 796–802, *United States v. Kōno Takeshi*, box 1563, UD 1321, RG 331, NACP.

30. See, for example, Toshimi Kumai, *The Blood and Mud in the Philippines: Anti-Guerrilla Warfare on Panay Island*, trans. Yukako Ibuki (Iloilo City, Philippines: Malones Press and Publishing House, 2009); and Jose Doromal, *The War in Panay: A Documentary History of the Resistance Movement in Panay during World War II* (Manila: Diamond Historical Publications, 1952).

31. Transcript, 86, *United States v. Kōno Takeshi*, box 1563, UD 1321, RG 331, NACP.

32. Ibid., 90–188.

33. Ibid., 116–290.

34. Ibid., 503–15.

35. Transcript, 185–90, 195–201, *United States v. Tozuka Ryoichi*, box 1565, UD 1321, RG 331, NACP.

36. Specifications, and transcript, 354, *United States v. Otsuka Noriyuki and Kuwano Tadataka*, box 1564, UD 1321, RG 331, NACP.

37. Transcript, 354, *United States v. Otsuka Noriyuki and Kuwano Tadataka*, box 1564, UD 1321, RG 331, NACP.

38. Ibid., 657–72.

39. Ibid., 802–30.

40. Transcript, 311–21, *United States v. Yamaguchi Masakazu*, box 1576, UD 1321, RG 331, NACP.

41. Transcript, 2852–64, 2899–966, 3528–31, *United States v. Yamaguchi Masakazu*, boxes 1577–78, UD 1321, RG 331, NACP.

42. Ibid., 3529.

43. Ibid., 3529–30.

44. Ibid., 3530, 3600–3601.

45. This summary is drawn largely from the account given in Robert Ross Smith, *Triumph in the Philippines* (Washington, DC: Office of the Chief of Military History, Department of the Army, 1963).

46. For a summary of the Yamashita trial, see Totani, *Justice in Asia*, 33–40.

47. Transcript, 33, *United States v. Toyonaga Tsunao*, box 1557, UD 1321, RG 331, NACP.

48. Specifications, and transcript, 51–52, 55–69, *United States v. Fujishige Masatoshi* et al., box 1558, UD 1321, RG 331, NACP.

49. Transcript, 55–69, *United States v. Fujishige Masatoshi* et al., box 1558, UD 1321, RG 331, NACP.

50. Ibid., 294–304.

51. Ibid., 95–100, 102–4.

52. Transcript, 100–124, case no. 32, *Philippines v. Ichimura Isao*, box 1694, UD 1323, RG 331, NACP.

53. Transcript, 113–18, 142–48, case no. 44, *Philippines v. Satō Matazō*, box 1697, UD 1323; and transcript, 40–67, case no. 5, *Philippines v. Kudō Chūshirō*, box 1729, UD 1328, RG 331, NACP.

54. Transcript, 1269–1323, *United States v. Fujishige Masatoshi* et al., box 1558, UD 1321, RG 331, NACP.

55. Dower, *Embracing Defeat*, 48–50; Beatrice Trefalt, *Japanese Army Stragglers and Memories of the War in Japan, 1950–1975* (London: Routledge-Curzon, 2003), 34–37.

56. Specifications, case no. 61, *Philippines v. Ainoda Hajime* et al., box 1705, UD 1323, RG 331, NACP.

57. Transcript, 13–14, 19–300, case no. 61, *Philippines v. Ainoda Hajime* et al., box 1705, UD 1323, RG 331, NACP.

58. Ibid., 19–33, 55–59, 66–76, 87–94, 108–20.

59. Three of the seventeen defendants were acquitted; of the fourteen found guilty, ten were sentenced to death and four to life in prison. See ibid., 185–208, 291–97, 382–93.

60. Ibid., exhibit 33 (statement text in English).

61. Tsuji Chōichi, *Yūhei Montenrupa* (Tokyo: Senshi Kankōkai, Hatsubai Seiunsha, 1984), 41–75, 111–17.

62. Senate Committee on Military Affairs, *Sack of Manila* (Washington, DC: US Government Printing Office, 1945), 2, in National Archives Library, NACP.

63. Teodoro Locsin, "Do You Want to Do Business with the Japs?," *Philippines Free Press*, September 2, 1949, 2.

64. US Embassy Manila cable no. 781, September 12, 1949, enclosure no. 2, "Issues and Men," *Daily News*, September 9, 1949, decimal 350, Manila Embassy Security Segregated Classified General Records, 1946–52, box 15, entry 3101, RG 84, NACP. See John Dower, *War without Mercy: Race and Power in the Pacific War* (New York: Pantheon Books, 1986), for a thoughtful examination of the racist caricatures employed by both sides.

Chapter 2. Rising to the Challenge

1. In 1942, prior to the surrender of Filipino and American forces, then Commonwealth vice president Osmeña and president Manuel Quezon had fled to the United States to form a government in exile; with Quezon's death there in 1944, Osmeña assumed the presidency.

2. United Nation War Crimes Commission, *History of the United Nations War Crimes Commission and the Development of the Laws of War* (London: HMSO, 1948), 109–34; David M. Crowe, *War Crimes, Genocide, and Justice: A Global History* (New York: Palgrave Macmillan, 2014), 153.

3. Office of the Judge Advocate General, "A History of the War Crimes Office, 25 September–30 June 1945," document L-341, War Crimes Division, Law Library Files, 1944–49, box 57, entry A1 135, RG 153, NACP.

4. Nagai Hitoshi, "The Tokyo War Crimes Trial," in Ikehata and Yu-Jose, *Philippines-Japan Relations*, 262–65.

5. Supreme Commander for the Allied Powers, Monograph 5, "Trials of Class 'B' and 'C' War Criminals," in *History of the Nonmilitary Activities of the Occupation of Japan* (Wilmington, DE: Scholarly Resources, 1989), microform, 41–42.

6. Ibid., 41–44.

7. Piccigallo, *Japanese on Trial*, 34–38; SCAP, Monograph 5, 215–22.

8. The Yokohama war crimes trials conducted by the US Eighth Army included some cases of alleged atrocities committed by Japanese soldiers in the Philippines; consequently, evidence of war crimes in the Philippines was presented in at least four different venues: US trials in Manila and Yokohama, Philippine trials in Manila, and the International Military Tribunal for the Far East in Tokyo.

9. AFWESPAC's successor organization, the Philippines-Ryukyus Command (PHILRYCOM), maintained custody of war crimes suspects and convicted war criminals for a period of time after the US trials were concluded.

10. SCAP, Monograph 5, 41–43.

11. Ibid., 44.

12. Ryan, *Yamashita's Ghost*, 61.

13. "General Yamashita, Found Guilty, Sentenced to Hang until Dead," *Manila Times*, December 8, 1945, 1.

14. See, for example, Cohen, "Beyond Nuremburg"; and Ryan, *Yamashita's Ghost*.

15. Teodoro Agoncillo, *The Fateful Years: Japan's Adventure in the Philippines, 1941–1945* (Quezon City: R. P. Garcia Publishing Company, 1965), 2:902.

16. Hayashi, *BC-kyū senpan saiban*, 83; Maj. Chas. E. Good, Manila Provost Marshal Command, memo, September 15, 1948, folder 11, Miscellaneous File, 1945–49, Legal Section Manila Branch, box 1976, UD 1253, RG 331, NACP; teletype conference, PHILRYCOM item no. 68, June 19, 1947, Radio Messages, 1945–51, SCAP Legal Section, Administrative Division, box 1353, UD 1268, RG 331, NACP.

17. Beginning in 1946 the Philippines did take part in the Tokyo trial of Japan's leaders, providing one of the eleven Allied judges (Delfin Jaranilla) and a prosecutor (Pedro Lopez); one significant intersection between the international proceeding and the national trials occurring at Manila was the mutual reliance on investigative reports of atrocities committed during the Japanese occupation (and the use of the Yamashita trial transcript at the Tokyo trial). For an overview of the Philippine role in the Tokyo trial, see Nagai, "The Tokyo War Crimes Trial," 261–98.

18. Piccigallo, *Japanese on Trial*, 197–98.

19. Nagai Hitoshi, *Firipin to tai-Nichi senpan saiban: 1945–1953-nen* (Tokyo: Iwanami Shoten, 2010), 202.

20. Memo for Chief, Legal Section, January 27, 1947, file 000.5C War Crimes Philippines, decimal file, 1945–51, SCAP Legal Section, Law Division, box 1413, UD 1289, RG 331, NACP.

21. War Department cable no. 71704, January 16, 1947, file 151-6, book 3, box 248, War Department cable no. WARX 91119, January 31, 1947, folder 15-6, book 3, box 248, Hubbert to Eberle, memo, May 7, 1947, file 151-6, book 4, box 249, and "Informal Discussion," 2nd Lt. Donald I. McPherson et al., February 24, 1947, folder 116-20c, box 112, War Crimes Branch, General Administrative Records (Set-up Files), 1944–49, entry A1 145, RG 153, NACP; Yard to Carpenter, memo, December 2, 1946, folder 16, Manila Correspondence, Miscellaneous File, 1946–49, Law Division, Legal Section, box 1429, UD 1290, RG 331, NACP.

22. Terminal report, 4, War Crimes Trials Division, Philippines-Ryukyus Command, May 9, 1947, folder 34, Legal Section Manila Branch Miscellaneous File, 1945–49, box 2023, UD 1362, RG 331, NACP.

23. Legal Section to Chief of Staff, check sheet memo, May 6, 1947, and attachments, folder War Crimes Trials in Manila, Miscellaneous Classified Files, 1945–52, SCAP Legal Section, Law Division, box 1434, UD 1294, RG 331, NACP; teletype conferences, PHILRYCOM item no. 51, February 20, 1947, and PHILRYCOM item no. 63, March 27, 1947, Radio Messages, 1945–51, SCAP Legal Section, Administrative Division, box 1353, UD 1268, RG 331, NACP.

24. Legal Section to Chief of Staff, check sheet memo, May 6, 1947, folder War Crimes Trials in Manila, Miscellaneous Classified Files, 1945–52, SCAP Legal Section, Law Division, box 1434, UD 1294, and Legal Section, memo, July 8, 1947, file 000.5C War Crimes Philippines, decimal file, 1945–51, SCAP Legal Section, Law Division, box 1413, UD 1289, RG 331, NACP.

25. An earlier executive order, no. 64, dealt with Philippine cooperation in US-led trials. Once the Philippines gained independence in July 1946, EO 64 became obsolete and was explicitly repealed by EO 68. Copies of EO 68 were included in the transcript record of each trial.

26. S. Melville Hussey, Legal Section Manila Branch, to Chief, Legal Section, letter and attachments, March 24, 1948, folder Manila Correspondence, War Crimes File 1945–49, SCAP Legal Section, Administrative Division, box 1349, UD 1267, RG 331, NACP; Ricardo Trota Jose, "The Philippine War Crimes Trials," *Social Science Information*, 33–34; transcript, 221, case no. 16, *Philippines v. Tone Seiichi*, box 1691, UD 1323, RG 331, NACP; "Butcher of Bay to Be Arraigned," *Manila Times*, July 31, 1947, 1.

27. Teletype conferences, PHILRYCOM item no. 63, July 31, 1947, FEC item no. 6, February 4, 1948, and PHILRYCOM item no. 71, August 28, 1947, Radio Messages, 1945–51, SCAP Legal Section, Administrative Division, box 1353, UD 1268, RG 331, NACP.

28. Teletype conferences, PHILRYCOM item no. 63, September 4, 1947, and PHILRYCOM item no. 65, September 11, 1947, Radio Messages, 1945–51, SCAP Legal Section, Administrative Division, box 1353, UD 1268, RG 331, NACP.

29. Teletype conference, Tokyo item no. 14, May 29, 1947, Radio Messages, 1945–51, SCAP Legal Section, Administrative Division, box 1353, UD 1268, RG 331, NACP.

30. Sugamo prisoner files, Central Command, 8132nd Army Unit / Sugamo Prison Detachment, UD UP 39, Records of General Headquarters, Far East Command, Supreme Commander Allied Powers and United Nations Command, RG 554, NACP.

31. Legal Section Tokyo to Legal Section Manila Branch, check sheet memo, March 18, 1948, and Legal Section Manila Branch to Legal Section Tokyo, check sheet memo, March 24, 1948, folder Manila Correspondence, War Crimes File 1945–49, SCAP Legal Section Administrative Division, box 1349, UD 1267, RG 331, NACP.

32. Fred Ruiz Castro and Guillermo S. Santos, "A Report on War Crimes Trials in the Philippines," *Lawyers' Journal* 15, no. 10 (October 1950): 471–72; Jose, "The Philippine War Crimes Trials, 1947–1949," *Social Science Information* 33; *United States v. Yamaguchi Masakazu*, box 1576, UD 1321, RG 331, NACP.

33. Transcript, 1–7, case no. 5, *Philippines v. Kudō Chūshirō*, box 1729, UD 1328, RG 331, NACP; "Jap Pleads Not Guilty," *Manila Bulletin*, August 2, 1947, 1.

34. See, for example, teletype conference, PHILRYCOM item no. 78, Tokyo item no. 37, and Tokyo item no. 42, April 24, 1947, Radio Messages, 1945–51, SCAP Legal Section, Administrative Division, box 1353, UD 1268, RG 331, NACP.

35. Legal Section to Chief of Staff, check sheet memo, May 6, 1947, folder War Crimes Trials in Manila, Miscellaneous Classified Files, 1945–52, SCAP Legal Section, Law Division, box 1434, UD 1294, and Japanese General Officers to Commander in Chief, AFWESPAC, October 30, 1946, folder Manila, Lawyers/Interpreters, SCAP Legal Section, Administrative Division, box 1229, UD 1226, RG 331, NACP.

36. Teletype conference, Tokyo item no. 42, April 24, 1947, Radio Messages, 1945–51, SCAP Legal Section, Administrative Division, box 1353, UD 1268, RG 331, NACP.

37. Yokoyama, one of the highest-ranking Japanese officers facing trial in a Philippine courtroom, had commanded the Shimbu Army under General Yamashita during the last stages of the war; he faced over fifty counts of having directed or permitted subordinates to commit atrocities on Luzon and was later convicted and sentenced to death. See case no. 48, *Philippines v. Yokoyama Shizuo*, boxes 1698–99, UD 1323, RG 331, NACP.

38. Legal Section to Chief of Staff, attachment to check sheet memo, May 6, 1947, folder War Crimes Trials in Manila, Miscellaneous Classified Files, 1945–52, SCAP Legal Section, Law Division, box 1434, UD 1294, RG 331, NACP.

39. Legal Section to Chief of Staff, attachments to check sheet memo, July 8, 1948, folder War Crimes Trials in the Philippines, Miscellaneous Classified Files, 1945–52, SCAP Legal Section, Law Division, box 1434, UD 1294, RG 331, NACP.

40. Teletype conference, PHILRYCOM item no. 56, August 8, 1947, Radio Messages, 1945–51, SCAP Legal Section, Administrative Division, box 1353, UD 1268, RG 331, NACP.

41. US Embassy Manila cable no. 1353, November 26, 1947, and enclosures, decimal 740.00116 PW/11-2647, Central Decimal File 1945–49, box 3632, RG 59, NACP; Legal Section to Chief of Staff, memo, December 11, 1948, folder Manila, P.I.: Lawyers and Interpreters, SCAP Legal Section, Administrative Division, box 1229, UD 1226, RG 331, NACP.

42. "Japanese Counsel Rebuffed: Quits Mass War Crimes Trial," *Manila Chronicle*, November 18, 1947, 1.

43. Transcript, 143–44, 272, case no. 12, *Philippines v. Nakamura Hideichi* et al., box 1690, UD 1323, RG 331, NACP.

44. US Embassy Manila cable no. 1353, November 26, 1947, decimal 740.00116 PW/11-2647, Central Decimal File, 1945–49, box 3632, RG 59, NACP; Jose, "The Philippine War Crimes Trials, 1947–1949," *Social Science Information*, 35.

45. See, for example, case no. 1, *Philippines v. Fujita Takefumi*, box 1728, and case no. 5, *Philippines v. Kudō Chūshirō*, box 1729, UD 1328, RG 331, NACP.

46. Transcript, 581–82, case no. 26, *Philippines v. Ogawa Eitarō*, box 1693, UD 1323, RG 331, NACP.

47. S. Melville Hussey to SCAP Legal Section Tokyo, memo, January 8, 1948, folder 16, Manila Correspondence, Miscellaneous File, 1946–49, SCAP Legal Section, Law Division, box 1429, UD 1290, RG 331, NACP.

48. Memo, "Matter Concerning the Philippine War Crimes Trials," May 6, 1949, 1:118–24, disclosure 14, D'130 2-5-2, JDRO.

49. Legal Section Manila Branch to Legal Section Tokyo, check sheet memo, August 20, 1948, folder Manila, P.I.: Lawyers and Interpreters, SCAP Legal Section, Administrative Division, box 1229, UD 1226, RG 331, NACP.

50. Kuroda Shigenori, "Montenrupa: Hitō senpan gokusha no taikenki," *Daiyamondo* 40, no. 17 (May 1952): 130. At the start of his trial Kuroda had asked to be represented by American lawyers, but his request was denied. See transcript, 7–10, case no. 50, *Philippines v. Kuroda Shigenori*, box 1699, UD 1323, RG 331, NACP.

51. See, for example, transcript, 161, case no. 1, *Philippines v. Fujita Takefumi*, box 1728, UD 1328, RG 331, NACP.

52. Teletype conference, PHILRYCOM item no. 55, August 8, 1947, Radio Messages, 1945–51, SCAP Legal Section, Administrative Division, box 1353, UD 1268, RG 331, NACP.

53. Transcript, 149, case no. 6, *Philippines v. Kodama Yoshiaki*, box 1729, UD 1328, RG 331, NACP.

54. Ibid., 254–55.

55. Transcript, 218, case no. 1, *Philippines v. Fujita Takefumi*, box 1728, UD 1328, RG 331, NACP.

56. Transcript, 864–65, case no. 18, *Philippines v. Matsuzaki Hideichi*, box 1691, UD 1323, RG 331, NACP.

57. Transcript, 576, case no. 24, *Philippines v. Matsuda Junzō*, box 1693, UD 1323, RG 331, NACP.

58. Yokoyama Misayo, "Kansha no kotoba," in *Nokosareta hitobito: Hitō senpan shikeishū no shuki*, ed. Okamoto Torao (Tokyo: Sumashobō, 1952), 2.

59. Satō Sō, *Onshū o koete: Hitō B-kyū senpan no shuki* (Tokyo: Nihon Kōgyō Shinbunsha, 1981), vi.

60. Memo, "Handling of Philippine War Crimes Tribunals, Especially the [name blacked out] Case," April 4, 1949, 1:104–9, and report, "Matter Concerning the Philippine War Crimes Trials," May 6, 1949, 1:118–24, disclosure 14, D'130 2-5-2, JDRO.

61. Specifications, and transcript, 41, case no. 14, *Philippines v. Harada Shimpei* et al., box 1690, UD 1323, RG 331, NACP; Harada Petition to Board of Review, August 1948, Harada Petition to President of the Philippines, December 17, 1949, and Defense Panel Chief, check sheet memo, September 20, 1948, Review File, bundle no. 12, *Philippines v. Harada Shimpei* et al., Japanese War Crime Records, Case Files, NAP.

62. Japanese Prisoner Stockade to Defense Panel Chief Capt. Pedro Serran, September 15, 1948 (English text in file), bundle no. 12, *Philippines v. Harada Shimpei* et al., Japanese War Crime Records, Case Files, NAP.

63. Jose Abad Santos had served as secretary of justice in the Philippine Commonwealth government before his appointment to the Supreme Court; he was named chief justice in late December 1941 shortly after the Japanese attack on the Philippines. He was captured by Japanese forces in April 1942 and executed some days later.

64. Transcript, 121–29, 377–94, 593, 769, case no. 64, *Philippines v. Hayashi Yoshihide and Kawaguchi Kiyotake*, boxes 1705–6, UD 1323, RG 331, NACP.

65. Teletype conference, PHILRYCOM item no. 76, October 2, 1947, Radio Messages, 1945–51, SCAP Legal Section, Administrative Division, box 1353, UD 1268, S. Melville Hussey to SCAP Legal Section Tokyo, memo, January 8, 1948, folder 16, Manila Correspondence, Miscellaneous File, 1946–49, SCAP Legal Section, Law Division, box 1429, UD 1290, and Chief Legal Section, memo for the record, October 17, 1947, folder Manila, P.I.: Lawyers and Interpreters, SCAP Legal Section, Administrative Division, box 1229, UD 1226, RG 331, NACP.

66. See, for example, transcript, 36–37, case no. 71, *Philippines v. Ogawa Somin* et al., box 1708, UD 1323, RG 331, NACP.

67. Chief Interpreter Andres Castro to Chief, NWCO, memo, June 4, 1948, attachment to check sheet memo, August 20, 1948, Legal Section Manila Branch to Legal Section Tokyo, and curriculum vitae for Asami Shingo and Saito Noboru, folder Manila, P.I.: Lawyers and Interpreters, SCAP Legal Section, Administrative Division, box 1229, UD 1226, RG 331, NACP.

68. The files did not indicate whether the Japanese government responded favorably to appeals for salary increases. See check sheet memos, May 6, 1948, and August 20, 1948, Legal Section Manila Branch to Legal Section Tokyo, folder Manila, P.I.: Lawyers and Interpreters, SCAP Legal Section, Administrative Division, box 1229, UD 1226, RG 331, NACP.

69. Kuroda to MacArthur, November 16, 1948, SCAP Legal Section to Chief of Staff, memo, December 11, 1948, and GHQ SCAP, memo, January 8, 1949, folder Manila, P.I.: Lawyers and Interpreters, SCAP Legal Section, Administrative Division, box 1229, UD 1226, RG 331, NACP.

70. Teletype conference, FEC item no. 1, and FEC item no. 37, September 25, 1947, Radio Messages, 1945–51, SCAP Legal Section, Administrative Division, box 1353, UD 1268, RG 331, NACP.

71. Executive Officer, LSMB, to Chief, Defense Panel, memo, November 5, 1948, folder Manila, P.I.: Lawyers and Interpreters, SCAP Legal Section, Administrative Division, box 1229, UD 1226, RG 331, NACP.

72. Transcript, 372–76, case no. 5, *Philippines v. Kudō Chūshirō*, box 1729, UD 1328, RG 331, NACP.

73. Transcript, 512–13, 551–52, case no. 3, *Philippines v. Takahashi Sadakichi*, box 1729, UD 1328, RG 331, NACP.

74. Transcript, 478–91, case no. 4, *Philippines v. Nakano Shizuo*, box 1729, UD 1328, RG 331, NACP.

75. Teletype conferences, PHILRYCOM item no. 67, FEC item no. 18, September 18, 1947, FEC item no. 1, PHILRYCOM item no. 69, September 25, 1947, and FEC item no. 4, October 2, 1947, Radio Messages, 1945–51, Legal Section, Administrative Division, box 1353, UD 1268, RG 331, NACP.

76. Teletype conference, PHILRYCOM item no. 51, October 31, 1947, Radio Messages, 1945–51, Legal Section, Administrative Division, box 1353, UD 1268, and Maj. Theodore King to William Yard, November 4, 1947, folder 16, Manila Correspondence, Miscellaneous File, 1946–49, Legal Section, Law Division, box 1429, UD 1290, RG 331, NACP.

77. Chief of NWCO to Executive Officer, Legal Section Manila Branch, memo, December 15, 1947, folder 16, Manila Correspondence, Miscellaneous File, 1946–49, SCAP Legal Section, Law Division, box 1429, UD 1290, Legal Section to Chief of Staff, check sheet memo, March 19, 1948, folder Manila, P.I.: Lawyers and Interpreters, SCAP Legal Section, Administrative Division, box 1229, UD 1226, and Dollete to Reinhard,

memo, May 11, 1948, Miscellaneous Subject File, 1945–49, Legal Section, Administrative Division, box 1225, UD 1225, RG 331, NACP.

78. Manila War Crimes Defense Office, Tokyo, to Major Fojas, Chief of National War Crimes Office, P.I., memo, January 31, 1948, 1:40–43, and Tokyo Branch, Manila War Crimes Defense Office, memo, February 1948, 2:28–31, disclosure 14, D'130 2-5-2, JDRO.

79. S. Melville Hussey to Col. Alva Carpenter, March 24, 1948, and attachments, folder Manilla [*sic*] Correspondence, War Crimes File, 1945–49, SCAP Legal Section, Administrative Division, box 1349, UD 1267, RG 331, NACP.

80. There were rare exceptions to the ban on calling witnesses from Japan, and they involved the trials of general officers. See transcript, 131–85, case no. 64, *Philippines v. Hayashi Yoshihide and Kawaguchi Kiyotake*, box 1705, UD 1323, transcript, 241–42, case no. 67, *Philippines v. Masuoka Kensichi*, box 1707, UD 1323, and CINCFE to PHILRYCOM, cable, April 25, 1949, folder Manila, P.I.: Lawyers and Interpreters, SCAP Legal Section, Administrative Division, box 1229, UD 1226, RG 331, NACP.

81. S. Melville Hussey to SCAP Legal Section Tokyo, memo, January 8, 1948, folder 16, Manila Correspondence, Miscellaneous File, 1946–49, SCAP Legal Section, Law Division, box 1429, UD 1290, and CLO no. 8685, November 7, 1947, folder Manila, P.I.: Lawyers and Interpreters, Witnesses File, 1946–49, SCAP Legal Section, Administrative Division, box 1229, UD 1226, RG 331, NACP.

82. Teletype conference, FEC item no. 27, September 25, 1947, Radio Messages, 1945–51, Legal Section, Administrative Division, box 1353, UD 1268, RG 331, NACP.

83. Memo, "Handling of Philippine War Crimes Tribunals, Especially the [name blacked out] Case, April 4, 1949, 1:104–9, disclosure 14, D'130 2-5-2, JDRO.

84. Yokoyama Shizuo, "Sono goro no gokusō seikatsu o kataru," *Shūkyō Kōron* 23, no. 6 (August 1953): 4.

85. Minear, *Victors' Justice*, 118–24.

Chapter 3. The Trials

1. "Kudo Enters Not Guilty Plea," *Manila Times*, August 2, 1947, 1; "Jap Pleads Not Guilty," *Manila Bulletin*, August 2, 1947, 1.

2. Data on the Philippine-led war crimes trials are derived from case nos. 1 through 71, Philippines Versus Various Japanese War Criminals, Case File, 1947–49, SCAP Legal Section, Prosecution Division, UD 1323 and UD 1328, RG 331, NACP; and People of the Philippines v. Japanese Soldiers, Japanese War Crime Records, Case Files, NAP. Various sources (e.g., Hayashi, *BC-kyū senpan saiban*; Piccigallo, *The Japanese on Trial*; and Nagai, *Firipin to tai-Nichi senpan saiban*) have provided conflicting data on the numbers of trials and defendants, but Philippine Archives files confirm that the Philippine government convened seventy-three trials, defined as a proceeding in which at least one defendant was arraigned, and that 155 defendants were arraigned in those trials. Even so, there may technically have been a seventy-fourth trial—the transcript of

the Hoshino Takashi trial makes reference to an earlier proceeding that had been aborted before a verdict had been reached. See transcript, 44–49, case no. 41, *Philippines v. Hoshino Takashi*, box 1696, UD 1323, RG 331, NACP.

3. Legal Section, memo for chief, January 27, 1947, file War Crimes Philippines, decimal file, 1945–51, SCAP Legal Section, Law Division, box 1413, UD 1289, RG 331, NACP.

4. This did not preclude the prosecutor from arguing that the suspect was merely pretending not to understand Japanese, given his service in the Japanese army and his presumed ability to communicate with his comrades. Defense counsel responded that he had been unable to communicate with the accused and was backed up by the superintendent of the prison where the accused was being held. See transcript, 4–7, 16–19, case no. 61, *Philippines v. Ainoda* et al., box 1705, UD 1323, RG 331, NACP.

5. NWCO to Legal Section Manila Branch, memo, September 22, 1949, and Legal Section Tokyo to G-2, Japanese Liaison, memo, November 18, 1949, folder Manila, P.I.: Lawyers and Interpreters, SCAP Legal Section, Administrative Division, box 1229, UD 1226, RG 331, NACP.

6. For example, the largest trial held by the Australians involved ninety-two defendants, and the British indicted forty-four defendants in a trial convened in Singapore. See Wilson et al., *Japanese War Criminals*, 68.

7. Specifications, special orders no. 291, December 1, 1948, and transcript, 1, case no. 50, *Philippines v. Kuroda Shigenori*, box 1699, UD 1323, RG 331, NACP.

8. Source for military service and rank is Itō et al., *Monten*, 47–51.

9. Case no. 49, *Philippines v. Furuse Takasue*, box 1699, case no. 71, *Philippines v. Ogawa Somin* et al., boxes 1708–9, and case no. 31, *Philippines v. Shimamura Katsuji* et al., box 1694, UD 1323, RG 331, NACP. One other naval officer, a lieutenant, was included in the Nakamura case. See case no. 12, *Philippines v. Nakamura Hideichi* et al., box 1690, UD 1323, RG 331, NACP.

10. Yu-Jose, *Japan Views the Philippines*, 157–165; Yu-Jose, "World War II," 79–80.

11. Those who retained their Japanese citizenship could be subject to indictment as war criminals; others born of Japanese fathers and Filipina mothers who had acquired Philippine citizenship might face prosecution as collaborators. The Japanese prewar communities essentially disappeared after the war as their surviving inhabitants returned to Japan.

12. Transcript, 8, 556, case no. 3, *Philippines v. Takahashi Sadakichi*, box 1729, UD 1328, RG 331, NACP.

13. Action of the Approving Authority, November 5, 1948, bundle no. 63, *Philippines v. Takahashi Sadakichi*, Japanese War Crime Records, Case Files, NAP.

14. Bundle no. 4, *Philippines v. Fukutake Kazuo*, Japanese War Crime Records, Case Files, NAP.

15. The ten defendants who in pleading guilty offered a defense of superior orders in hopes of mitigating their sentences were not uniformly successful. Three received term sentences, four were sentenced to life, and three received the death penalty (two of

these were sentenced to the more honorable "death by musketry"). Two of the three sentenced to death had admitted involvement in mass killings.

16. Transcript, 28–35, case no. 14, *Philippines v. Harada Shimpei* et al., box 1690, transcript, 14, case no. 28, *Philippines v. Miyake Tomomi*, box 1694, transcript, 29–41, 47–54, case no. 31, *Philippines v. Shimamura Katsuji* et al., box 1694, transcript, 19, case no. 34, *Philippines v. Hane Chōkichi*, box 1695, transcript, 9, 16–22, 41, case no. 46, *Philippines v. Satō Ichirō*, box 1697, transcript, 16, case no. 59, *Philippines v. Mizuno Akira and Ochiai Haruichi*, box 1704, transcript, 9–10, case no. 62, *Philippines v. Deguchi Motoaki*, box 1705, transcript, 593, 652–53, 705–10, 769, case no. 64, *Philippines v. Hayashi Yoshihide and Kawaguchi Kiyotake*, box 1706, and transcript, 33, case no. 33, *Philippines v. Sunahara Hiroshi* et al., box 1695, UD 1323, RG 331, NACP.

17. The authors of the most recent and thorough comparative study of the postwar trials in Asia found that, overall, the higher the military rank, the more severe the punishment. See Wilson et al., *Japanese War Criminals*, 95.

18. In this as in other aspects of the trials, the commissions served the same function as the American commissions that preceded them. For a discussion of the evolution of military commissions in the US armed forces, see Ryan, *Yamashita's Ghost*, 52–56.

19. There may well have been a third, although the evidence is tantalizingly slight. In the trial of defendant Hoshino Takashi, there is a rather cryptic reference to an earlier trial of the defendant that was cut short because of a challenge to the commission's "judicial temperament." See transcript, 44–49, case no. 41, *Philippines v. Hoshino Takashi*, box 1696, UD 1323, RG 331, NACP.

20. Transcript, 373–76, case no. 48, *Philippines v. Yokoyama Shizuo*, box 1698, and transcript, 4–8, case no. 54, *Philippines v. Tsuneoshi Yoshio*, box 1703, UD 1323, RG 331, NACP.

21. Transcript, 734, case no. 71, *Philippines v. Ogawa Somin* et al., box 1708, UD 1323, RG 331, NACP.

22. See, for example, transcript, 102, case no. 42, *Philippines v. Hatogai Yoshimasa*, box 1697, UD 1323, RG 331, NACP.

23. Transcript, 667–82, case no. 8, *Philippines v. Kita Heiji* et al., box 1688, and transcript, 134–41, case no. 19, *Philippines v. Nakanishi Shioji*, box 1691, UD 1323, RG 331, NACP.

24. See, for example, transcript, 515, case no. 58, *Philippines v. Koike Kaneyuke*, box 1704, UD 1323, RG 331, NACP.

25. Specifications, case no. 66, *Philippines v. Inamura Rokujonō*, box 1707, UD 1323, RG 331, NACP.

26. Specifications, case no. 50, *Philippines v. Kuroda Shigenori*, box 1699, UD 1323, RG 331, NACP.

27. Tsuji Yutaka, ed., *Montenrupa: Hitō yūshū no kiroku* (Tokyo: Asahi Shimbun Co., 1952), 196–97.

28. An eleventh defendant's case was suspended because he was dying of tuberculosis.

29. Transcript, 105, case no. 8, *Philippines v. Kita Heiji* et al., box 1688, UD 1323, RG 331, NACP.

30. Transcript, 197, case no. 11, *Philippines v. Morishita Tsuneo*, box 1689, UD 1323, RG 331, NACP.

31. Wilson et al., *Japanese War Criminals*, 81.

32. Ibid., 82.

33. See, for example, transcript, 202–19, case no. 6, *Philippines v. Kodama Yoshiaki*, box 1729, UD 1328, and transcript, 297–314, case no. 40, *Philippines v. Gotō Shōzō and Fujii Rokujirō*, box 1696, UD 1323, RG 331, NACP.

34. Bing Bing Jia, "The Plea of Superior Orders in the Hong Kong Trials," in Linton, *Hong Kong's War Crimes Trials*, 169–98; Cheah Wui Ling, "The Superior Orders Defence at the Post-war Trials in Singapore," in Sellars, *Trials for International Crimes*, 104. For examples of US trials, see transcript, 315–44, *United States v. Otsuka Noriyuki and Kuwano Tadataka*, and transcript, 407–8, *United States v. Fujii Hajime*, box 1566, UD 1321, RG 331, NACP.

35. How to handle claims of obedience to superior orders as a defense was the subject of much discussion by the Allies, who ultimately could not decide on how exactly to define the circumstances in which such claims might be considered but did agree that such pleas could not in principle completely exonerate the offenders. See United Nations War Crimes Commission, *History*, 274–88.

36. In the case of Fujii Hajime, for example, the defendant's impassioned plea that he had no choice but to obey the orders handed down by his superiors fell on deaf ears; he was found guilty and sentenced to death. Transcript, 407–10, *United States v. Fujii Hajime*, box 1566, UD 1321, RG 331, NACP.

37. Yokoyama, "Sono goro," 3–4; Owari Saburō to wife, undated (English translation in file), bundle no. 17, *Philippines v. Ichimura Isao and Owari Saburō*, Japanese War Crime Records, Case Files, NAP.

38. Teletype conference, FEC item no. 8, August 28, 1947, Radio Messages, 1945–51, SCAP Legal Section, Administrative Division, box 1353, UD 1268, RG 331, NACP.

39. Transcript, 390, case no. 8, *Philippines v. Kita Heiji* et al., box 1688, and transcript, 423, case no. 10, *Philippines v. Shimizu Hisamitsu and Uemura Masao*, box 1689, UD 1323, RG 331, NACP.

40. Specifications, and transcript, 555–87, case no. 8, *Philippines v. Kita Heiji,* et al., box 1688, UD 1323, RG 331, NACP.

41. Transcript, 236–41, 269–75, 460, 867, case no. 18, *Philippines v. Matsuzaki Hideichi*, box 1691, UD 1323, RG 331, NACP. The Quirino letter was not included in the copy of the transcript in the US National Archives but was included in transcript, exhibit B, bundle no. 35, *Philippines v. Matsuzaki Hideichi*, Japanese War Crime Records, Case Files, NAP.

42. Transcript, 285–86, 651–61, 667–70, 689–90, case no. 10, *Philippines v. Shimizu Hisamitsu and Uemura Masao*, box 1689, UD 1323, RG 331, NACP.

43. See, for example, transcript, 402, case no. 22, *Philippines v. Murata Masaaki*, box 1692, UD 1323, RG 331, NACP. The notion that the Japanese were "nice" to members of the Filipino elite was also voiced by the American prosecutor in the Kuroda case. See transcript, 3049–50, case no. 50, *Philippines v. Kuroda Shigenori*, box 1702, UD 1323, RG 331, NACP.

44. Case no. 29, *Philippines v. Taninaka Katsuyoshi*, box 1694, UD 1323, RG 331, NACP.

45. Transcript, 438, case no. 4, *Philippines v. Nakano Shizuo*, box 1729, UD 1328, RG 331, NACP.

46. Transcript, 40–42, case no. 1, *Philippines v. Fujita Takefumi*, box 1728, UD 1328, RG 331, NACP.

47. Transcript, 580–82, case no. 69, *Philippines v. Fujimoto Takao*, box 1708, UD 1323, RG 331, NACP.

48. For examples of the prosecution's strategy, see transcript, 491–92, case no. 13, *Philippines v. Uemura Eichirō and Arai Hatsuyoshi*, box 1690, and transcript, 383–96, case no. 19, *Philippines v. Nakanishi Shioji*, box 1692, UD 1323, RG 331, NACP.

49. Transcript, 253–418, 611–12, case no. 55, *Philippines v. Nakamura Fumio*, box 1703, UD 1323, RG 331, NACP.

50. Transcript, 382–93, case no. 61, *Philippines v. Ainoda Hajime* et al., box 1705, UD 1323, RG 331, NACP; Tsuji, *Yūhei Montenrupa*, 113–14.

51. Transcript, 288–89, and defense exhibit E, case no. 37, *Philippines v. Satō Sō*, box 1696, UD 1323, RG 331, NACP; file, Satō Sō, Sugamo Prison Detachment, box 136, UD UP 39, RG 554, NACP.

52. Transcript, 277–308, case no. 69, *Philippines v. Fujimoto Takao*, box 1707, UD 1323, RG 331, NACP.

53. Transcript, 244, *United States v. Tabuo Chikanori*, box 1559, and transcript, 174–75, *United States v. Shin Fusataro*, box 1566, UD 1321, RG 331, NACP.

54. Transcript, 10, case no. 23, *Philippines v. Teramoto Tukuji [Tokuji]*, box 1692, UD 1323, RG 331, NACP.

55. Transcript, 16–49, case no. 17, *Philippines v. Mori Kenkichi*, box 1691, transcript, 115–19, case no. 71, *Philippines v. Ogawa Somin* et al., box 1708, and transcript, 16, case no. 20, *Philippines v. Seki Sakuyoshi and Hamada Kazuo*, box 1692, UD 1323, RG 331, NACP.

56. Transcript, 61–63, 108–20, case no. 61, *Philippines v. Ainoda Hajime* et al., box 1705, and transcript, 346–52, case no. 71, *Philippines v. Ogawa Somin* et al., box 1708, UD 1323, RG 331, NACP.

57. Case no. 44, *Philippines v. Satō Matazō*, box 1697, UD 1323, RG 331, NACP; review board report, 24–33, bundle no. 55, *Philippines v. Satō Matazō*, Japanese War Crime Records, Case Files, NAP.

58. For example, the prosecution in its closing statement in the case against Itō Masayasu disparaged the efforts of the defendant to produce an alibi as a common resort among Japanese war criminals. See prosecution closing statement, case no. 25,

Philippines v. Itō Masayasu, box 1693, UD 1323, RG 331, NACP. See also transcript, 496, case no. 13, *Philippines v. Uemura Eichirō and Arai Hatsuyoshi*, box 1690, UD 1323, RG 331, NACP.

59. See, for example, Kumai, *Blood and Mud*, 132–36; and Satō, *Onshū o koete*, 30–34.

60. The Tatishi ("Tateishi" if using the Japanese character reading) family represents in microcosm the tangled circumstances and outcomes for Japanese civilians after the war ended. Vicente's father, Masajiro, had immigrated to the Philippines before the war and was baptized Raymundo Cantos before his marriage to a Filipina; he retained his Japanese citizenship and died in a camp in Davao in 1945. Vicente's older brother Teodoro Cantos was initially tried for war crimes by an American tribunal and sentenced to death; he appealed that conviction on the grounds that he was a naturalized Filipino citizen. Turned over to the Philippine government by the American authorities, he was subsequently convicted of treason and murder by a Philippine court and sentenced to death. His sentence was later commuted to life by the Supreme Court of the Philippines, and he was released in July 1953 along with other collaborators as part of a general amnesty. Vicente used the name Tatishi and spent part of his youth in Japan before returning to the Philippines at age fourteen, but he testified that he spoke only Visayan and learned Japanese only after his imprisonment. Transcript, 499–515, case no. 53, *Philippines v. Matsuda Ichiji* et al., box 1703, and transcript, 163–68, case no. 63, *Philippines v. Takano Chōyō*, box 1705, UD 1323, RG 331, NACP; review board report, *United States v. Teodoro Tatishi*, box 1575, UD 1321, RG 331, NACP; "Freed Jap POWs, PI Collaborators Listed," *Evening News* (Manila), July 4, 1953, 5; "Court Denies Tatishi Plea," *Manila Bulletin*, December 18, 1946, 4; Republic of the Philippines Supreme Court, GR no. L-1661, April 28, 1949, *in re People of the Philippines v. Teodoro Cantos*.

61. Specifications, transcript, 19–34, 262, 328, 378, 386–87, 499, 576–77, 702–4, and commission rationale, case no. 53, *Philippines v. Matsuda Ichiji* et al., box 1703, UD 1323, RG 331, NACP.

62. Transcript, 506–9, case no. 11, *Philippines v. Morishita Tsuneo*, boxes 1689–90, and transcript, 209–24, case no. 51, *Philippines v. Doi Kunio*, box 1702, UD 1323, RG 331, NACP.

63. Okamoto, *Nokosareta hitobito*, letters and essays section, 221–24; specifications, and transcript, 9, 65, 203–4, 339–41, case no. 46, *Philippines v. Satō Ichirō* et al., box 1697, UD 1323, RG 331, NACP.

64. Ryan, *Yamashita's Ghost*, 99.

65. Transcript, 202–3, case no. 1, *Philippines v. Fujita Takefumi*, box 1728, UD 1323, RG 331, NACP.

66. Transcript, 168, case no. 26, *Philippines v. Ogawa Eitarō*, box 1693, UD 1323, RG 331, NACP.

67. Transcript, 372, case no. 12, *Philippines v. Nakamura Hideichi* et al., box 1690, UD 1323, RG 331, NACP.

68. Transcript, 46–48, case no. 7, *Philippines v. Satō Sō*, box 1688, UD 1323, RG 331, NACP. In another case, the defense attorney likewise declined to be present when the

prosecution proposed holding a deposition but did not explain his reasoning. See exhibit 6A, case no. 53, *Philippines v. Matsuda Ichiji* et al., box 1703, UD 1323, RG 331, NACP.

69. Transcript, 11–29, case no. 16, *Philippines v. Tone Seiichi*, box 1691, UD 1323, RG 331, NACP.

70. Transcript, 563, case no. 23, *Philippines v. Teramoto Tukuji [Tokuji]*, box 1693, UD 1323, RG 331, NACP.

71. Transcript, 386–93, case no. 31, *Philippines v. Shimamura Katsuji*, box 1694, UD 1323, RG 331, NACP; bundle no. 23, *Philippines v. Kobayashi Kesaki*, Japanese War Crime Records, Case Files, NAP.

72. The Kudō Chūshirō case offers a useful example. The defense actually succeeded in bringing over one witness from Japan to testify, and he corroborated parts of Kudō's proffered alibi that he had not been in the town of Bay during the commission of the atrocities with which he was charged. But when questioned by the prosecution and commission members, the witness acknowledged that Kudō could have been ordered to Bay without the witness's knowledge. See transcript, 232–40, case no. 5, *Philippines v. Kudō Chūshirō*, box 1729, UD 1328, RG 331, NACP.

73. Transcript, 66–160, 200–205, 242–46, 267–69, 292–95, and commission rationale, 11, case no. 46, *Philippines v. Satō Ichirō* et al., box 1697, UD 1323, RG 331, NACP.

74. Transcript, 2121–26, case no. 71, *Philippines v. Ogawa Somin* et al., box 1709, UD 1323, RG 331, NACP.

75. Commission rationale, case no. 52, *Philippines v. Kurasawa Tooru*, box 1703, UD 1323, RG 331, NACP.

76. For a discussion of this distinction, see Chantal Meloni, "Command Responsibility: Mode of Liability for the Crimes of Subordinates or Separate Offence of the Superior?," *Journal of International Criminal Law* 5 (2007): 621–23.

77. Transcript, 22–360, case no. 47, *Philippines v. Hatayama Yoshimi* et al., box 1697, UD 1323, RG 331, NACP.

78. Transcript, 333, case no. 51, *Philippines v. Doi Kunio*, box 1702, UD 1323, RG 331, NACP.

79. Transcript, 550, case no. 56, *Philippines v. Omura Yasuo*, box 1703, and transcript, 867, case no. 18, *Philippines v. Matsuzaki Hideichi*, box 1691, UD 1323, RG 331, NACP.

80. Transcript, 590–93, and prosecution and defense briefs, case no. 4, *Philippines v. Nakano Shizuo*, box 1729, UD 1328, RG 331, NACP.

81. David Cohen notes that the test for determining a de facto superior-subordinate relationship is assessing whether the commander has effective control over his men, that is, the "power to prevent or punish." See David J. Cohen, "The Singapore War Crimes Trials and Their Relevance Today," *Singapore Law Review* 31 (2013): 7–8.

82. Lt. Gen. Kuroda Shigenori (commander of the Fourteenth Army from May 1943 to September 1944) and Maj. Gen. Masuoka Kensichi (Kempeitai commander from February 1945 to the end of the war) were both charged with multiple counts of the

willful failure to prevent their subordinates from committing atrocities. In large measure, these trials followed the precedent set by US prosecutors in the trial of Yamashita Tomoyuki, with an emphasis on the argument that the abuses were so widespread that the defendants could not plead ignorance as a legitimate defense. The outcomes, however, differed: Kuroda was found guilty and sentenced to life, whereas Masuoka was acquitted of the command responsibility charges he faced (he was convicted of one separate count). The commission in Masuoka's case concluded that "the accident of command cannot alone be made the basis of responsibility for war crimes." See case no. 50, *Philippines v. Kuroda Shigenori*, boxes 1699–1702, and transcript, 393, case no. 67, *Philippines v. Masuoka Kensichi*, box 1707, UD 1323, RG 331, NACP.

83. Transcript, 6–8, 9–33, 71–87, 119–33, 223–26, and prosecution exhibits 3 and 4, case no. 1, *Philippines v. Fujita Takefumi*, box 1728, UD 1328, RG 331, NACP.

84. Transcript, 772–75, case no. 1, *Philippines v. Fujita Takefumi*, box 1728, UD 1328, RG 331, NACP.

85. Higher-ranking Kempeitai officers with command responsibilities at Fort Santiago had already been put on trial by the US military for the suffocation deaths, among other charges (see chapter 1).

86. Specifications, transcript, 12–25, 84–94, 100–133, 137–61, and exhibits 6 and 7, case no. 8, *Philippines v. Kita Heiji* et al., box 1688, UD 1323, RG 331, NACP.

87. Specifications, and transcript, 221–313, 398–406, 477–550, case no. 8, *Philippines v. Kita Heiji* et al., box 1688, UD 1323, RG 331, NACP.

88. Transcript, 721, case no. 8, *Philippines v. Kita Heiji* et al., box 1688, UD 1323, RG 331, NACP.

89. Ibid., 762–63.

90. Ibid., 782–85.

91. Specifications, and transcript, 31–829, case no. 71, *Philippines v. Ogawa Somin* et al., box 1708, UD 1323, RG 331, NACP.

92. Transcript, 902–31, case no. 71, *Philippines v. Ogawa Somin* et al., box 1708, UD 1323, RG 331, NACP.

93. Ibid., 1270–1302.

94. Ibid., 1443–52, 1777–89.

95. Ibid., 1967–2077.

96. Ibid., 2148–55.

97. Specifications, and transcript, 267–308, 389–93, case no. 67, *Philippines v. Masuoka Kensichi*, box 1707, UD 1323, RG 331, NACP.

98. Four of the defendants in a third trial had given prior statements claiming they had acted in self-defense, but this was not a defense pursued at trial, and in his closing remarks the prosecutor discounted such a claim as purely self-serving. See exhibits 25A, 27A, 28A, 31A, and prosecutor closing statement, 10, case no. 61, *Philippines v. Ainoda Hajime* et al., box 1705, UD 1323, RG 331, NACP.

99. Specifications, and transcript, 326–72, 549–51, case no. 7, *Philippines v. Satō Sō*, box 1688, UD 1323, RG 331, NACP.

100. Judge Advocate General, *War Department Basic Field Manual: Rules of Land Warfare, FM 27-10* (Washington, DC: US Government Printing Office, 1940), para. 351, in box 106, War Crimes Division, Law Library Files, 1944–49, entry A1 135, RG 153, NACP.

101. See, for example, transcript, 362–64, case no. 9, *Philippines v. Mihara Kikuichi*, box 1688, and transcript, 1131, case no. 10, *Philippines v. Shimizu Hisamitsu and Uemura Masao*, box 1689, UD 1323, RG 331, NACP.

Chapter 4. Awaiting Their Fate

1. Kagao Shūnin, "Ikite iru Hitō senpan," *Kaizō* 32, no. 7 (June 1951): 132–39.
2. The text of EO 68 was made a part of the official record of each war crimes trial.
3. See, for example, bundle no. 3, *Philippines v. Deguchi Motoaki*, and bundle no. 10, *Philippines v. Gotō Shōzō and Fujii Rokujirō*, Japanese War Crime Records, Case Files, NAP.
4. Review file documents, bundle no. 47, *Philippines v. Nakanishi Shioji*, Japanese War Crime Records, Case Files, NAP.
5. Records of the war crimes trials have been preserved at the National Archives of the Philippines, but not all of the case files contain postsentence review documentation, so this conclusion is based on those board reports that are available.
6. Review board report, 24, bundle no. 14, *Philippines v. Hatogai* et al., Japanese War Crime Records, Case Files, NAP.
7. Review board report, 27–30, bundle no. 24, *Philippines v. Kobayashi Masatake* et al., Japanese War Crime Records, Case Files, NAP.
8. Review board report, 85–88, and recommendations, bundle no. 50, *Philippines v. Ogawa Somin* et al., Japanese War Crime Records, Case Files, NAP.
9. Review board report, bundle no. 60, *Philippines v. Shimizu Hisamitsu and Uemura Masao*, Japanese War Crime Records, Case Files, NAP.
10. Torres to Army Chief of Staff Castaneda, January 28, 1949, bundle no. 60, *Philippines v. Shimizu Hisamitsu and Uemura Masao*, Japanese War Crime Records, Case Files, NAP.
11. Specifications, transcript, 12–14, 46–56, 87–93, 271, 314, 437–40, 531, 571–72, 574, and defense exhibits A, C, and E, case no. 44, *Philippines v. Satō Matazō*, box 1697, UD 1323, RG 331, NACP.
12. Review board report, 24–33, Military Commission Orders no. 5, October 16, 1950, and Board of Review to SGS, message, October 9, 1950, bundle no. 55, *Philippines v. Satō Matazō*, Japanese War Crime Records, Case Files, NAP.
13. Transcript, 130–37, 321–22, case no. 61, *Philippines v. Ainoda Hajime* et al., box 1705, UD 1323, RG 331, NACP.
14. Case no. 55, *Philippines v. Nakamura Fumio*, box 1703, UD 1323, RG 331, NACP.
15. Board of review report, 22–23, and recommendations, bundle no. 10, *Philippines v. Gotō Shōzō and Fujii Rokujirō*, Japanese War Crime Records, Case Files, NAP.

16. Board of review report, 50–55, bundle no. 26, *Philippines v. Koike Kaneyuki*, Japanese War Crime Records, Case Files, NAP.

17. Board of review report, 8–14, bundle no. 12, *Philippines v. Harada Shimpei* et al., and board of review report, dissenting opinion, 2, 9, bundle no. 56, *Philippines v. Satō Sō*, Japanese War Crime Records, Case Files, NAP.

18. Board of review report, and action of reviewing authority (unsigned), May 20, 1952, bundle no. 24, *Philippines v. Kobayashi Masatake* et al., Japanese War Crime Records, Case Files, NAP; Itō et al., *Monten*, 49.

19. Review file, bundle no. 22, *Philippines v. Kita Heiji* et al., Japanese War Crime Records, Case Files, NAP; transcript, 1–7, 247, 367–69, 782–84, case no. 8, *Philippines v. Kita Heiji* et al., box 1688, UD 1323, RG 331, NACP.

20. Transcript, 5–6, 11, 593, case no. 4, *Philippines v. Nakano Shizuo*, box 1729, UD 1328, RG 331, NACP; board of review report, 26–27, and action of the reviewing authority, April 10, 1948, bundle no. 48, *Philippines v. Nakano Shizuo*, Japanese War Crime Records, Case Files, NAP.

21. See, for example, bundle no. 48, *Philippines v. Nakano Shizuo*, bundle no. 49, *Philippines v. Ogawa Eitarō*, bundle no. 18, *Philippines v. Itō Masayasu*, bundle no. 61, *Philippines v. Shirota Gintarō*, and bundle no. 72, *Philippines v. Yamashita Suekichi*, Japanese War Crime Records, Case Files, NAP.

22. For example, a local paper reported in February 1951 that the secretary of justice had forwarded (only) ten cases to the president for his review. See "EQ to Review Cases of Japs," *Manila Chronicle*, February 6, 1951, 1–2.

23. Specifications, and transcript, 183, 192–96, 282, 867, case no. 18, *Philippines v. Matsuzaki Hideichi*, box 1691, UD 1323, RG 331, NACP.

24. "Hitō kara Matsuzaki moto chūsara kaeru," *Nihon Keizai Shimbun*, March 29, 1951, 3; Carlos Quirino, *Apo Lakay: The Biography of President Elpidio Quirino of the Philippines* (Manila: Total Book World, 1987), 66; Nihon no Firipin Senryōki ni Kansuru Shiryō Chōsa Fōramu, ed., *Nihon no Firipin senryō: Intabyū kiroku* (Tokyo: Ryūkei Shosha, 1994), 211, 247–49; Republic of the Philippines, *Official Gazette* 47, no. 2 (February 1951): xiv; press release, 2-10-4, Office of the President of the Philippines, February 10, 1951, attachment to check sheet memo, March 6, 1951, decimal 694.0026/3-651, box 3020, Central Decimal File, 1950–54, RG 59, NACP; memo, "Information Concerning Philippine War Criminals Issue," September 27, 1949, 1:158–61, disclosure 14, D'130 2-5-2, JDRO.

25. Charge, specifications, and transcript, 49, 555, 578, 756, 784–85, case no. 8, *Philippines v. Kita Heiji* et al., box 1688, UD 1323, RG 331, NACP.

26. Chairman of Board of Review to SGS, memo, October 7, 1950, Nanadiego to Chairman, Board of Review, memo, March 21, 1950, and conditional pardon, February 8, 1952, bundle no. 22, *Philippines v. Kita Heiji* et al., Japanese War Crime Records, Case Files, NAP; "Kita moto chūi mo tokusha," *Asahi Shimbun*, February 15, 1952, 3.

27. Transcript, 1795–96, 1899, 2010, 2032, case no. 50, *Philippines v. Kuroda Shigenori*, box 1702, UD 1323, RG 331, NACP; "Firipin no inshō," *Mainichi Shimbun*, March 10,

1952, 2; "Kuroda Japan-Bound: Occupation General Bids Quirino Good-Bye," *Manila Times*, January 30, 1952, 1.

28. Kuroda, "Montenrupa," 133; "Kuroda Japan-Bound," *Manila Times*, January 30, 1952, 1; "EQ at Clark Field," *Manila Times*, February 22, 1952, 1; "The President's Day," *Manila Chronicle*, January 30, 1952, 1; "The President's Day," *Manila Chronicle*, February 22, 1952, 1; "Tsushima zenken, Kirino daitōryō to kaiken," *Asahi Shimbun*, January 29, 1952, 1; "Kuroda moto chūjō, Kirino daitōryō ni aisatsu," *Mainichi Shimbun*, January 30, 1952, 3; "'Nisenpan no onjō wa wasurenu': Kirino daitōryō, Kita-shi ni kataru," *Mainichi Shimbun*, February 22, 1952, 3; "Hitō kara Matsuzaki moto chūsara kaeru," *Nihon Keizai Shimbun*, March 29, 1951, 3.

29. "Extemporaneous Remarks of President Quirino to the Delegates to the International Council of Christian Churches Conference, Malacañan Palace, December 1, 1953, Republic of the Philippines," *Official Gazette* 47, no. 12 (December 1951): 6086.

30. "Tsushima zenken," *Asahi Shimbun*, January 29, 1952, 1; "Kita moto chūi mo tokusha," *Asahi Shimbun*, February 15, 1952, 3; "Hitō senpan zenin o naichi e," *Mainichi Shimbun*, February 21, 1952, 3; "'Nisenpan no onjō wa wasurenu,'" *Mainichi Shimbun*, February 22, 1952, 3; "Kuroda Japan-Bound," *Manila Times*, January 30, 1952, 1; "EQ at Clark Field," *Manila Times*, February 22, 1952, 1; "The President's Day," *Manila Chronicle*, January 30, 1952, 1.

31. The phrase the reporter heard while at the prison was "ishi ga nagarete ki no ha ga shizumu," literally translated as "[when] stones float and leaves sink" (Tsuji, *Montenrupa*, 20–25).

32. Transcript, 714–20, case no. 58, *Philippines v. Koike Kaneyuke*, box 1704, UD 1323, RG 331, NACP; "'Nisenpan no onjō wa wasurenu,'" *Mainichi Shimbun*, February 22, 1952, 3; "Genkei no kenpei o shakuhō," *Mainichi Shimbun*, July 10, 1953, evening edition, 7.

33. Fred Ruiz Castro to President of the Philippines, March 3, 1952, review file, bundle no. 26, *Philippines v. Koike Kaneyuki*, Japanese War Crime Records, Case Files, NAP.

34. Arai, "Montenrupa no atsui kaze," 250–51.

35. US Embassy Manila airgram no. A-329, July 26, 1948, file 711.6, Manila Embassy General Records, 1948, box 40, entry 3100A, RG 84, NACP; "I Who Am About to Die," *Philippines Free Press*, October 2, 1948, 16; US Embassy Manila dispatch no. 32, January 10, 1950, file War Criminals Vol. VII, Decimal File, 1945–51, SCAP Legal Section, Law Division, box 1413, UD 1289, RG 331, NACP.

36. "Reporter Gives Eyewitness Account of Kudo's Hanging," *Manila Bulletin*, August 14, 1948, 1; charge, specifications, and transcript, 1, 600, case no. 5, *Philippines v. Kudō Chūshirō*, box 1729, UD 1328, RG 331, NACP.

37. "Former Jap Terror Is Hanged, Buried," *Evening Herald*, August 14, 1948, 2; "Butcher of Bay Is Hanged," *Manila Times*, August 14, 1948, 1; "Another Jap War Criminal to Hang; Kudo Executed," *Manila Chronicle*, August 14, 1948, 6; Satō, *Onshū o koete*, 80.

38. Itō et al., *Monten*, log entry for August 14, 1949.

39. "I Who Am About to Die," *Philippines Free Press*, October 2, 1948, 16.

40. Specifications, and transcript, 1062, case no. 9, *Philippines v. Nakano Shizuo*, boxes 1688–89, UD 1323, RG 331, NACP; specifications, and transcript, 593, case no. 23, *Philippines v. Teramoto Tukuji [Tokuji]*, boxes 1692–93, UD 1323, RG 331, NACP; "2 More Japs Are Executed," *Manila Times*, November 11, 1948, 1; "Two Japs Swing at Muntinlupa," *Evening News*, November 11, 1948, 13; "2 Japs Hanged for War Crimes," *Manila Bulletin*, November 11, 1948, 2; "2 Jap Criminals Hanged in Prison," *Manila Chronicle*, November 11, 1948, 1.

41. US Embassy Manila cable no. 711, July 9, 1948, file 711.6, Manila Embassy General Records, 1946–61, box 40, entry 3100A, RG 84, NACP.

42. Legal Section to Chief of Staff, check sheet memo, May 6, 1947, folder War Crimes Trials in Manila, Miscellaneous Classified Files, 1945–52, SCAP Legal Section, Law Division, box 1434, UD 1294, and check sheet memo, July 8, 1947, file 000.5C, "War Crimes Philippines," Decimal File, 1945–51, SCAP Legal Section, Law Division, box 1413, UD 1289, RG 331, NACP.

43. Eleuterio Fojas to President of the Philippines, May 27, 1948, Roman Ozaeta to Director of Prisons, May 28, 1948, and Director of Prisons to Director, PHILRYCOM Prison Division, memo, June 2, 1948, folder Transfer of Condemned Prisoners to New Bilibid Prison, Miscellaneous File, 1945–49, SCAP Legal Section, Manila Branch, box 1975, UD 1353, RG 331, NACP.

44. This was at least the speculation of one Filipino commentator, who observed in early 1948 that convicted war criminals transferred to Sugamo Prison in Tokyo could be freed after Japan regained its independence. See Teodoro Locsin, "Day of Reckoning," *Philippines Free Press*, January 17, 1948, 19. This did not, in the event, turn out to be the case. The San Francisco Peace Treaty, signed in September 1951, stipulated that Allied governments retained control over decisions regarding the release of prisoners tried in their courts.

45. Petition, June 18, 1948, folder Transmittal of Petitions of Japanese, Investigative Reports for War Crimes, 1945–48, SCAP Legal Section, Administrative Division, box 898, UD 1182, RG 331, NACP.

46. Arai, "Montenrupa no atsui kaze," 252–53; Kagao Shūnin, "Montenrupa no namida," *Daihōrin* 20, no. 3 (March 1953): 6; Tsuji, *Yūhei Montenrupa*, 102; Kagao Shūnin, *Montenrupa ni inoru: Nippi senpan shikeishū to tomo ni* (Tokyo: Fuji Shoen, 1953), 109; Tsuji, *Montenrupa*, 135–38.

47. Asia Bureau, "Matters Concerning War Criminals in the Philippines," memo, November 12, 1952, 1:283–84, disclosure 14, D'130 3-1-1, JDRO; Kagao, "Ikite iru Hitō senpan," 134.

48. Asia Bureau, "Matters Concerning War Criminals," memo, November 12, 1952, 1:283–84, disclosure 14, D'130 3-1-1, JDRO; Tsuji, *Yūhei Montenrupa*, 102, 121, 132; Kuroda, "Montenrupa," 131–32; "Hitō senpan shūyōjo o tou," *Asahi Shimbun*, January 28, 1952, 3.

49. "Report Concerning the Status of the Philippines War Crimes Trials," June 9,

1949, 1:148–49, disclosure 14, D'130 2-5-2, JDRO; Tsuji, *Montenrupa*, 70; Mineo Shisuhiko, *Uminari ga kikoeru: Hitō senpan shikeishū kaigun seinen shōkō no ikan* (Tokyo: Fuesu Shuppan, 1966), 195.

50. Report, "Matter Concerning the Philippine War Crimes Trials," May 6, 1949, 1:118–24, disclosure 14, D'130 2-5-2, JDRO.

51. Kobayashi Hirotada, *Ten ni tou tegami: Mujitsu no senpan kyūsai ni hansei o sasageta Ueki Shinkichi* (Tokyo: Mainichi Shimbunsha, 2008), 60–65; "16 Convicts, 2 Prison Men Slain in Battle," *Manila Times*, May 27, 1950, 1.

52. Kagao, "Ikite iru Hitō senpan," 137; Tsuji, *Yūhei Montenrupa*, 102–4.

53. Kobayashi, in subsequent testimony before a Diet committee, also complained about the quality of the food in prison. Testimony of Kobayashi Yusaku, November 13, 1952, Welfare Committee Hearing, House of Councilors, Japan National Diet.

54. "Jap PWs Fed Well, Says Balagtas," *Manila Times*, November 5, 1952, 1; aide-mémoire, November 11, 1952, and Asia Bureau, "Matters Concerning War Criminals," November 12, 1952, 1:283–84, disclosure 14, D'130 3-1-1, JDRO.

55. Nakamura Kazunori to Maj. Charles W. Willoughby, Chief, Criminal Registry Division, Legal Section, SCAP, March 27, 1949, folder no. 24, "Reports from Manila Defence" [*sic*], and check sheet memos, SCAP Legal Section Tokyo, February 17 and March 1, 1949, folder no. 26, "Policy," Miscellaneous Subject File, 1945–50, SCAP Legal Section, Administrative Division, box 1225, UD 1225, RG 331, NACP.

56. It was the position of the Philippine government, concurred in by the US government, that because the Japanese incarcerated in Muntinlupa were classified as war criminals or war crimes suspects, they were not entitled to the pay that prisoners of war were ordinarily allowed. The failure to provide dentures was due to a lack of materials, a problem that was subsequently remedied by supplies from the Japanese Red Cross. See US Political Adviser Tokyo no. 761, May 16, 1950, and attachments, decimal 694.9626/5-1650, Central Decimal File, 1950–54, box 3023, RG 59, NACP; and check sheet memo, Legal Section, March 31, 1950, decimal War Crimes 000.5B, Decimal File, 1945–51, Legal Section, Law Division, box 1413, UD 1289, RG 331, NACP.

57. Office of the United States Political Adviser for Japan, no. 795, and attachments, November 15, 1949, file 321.4, Manila Embassy Security Segregated Classified General Records, 1944–52, box 15, entry 3101, RG 84, NACP.

58. Ilde Remolona, "Hitō no Nihonjin senpantachi: Sono seikatsu to kokoro no hi," *Nyū Eiji* 3, no. 8 (August 1951): 16–20.

59. Ibid., 17–18.

60. Nelson is much better known as the compiler of *Nelson's Japanese English Character Dictionary*. Tsuji, *Yūhei Montenrupa*, 99; Kagao, *Montenrupa ni inoru*, 109–12.

61. Tsuji, *Yūhei Montenrupa*, 121–22; "Returning War Criminals Invite Nun to Meet Them," *Nippon Times*, July 21, 1953, 1; Remolona, "Hitō no Nihonjin senpantachi," 20.

62. Kagao Shūnin, "Montenrupa shikei no ichiya," *Daihōrin* 20, no. 10 (October 1953): 6–7, 14; Kagao, *Montenrupa ni inoru*, 53–54.

63. Kagao, "Montenrupa shikei no ichiya," 8.

64. Ibid., 7–12; Kagao, *Montenrupa ni inoru*, 142–207.

65. Kagao, "Ikite iru Hitō senpan," 135.

66. Ibid., 134; testimony of Jimbō Nobuhiko, March 13, 1951, hearing, Special Committee on Overseas Repatriation, House of Councilors, Japan National Diet.

67. Okamoto, *Nokosareta hitobito*, letters and essays section, 9–11; Kagao, "Montenrupa shikei no ichiya," 9.

68. Kagao, "Ikite iru Hitō senpan," 136–37.

69. Nakajima Shōhei, "Shikeishū no inori," *Sunday Mainichi* 30 (August 19, 1951): 3–4.

70. Bundle no. 63, *Philippines v. Takahashi Sadakichi*, bundle no. 18, *Philippines v. Itō Masayasu*, bundle no. 49, *Philippines v. Ogawa Eitarō*, bundle no. 22, *Philippines v. Kita Heiji* et al., bundle no. 36, *Philippines v. Mihara Kikuichi*, and bundle no. 46, *Philippines v. Nakamura Hideichi* et al., Japanese War Crime Records, Case Files, NAP.

71. Elpidio Quirino, *The Memoirs of Elpidio Quirino* (Manila: National Historical Institute, 1990).

72. Action of the reviewing authority, May 18, 1948, review file, bundle no. 18, *Philippines v. Itō Masayasu*, and Defense Panel Office to the President of the Philippines, check sheet memo, December 7, 1948, review file, bundle no. 49, *Philippines v. Ogawa Eitarō*, Japanese War Crime Records, Case Files, NAP.

73. "Quirino Stresses View on Jap Trade," *Manila Times*, May 6, 1948, 1.

74. Memo, "Information Concerning Philippine War Criminals Issue," September 27, 1949, 1:158–61, disclosure 14, D'130 2-5-2, JDRO.

75. "Ask Mercy for Jap Criminals," *Manila Bulletin*, February 5, 1951, 1; John Nevin Sayre to Senator Herbert Lehman, February 9, 1951, decimal 694.9626/3-551, Central Decimal File, 1950–54, box 3023, RG 59, NACP.

76. Sayre to Lehman, February 9, 1951, and Assistant Secretary Jack McFall to Senator Lehman, March 20, 1951, decimal 694.9626/3-551, Central Decimal File, 1950–54, box 3023, RG 59, NACP; Ambassador Dulles and Philippine President Elpidio Quirino, memo of conversation, February 12, 1951, file 320, "International Political Relations," Manila Embassy General Records, 1946–61, box 20, entry 3100A, RG 84, NACP.

77. Yoshikawa Yōko, *Nippi baishō gaikō kōshō no kenkyū, 1949–1956* (Tokyo: Keisō Shobō, 1991), 23–25; Ohno Takushi, *War Reparations and Peace Settlement: Philippines-Japan Relations, 1945–1956* (Manila: Solidaridad Publishing House, 1986), 36–43; Kagao, "Montenrupa shikei no ichiya," 8.

Chapter 5. From Retribution to Resolution

1. When Philippine outcomes are compared with those for US trials as a whole, the disparity virtually disappears. According to data cited by Hayashi, the United States executed 10 percent of all those it put on trial in the Asia theater, compared with the

11 percent who were executed by the Philippine government. In fact, the United States and the Philippines executed the fewest Japanese, measured as a percentage of those tried. The British and the Dutch executed 23 and 22 percent, respectively, followed by China (17 percent), Australia (16 percent), and France (11 percent). See Hayashi, *BC-kyū senpan saiban*, 61; Chaen Yoshio, ed., *BC-kyū senpan Beigun Manira saiban shiryō* (Tokyo: Fuji Shuppan, 1986), 6, 162–80; and Manila Provost Marshal Command, Prison Division, Headquarters, Philippines-Ryukyus Command, "Master Roster of Executed War Criminals," undated, file Lists of Executed and Cemetery Plots, Miscellaneous File, 1945–49, Manila Branch, SCAP Legal Section Investigative Division, box 1971, UD 1353, RG 331, NACP.

2. State Department cable no. CA-5302, "Japanese War Criminals," March 25, 1954, folder Post-Treaty—Japanese War Criminals, 1954, box 24, and Parole and Clemency Board memo, "Japanese War Criminals," January 7, 1957, folder Disposition, 1954–57, box 23, Records of the Legal Adviser Relating to Japanese War Crimes, 1943–60, lot file 61 D 33, Records of the Legal Adviser Relating to War Crimes, RG 59, NACP; US Department of State, *Foreign Relations of the United States, 1958–1960* (Washington, DC: US Government Printing Office, 1994), 18:83.

3. "Senpan o shokei?," *Asahi Shimbun*, February 1, 1951, 3; "Hitō de senpan jyūyonmei jūsatsu," *Nihon Keizai Shimbun*, February 1, 1951, 3; Kagao, "Montenrupa shikei no ichiya," 13.

4. Kagao, "Montenrupa shikei no ichiya," 26; Kagao, "Ikite iru Hitō senpan," 134; "Firipin senpan no shikei enki chinjō," *Asahi Shimbun*, February 3, 1951, 1.

5. Kagao, "Montenrupa shikei no ichiya," 13–14; Tsuji, *Yūhei Montenrupa*, 152, 160–61; Tsuji, *Montenrupa*, 230–31; Kobayashi, *Ten ni tou tegami*, 116–17; "Firipin senpan no shikei enki chinjō," *Asahi Shimbun*, February 3, 1951, 1; "Horarete ita nijyū no boketsu: Montenrupa no hiwa," *Asahi Shimbun*, July 1, 1953, evening edition, 3.

6. Draft text of aide-mémoire, March 5, 1952, 1:255–57, disclosure 14, D'130 3-1-1, JDRO; "Genkei tangan ga sattō: Nihon no senpan kazoku kara," *Asahi Shimbun*, February 3, 1952, evening edition, 2; "EQ to Review Cases of Japs," *Manila Chronicle*, February 6, 1951, 2; "Hitō de senpan jyūyonmei jūsatsu," *Nihon Keizai Shimbun*, February 3, 1951, 3; "Pardon Due All Filipino, Jap War Criminals," *Evening News*, June 27, 1953, 1; "5 Million Jap Signatures to Release POW's Arrive," *Saturday Mirror*, June 27, 1953, 1.

7. "Kirino Hidaitōryō: Senpan o shinsa," *Nihon Keizai Shimbun*, February 7, 1951, 3; "Japs to Ask Diet to Intercede for War Criminals Facing Death in P.I.," *Manila Bulletin*, February 8, 1951, 4.

8. Press release, 2-10-4, Office of the President of the Philippines, February 10, 1951, attachment to check sheet memo, March 6, 1951, decimal 694.0026/3-651, box 3020, Central Decimal File, 1950–54, RG 59, NACP.

9. Memo, "Information Concerning Philippine War Criminals Issue," September 27, 1949, 1:158–61, disclosure 14, D'130 2-5-2, JDRO; transcript, 362–66, case no. 64, *Philippines v. Kawaguchi Kiyotake and Hayashi Yoshihide*, box 1705, UD 1323, RG 331, NACP; Tsuji, *Yūhei Montenrupa*, 130; memo, "Matter Concerning the Philippine War

Crimes Trials," May 6, 1949, 1:118–24, disclosure 14, D'130 2-5-2, JDRO; Kobayashi, *Ten ni tou tegami*, 148.

10. US Embassy Manila telegram no. 838, September 18, 1952, decimal 510, Manila Embassy Secret General Records, 1950–52, box 2, entry 3103, RG 84, NACP; US Embassy Manila cable no. 1240, December 9, 1948, decimal 694.9631/12-948, Central Decimal File, 1945–49, box 2918, RG 59, NACP; Willard A. Hanna, "Japan's Return to the Philippines," *AUFS Reports: East Asia Series* (Japan) 4, no. 12 (1955): 20.

11. Draft text of aide-mémoire, March 5, 1952, 1:255–57, draft text of note verbale, November 6, 1952, 1:278–79, and Manila cables, November 5 and November 6, 1952, 1:268–274, disclosure 14, D'130 3-1-1, JDRO.

12. Manila cable no. 84, January 27, 1953, 1:334, and Tokyo cable no. 22, June 16, 1953, 1:426–27, disclosure 14, D'130 3-1-1, JDRO.

13. Manila cable no. 46, November 28, 1952, 1:295, and Asia Bureau Third Section Chief Tobu to Asia Bureau Chief, message, July 21, 1952, 1:258–60, disclosure 14, D'130 3-1-1, JDRO.

14. "Senpan wa koku ni shamen," *Asahi Shimbun*, January 15, 1952, 3; "'Senpan wa hayaku kaeshitai': Kirino daitōryō senmei," *Asahi Shimbun*, February 26, 1952, 3.

15. US Embassy Tokyo dispatch no. 215, June 12, 1952, folder Post-Treaty—Japanese War Criminals, 1950–52, box 24, Records of the Legal Adviser Relating to Japanese War Crimes, 1943–60, lot file 61 D 33, Records of the Legal Adviser Relating to War Crimes, RG 59, NACP; "Kirino daitōryō no ikō," *Asahi Shimbun*, June 6, 1952, 3; "Kongo shikei wa okonowarenu," *Mainichi Shimbun*, June 20, 1952, evening edition, 2; "Senpan, jojo ni kaesu," *Mainichi Shimbun*, July 30, 1952, 3; "Hayaku wa kaesenu senpan," *Nihon Keizai Shimbun*, July 31, 1952, 7; Manila cable no. 117, December 24, 1952, 1:312, disclosure 14, D'130 3-1-1, JDRO.

16. Manila cable no. 130, December 29, 1952, 1:314, disclosure 14, D'130 3-1-1, JDRO.

17. Manila cable no. 129, December 29, 1952, 1:313; Manila cable no. 130, December 29, 1952, 1:317–18, and Tokyo cable no. 84, December 30, 1952, 1:315, disclosure 14, D'130 3-1-1, JDRO.

18. Manila cable no. 2, January 2, 1953, 1:317–18, disclosure 14, D'130 3-1-1, JDRO.

19. Manila cable no. 109, February 13, 1953, 1:338, Manila cable no. 69, February 17, 1953, 1:347–48, Manila cable no. 122, February 20, 1953, 1:350, Manila cable no. 289, June 3, 1953, 1:398, and Tokyo cable no. 22, June 16, 1953, 1:426–27, disclosure 14, D'130 3-1-1, JDRO.

20. Ohno, *War Reparations*, 35–54.

21. Quoted in ibid., 49.

22. Ibid., 68–71.

23. Ibid., 58–59, 73–76, 79–80; Yoshikawa, *Nippi baishō*, 57, 92–93; US Embassy Manila cable no. 394, October 3, 1952, decimal 694.96/10-352, Central Decimal File, 1950–54, box 3023, RG 59, NACP.

24. Secretary of Foreign Affairs Elizalde to President Quirino, December 12, 1952, file Foreign Affairs, Office of the Secretary, box 19, Elpidio Quirino Papers, Filipinas Heritage Museum, Manila, the Philippines; Ohno, *War Reparations*, 73–76.

25. Tsuji, *Montenrupa*, 133–34.

26. Ibid., 134.

27. US Political Adviser, Tokyo no. 418, September 17, 1951, decimal 694.9624/9-1751, Central Decimal File, 1950–54, box 3032, RG 59, NACP.

28. Editorial, "Reparations, Not Ransom," *Manila Times*, January 5, 1953, 4.

29. "Reparations May Decide POW Release," *Nippon Times*, January 4, 1953, 1; "Reparations vs. POW's," *Nippon Times*, January 5, 1953, 8; Elizalde to Quirino, January 19, 1953, folder Japanese Peace Treaty 1953, Japanese Peace Treaty: Far Eastern Commission, box 24, Quirino Papers; Kobayashi, *Ten ni tou tegami*, 234.

30. Manila cable no. 88, January 30, 1953, 1:330, disclosure 14, D'130 3-1-1, JDRO; agenda, January 16, 1953, Cabinet Agenda, January–December 1953, box 75, Quirino Papers.

31. Tsuji, *Montenrupa*, 223–24; Kagao, "Montenrupa no namida," 11; "Hitō senpan shūyōjo o tou," *Asahi Shimbun*, January 28, 1952, 3.

32. Kagao, "Montenrupa no namida," 12.

33. Tsuji, *Montenrupa*, 150–51; Kagao, "Montenrupa shikei no ichiya," 13–14; Kagao, "Montenrupa no namida," 7, 12–13; Kobayashi, *Ten ni tou tegami*, 117–18, 155–56.

34. Kagao, "Ikite iru Hitō senpan," 132–39; Kagao, "Montenrupa no namida," 6–13; Kagao Shūnin, "Montenrupa no senpan to tomo ni," *Fujin Kōron* 39:10, no. 437 (September 1953): 204–7; Kagao, "Montenrupa shikei no ichiya," 6–15.

35. Arai, "Montenrupa no atsui kaze," 252–54; Tsuji, *Yūhei Montenrupa*, 163–65; Montenrupa no Kai, "Aa, Montenrupa," *Seiron* 414 (September 2006): 23–29; Tōjima Kazuko, "Nippi yūkō no ishizue ni: 'Montenrupa no yo wa fukete,'" *Energy Review* 20:2, no. 229 (February 2000): 36.

36. "Lifesaving Song Rekindles Wartime Memories," *Kyodo News*, July 30, 1999, http://findarticles.com/p/articles/mi_mOWDQ/is_1999_August_2/ai_55364580/.

37. The names of the society and the newsletter were not just a partial phonetic rendering of "Muntinlupa"; the characters "mon" (問) and "ten" (天) could be construed to mean "appeal to heaven." The group went through several evolutions, beginning with a families' association that later merged with a more tightly knit group of prison returnees to form a broader organization that adopted the name Montenkai and then was later renamed Montenrupa no Kai for wider name recognition. Kobayashi, *Ten ni tou tegami*, 11–17, 24–26, 36–37, 50–52, 226, 243, 249–51.

38. Ueki's leak did not go unnoticed by his superiors; his boss chastised him for putting the jobs of his colleagues at risk by possibly angering SCAP officials and directed him to apologize to the head of the bureau; fortunately for Ueki, the bureau chief supported him. Kobayashi, *Ten ni tou tegami*, 110–14.

39. Ibid., 11–17, 36–37, 50–52, 143–46; Nakajima, "Shikeishū no inori," 3–8.

40. "Firipin no genjō," *Asahi Shimbun*, February 20, 1950, 1.

41. See, for example, "Hitō no tai-Nichi kanjō o saguru," *Mainichi Shimbun*, February 3, 1952, 1; "Hikoku senpan: Kangeki no owakare paatei," *Mainichi Shimbun*, July 12, 1953, 7; "Goei keikan wa shinsetsu," *Asahi Shimbun*, January 28, 1952, 3; "Firipin hito no kokoro," *Asahi Shimbun*, February 4, 1952, 3; "Akuma wa wasureyō: Manira no tai-Nichi kanjō yawaragu," *Asahi Shimbun*, July 9, 1953, evening edition, 3.

42. "Goei keikan wa shinsetsu," *Asahi Shimbun*, January 28, 1952, 3; "Firipin hito no kokoro," *Asahi Shimbun*, February 4, 1952, 3.

43. "Genki na Kuroda moto chujō: Senpan no unmei, baishō to kankei bimyō," *Mainichi Shimbun*, January 27, 1952, 1.

44. Tsuji, *Montenrupa*, 101–17; "Goei keikan wa shinsetsu," *Asahi Shimbun*, January 28, 1952, 3; "Firipin hito no kokoro," *Asahi Shimbun*, February 4, 1952, 3.

45. "Firipin hito no kokoro," *Asahi Shimbun*, February 4, 1952, 3.

46. Kagao, "Montenrupa no namida," 7; "Enjo no te nobeta hisoka no hitobito," *Asahi Shimbun*, June 28, 1953, 7; "Montenrupa e kazoku no kao," *Mainichi Shimbun*, March 29, 1953, 6; Kobayashi, *Ten ni tou tegami*, 207–8.

47. Memo, "Sentence Commutation for War Criminals in the Philippines," September 27, 1951, 1:252, disclosure 14, D'130 3-1-1, JDRO.

48. Kagao, "Ikite iru Hitō senpan," 139; Kobayashi, *Ten ni tou tegami*, 134, 137, 155, 161; Okamoto, *Nokosareta hitobito*, letters and essays section, 188; Tsuji, *Montenrupa*, 6; US Embassy Manila dispatch no. 1241, March 20, 1952, decimal 350, Political Affairs, 1952, Manila Embassy Security Segregated Classified General Records, 1946–52, box 29, entry 3101, RG 84, NACP.

49. Kobayashi, *Ten ni tou tegami*, 161; "Baishō mondai kidō ni noru," *Asahi Shimbun*, January 1, 1953, 2; "Hitō no Juran-shi namida de yakusoku," *Mainichi Shimbun*, January 11, 1952, 3; "Kazokutachi ni kokoro kara no yorokobi o Oshiasu giin ga honsha ni messeji," *Mainichi Shimbun*, July 4, 1953, 7; Tsuji, *Montenrupa*, 243–44, 246–47.

50. "Senpan no genkei to Nihon sōkan," *Asahi Shimbun*, February 16, 1952, 2; "Mission to Japan," *Manila Times*, February 16, 1952, 1–2; Tsuji, *Montenrupa*, 241; Kagao, "Montenrupa no namida," 7, 12.

51. Memo, "Information Concerning Philippine War Criminals Issue," September 27, 1949, 1:158–61, disclosure 14, D'130 2-5-2, JDRO; Kobayashi, *Ten ni tou tegami*, 140.

52. Kagao, *Montenrupa ni inoru*, 110–11; Nishimura Kanichi, "Montenrupa no dōfuku o tazunete," *Nyū Eiji* 5, no. 4 (April 1954): 60–64; Remolona, "Hitō no Nihonjin senpantachi," 16–17; A. N. Nelson to Marciano Roque, May 11, 1951, bundle no. 32, *Philippines v. Masaki Shiochi* et al., Japanese War Crime Records, Case Files, NAP.

53. US Embassy Manila cable no. 3904, June 30, 1953, folder Post-Treaty—Japanese War Criminals, 1953, box 24, Records of the Legal Adviser Relating to Japanese War Crimes, 1943–60, lot file 61 D 33, Records of the Legal Adviser Relating to War Crimes, RG 59, NACP; Manila cable no. 332, June 28, 1953, 1:506, disclosure 14, D'130 3-1-1, JDRO. As one Manila newspaper noted, the presidential action was not technically an "amnesty," which would have required congressional concurrence, but rather a decision

to grant individual pardons. "105 Pardoned Jap Prisoners Signed Away by Neri at Rites," *Manila Bulletin*, July 7, 1953, 1.

54. Republic of the Philippines, *Official Gazette* 49, no. 7 (July 1953): xcvii–xcix.

55. Manila cable no. 332, June 28, 1953, 1:506, and Manila cable no. 334, June 29, 1953, 1:527, disclosure 14, D'130 3-1-1, JDRO.

56. Manila cable no. 336, June 30, 1953, 1:534, disclosure 14, D'130 3-1-1, JDRO; "Japs Okay Cash Reps," *Manila Times*, June 30, 1953, 1; editorial, "Good Faith," *Manila Times*, July 3, 1953, 4; "Japanese Gov't Reported Evaluating Ability to Pay Reparations in Cash," *Manila Bulletin*, July 1, 1953, 3; "Neri Counsels against Optimism over Reparations Issue with Japan," *Manila Bulletin*, July 22, 1953, 1; "The Local Scene," *Philippines Free Press*, July 4, 1953, 52; Yoshikawa, *Nippi baishō*, 133.

57. Press release no. 7-6-6, July 6, 1953, Office of the President of the Philippines, decimal 694.9624/7-653, Central Decimal File, 1950–54, box 3023, RG 59, NACP; Acting Secretary of Foreign Affairs Felino Neri to Chief of Japanese Mission Nakagawa Toru, note, July 4, 1953, and Nakagawa to Neri, note, July 4, 1953, 1:580–83, disclosure 14, D'130 3-1-1, JDRO; "Hikoku senpan no tokusha: Kyō seishiki oboegaki o kōkan," *Asahi Shimbun*, July 6, 1953, evening edition, 3.

58. "Hikoku no senpan kokoku e," *Asahi Shimbun*, July 15, 1953, evening edition, 3; "110 War Criminals Reach Yokohama," *Manila Bulletin*, July 23, 1953, 2; Kobayashi, *Ten ni tou tegami*, 270–72; Manila cable no. 366, July 8, 1953, 1:455, and Manila cable no. 384, July 14, 1953, 1:492, disclosure 14, D'130 3-1-1, JDRO.

59. Editorial, "Honored Ashes," *Manila Times*, July 5, 1953, 4.

60. Manila cable no. 361, July 7, 1953, 1:441, disclosure 14, D'130 3-1-1, JDRO.

61. Memo, "Final Disposition and Policies Governing Burial and Graves Registration of Executed War Criminals," Col. R. M. Levy to Commanding Generals, Eighth Army and Philippine Command, August 13, 1948, and Quartermaster, Far East Command, check sheet memo, August 6, 1948, file 000.5E War Criminals, Decimal File 1945–51, SCAP Legal Section, Law Division, box 1413, UD 1289, RG 331, NACP; US Embassy Manila cable no. 114, July 14, 1953, folder Post-Treaty—Japanese War Criminals, 1953, box 24, Records of the Legal Adviser Relating to Japanese War Crimes, 1943–60, lot file 61 D 33, Records of the Legal Adviser Relating to War Crimes, RG 59, NACP; "Hanjiranu rokujūnana no itai," *Asahi Shimbun*, July 15, 1953, 7.

62. Manila cable no. 548, November 24, 1953, 2:83, disclosure 14, D'130 3-1-1, JDRO; "Inori—matta kono hi: Hikoku senpan kazoku no yorokobi," *Asahi Shimbun*, June 28, 1953, 7; "'Zetsubō' koete, 'bakushō': Kanrui ni urumu hyakuroku senpan," *Asahi Shimbun*, July 4, 1953, 7; "Shi no kunō kara ikiru muzukashisa e," *Asahi Shimbun*, July 12, 1953, 7; "'Ima wa natsukashi Manira': Hakusan Maru senjō no senpantachi," *Asahi Shimbun*, July 16, 1953, 7; "Hakusan Maru, Yokohama kōgai ni teihaku," *Asahi Shimbun*, July 22, 1953, 7; "Shamen ikō nashi: Sugamo no Hikoku senpan," *Asahi Shimbun*, November 24, 1953, 7; "Ima nizukuri o owawara: Montenrupa ikotsu 17 karada mo tomo ni kaeru," *Mainichi Shimbun*, July 14, 1953, 7; "Hakusan Maru kinō Manira shukkō," *Mainichi Shimbun*, July 16, 1953, 7; "Sugamogumi to shakuhōgumi to," *Mainichi Shimbun*, July 22, 1953, 3; Dower, *Embracing Defeat*, 515.

63. "Yorokobi niwaku Montenrupa," *Asahi Shimbun*, June 30, 1953, evening edition, 3; "Hikoku Sugamo no senpan o shamen," *Asahi Shimbun*, December 29, 1953, 1.

64. Manila cable no. 559, November 27, 1953, 2:86, Manila cable no. 577, December 5, 1953, 1:95, Manila cable no. 588, December 8, 1953, 2:96, English text of Yoshida letter, December 11, 1953, and report, "Decision Concerning Recommendation for Clemency," December 2, 1953, 2:106–10, disclosure 14, D'130 3-1-1, JDRO.

65. Yoshikawa, *Nippi baishō*, 136–41; "Jap Rep Bid Unacceptable," *Manila Times*, December 11, 1953, 1; "Baishō nakuba shamen sezu," *Mainichi Shimbun*, December 11, 1953, 1.

66. Manila cable no. 604, December 12, 1953, 2:126, disclosure 14, D'130 3-1-1, JDRO.

67. Agenda, December 23, 1953, Cabinet Agenda, January–December 1953, box 75, Quirino Papers.

68. Manila cable no. 630, December 23, 1953, 2:128, Manila cable no. 636, December 26, 1953, 2:135, and Manila cable no. 642, December 28, 1953, 2:136, disclosure 14, D'130 3-1-1, JDRO.

69. Jorge R. Coquia, *The Philippine Presidential Election of 1953* (Manila: University Publishing Co., 1955), 97–99, 159–61; Ohno, *War Reparations*, 58–59.

70. Yoshikawa, *Nippi baishō*, 133; Coquia, *The Philippine Presidential Election*, 68–70.

71. Editorial, "Feeling toward Japan," *Manila Bulletin*, July 1, 1953, 12.

72. Report, Senate Committee on Investigation (Blue Ribbon), May 19, 1954, folder Magalona, Enrique, Congress of the Philippines, Senate, box 40, Quirino Papers.

73. Yoshikawa Yōko, "War Reparations Implementation, Reparations-Secured Loans and a Treaty of Commerce," in Ikehata and Yu-Jose, *Philippines-Japan Relations*, 380.

74. One informed observer, Willard Hanna, wrote in late 1955 of the gradual "changed mood" in Philippines-Japan relations, a mood that was marked by a lessening of Filipinos' bitter hatred of Japanese and Japanese appreciation of the reasons for Filipino anger and the need to find ways to "repay old debts" ("Japan's Return," 1–3).

Chapter 6. Constructing Narratives and Assessing Impact

1. Congressman Miguel Tolentino to President Sergio Osmeña, March 31, 1945, series II, box 10, folder Bills 1, 2, 6, 27, Sergio Osmeña Papers, National Library of the Philippines, Manila.

2. See, for example, speech, "The Devil and the Deep Sea," October 22, 1949, box 4, Jorge C. Bocobo Papers, University of the Philippines, Diliman; and "Remarks," Vicente G. Sinco, San Francisco Press Club, September 1951, box 10, Presidential Papers Collections, University of the Philippines, Diliman.

3. Satō, *Onshū o koete*, 7.

4. Castro and Santos, "A Report," 471.

5. Report of intercepted letters from POW Fujii Hajime, case no. 1486, January 10,

1947 (English translation in file), Investigation Reports, 1945–49, SCAP Legal Section, Investigative Division, box 1749, UD 1330, RG 331, NACP.

6. US Embassy Manila cable no. 1041 and attachments, July 31, 1947, decimal 740.00116 PW/7-3147, Central Decimal File, 1945–49, box 3632, RG 59, NACP; US Embassy Manila cable no. 1353, November 26, 1947, decimal file 711.6, Manila Embassy General Records, 1946–61, box 22, entry 3100A, RG 84, NACP.

7. Transcript, 552, case no. 3, *Philippines v. Takahashi Sadakichi*, and transcript, 598, case no. 5, *Philippines v. Kudō Chūshirō*, box 1729, UD 1328, RG 331, NACP.

8. Transcript, 452–53, case no. 57, *Philippines v. Itō Saburō*, box 1704, UD 1323, RG 331, NACP.

9. Editorial, *Liberty News*, November 11, 1947, attachment to US Embassy Manila cable no. 1353, November 26, 1947, decimal 740.00116 PW/11-2647, Central Decimal File, 1945–49, box 22, RG 59, NACP.

10. "Letter to Madame Tojo," *Philippines Free Press*, December 11, 1948, 60F–G.

11. Teodoro Locsin, "Day of Reckoning," *Philippines Free Press*, January 17, 1948, 35.

12. Owari Saburō to Kiyoko, undated (English translation in file), bundle no. 17, *Philippines v. Ichimura Isao and Owari Saburō*, Japanese War Crime Records, Case Files, NAP. For other letters, see Sugamo Isho Hensankai, ed., *Seiki no isho* (Tokyo: Sugamo Isho Hensankai Kanko Jimusho, 1953), 575, 592, 594–95, 607–14, 622.

13. See, for example, Tsuji, *Yūhei Montenrupa*, 113–14.

14. Kuroda, "Montenrupa," 130–31.

15. Mineo, *Uminari ga kikoeru*, 122–23, 174.

16. Owari Saburō to brother, undated (English translation in file), bundle no. 17, *Philippines v. Ichimura Isao and Owari Saburō*, Japanese War Crime Records, Case Files, NAP.

17. Memo, "Matter Concerning Report on Philippine War Crimes Trials," May 6, 1949, and report, "Matter Concerning the Philippine War Crimes Trials," May 6, 1949, 1:117–24, disclosure 14, D'130 2-5-2, JDRO.

18. Sugamo Isho Hensankai, *Seiki no isho*, 592–93.

19. Yoshimura, Chief of War Crimes Section, to Captain Dollete, February 17, 1949, 2:395–96, disclosure 14, D'130 2-5-2, JDRO.

20. Although "Nakamura" is blacked out in the available Japanese Foreign Ministry memos and other documents discussing the case, it is clear from the context that it was the Nakamura case that was being discussed. See memo, "Matter Concerning Letter to Philippine War Crimes Office Investigations Section Chief Dollete," February 17, 1949, 1:84–86, disclosure 14, D'130 2-5-2, JDRO.

21. Satō, *Onshū o koete*, ii, 41–42, 61, 75, 84, 91–92.

22. Teletype conference, FEC item no. 2, October 16, 1947, Radio Messages, 1945–51, SCAP Legal Section, Administrative Division, box 1353, UD 1268, RG 331, NACP.

23. US Embassy Manila cable no. 550, May 28, 1948, decimal 694.9631/5-2848, US Embassy Manila cable no. 793, August 4, 1948, decimal 694.9631/8-448, US Embassy

Manila cable no. 812, August 11, 1948, decimal 694.9631/8-1148, US Embassy Manila cable no. 830, August 17, 1948, decimal 694.9631/8-1748, and US Embassy cable no. 857, August 25, 1948, decimal 694.9631/8-2548, Central Decimal File, 1945–49, box 2918, RG 59, NACP; "Quirino Stresses View on Jap Trade," *Manila Times*, May 6, 1948, 1.

24. "Resume Trade with Japan? Most Free Press Readers Find the Idea Repulsive," *Philippines Free Press*, March 15, 1947, 26–27.

25. Felipe Lagon, "The No's Have It," *Philippines Free Press*, May 22, 1948, 44–45.

26. US Embassy Manila cable no. 925, September 14, 1948, decimal 800/891, Manila Embassy General Records, 1946–61, box 41, entry 3100A, RG 84, NACP.

27. Ibid.

28. Speech, "The Devil and the Deep Sea," October 22, 1949, and letter/article for *Herald* newspaper, "Reparations from Japan," November 15, 1949, box 4, Bocobo Papers. Bocobo's postwar perspective represented a marked turnaround for one who before the war had seen much to admire in Japan.

29. "Report of Ambassador Jessup's Meeting with Japanese Businessmen," January 20, 1950, Tokyo no. 82, section II(g), Official Chronological File, 1948–53, Records of Ambassador-at-Large Philip C. Jessup, lot file no. 53 D 470, Official Lot Files, box 2, RG 59, NACP; US Embassy Manila cable no. 857, August 25, 1948, decimal 694.9631/8-2548, Central Decimal File, 1945–49, box 2918, RG 59, NACP.

30. Kobayashi, *Ten ni tou tegami*, 124–25, 155; "Firipin hito no kokoro," *Asahi Shimbun*, February 4, 1952, 3.

31. Rafael A. Bautista, "'Never the Twain Shall Meet?': A Letter to a Prewar Japanese Friend," *Philippines Free Press*, April 27, 1946, 11, 19; "A Letter from Harry," *Philippines Free Press*, June 23, 1951, 25.

32. Ernesto Deza, letter to *Philippines Free Press*, June 1, 1946, 14; J. Silva de la Cruz, "Two Japanese Waifs," *Philippines Free Press*, March 22, 1947, 21; E. Acayan Gonzales, "One Japanese Who Deserves NO Hate," *Philippines Free Press*, June 7, 1947, 19.

33. Alvaro Basilides, "Yes, Let Us Trade with Japan," *Philippines Free Press*, June 12, 1948, 50–51.

34. Enrique B. Santos, "Conquerors No More," *This Week Magazine* (*Manila Chronicle*), December 3, 1950, 9–12.

35. Asia Bureau, "Matters Concerning the War Criminals," memo, November 12, 1952, 1:283–84, Manila cable no. 88, January 30, 1953, 1:330, and Manila cable no. 348, July 3, 1953, 1:555, disclosure 14, D'130 3-1-1, JDRO.

36. Dower, *Embracing Defeat*, 506–7; Awaya Kentarō, *Shiryō Nihon gendaishi 2: Haisen chokugo no seiji to shakai* (Tokyo: Otsuki Shoten, 1981), 207–10; editorial, *Chuka Kokusai*, November 19, 1948, and editorial, *Kobe Shimbun*, November 29, 1948, Press Translations, Miscellaneous File, 1945–49, SCAP Legal Section, Office of the Chief, box 840, UD 1175, RG 331, NACP.

37. Letter, unsigned and undated (ca. 1948), bundle no. 17, *Philippines v. Ichimura Isao and Owari Saburō*, Japanese War Crime Records, Case Files, NAP; Tsuji, *Montenrupa*, 190; Kagao, "Montenrupa no senpan to tomo ni," 205.

38. "Kudō ni shikei no hanketsu," *Asahi Shimbun*, November 7, 1947, 2; "Tsuneoka moto shōsa kōshukei," *Asahi Shimbun*, December 17, 1948, 2.

39. "'Mujitsu' no uttae saiyō: Hikoku daitōryō ga torihakarai," *Asahi Shimbun*, March 2, 1950, 3. Saitō was among those executed, while Itō was eventually granted amnesty.

40. Kagao, "Ikite iru Hitō senpan," 132–39.

41. "Letter from Japan," *Philippines Free Press*, May 5, 1951, 16.

42. "Mrs. Kora and Her Appeal," *Philippines Free Press*, June 9, 1951, 20.

43. Kobayashi, *Ten ni tou tegami*, 145–46; Nakajima, "Shikeishū no inori," 3.

44. Kobayashi, *Ten ni tou tegami*, 143–45; Fujita Takefumi, "Hitō no shikeishū bochi," *Bungei Shunjū* 29, no. 13 (October 1951): 126–34; transcript, 772–75, case no. 1, *Philippines v. Fujita Takefumi*, box 1728, UD 1328, RG 331, NACP.

45. Tsuji, *Montenrupa*, 65–74; "Kai-inutachi mo 'shakuhō,'" *Asahi Shimbun*, July 13, 1953, 5; specifications, and transcript, 6, 9, 33, case no. 69, *Philippines v. Fujimoto Takao*, box 1707, UD 1323, RG 331, NACP.

46. Tsuji, *Montenrupa*, 75–98; "Futatabi fumenu haha no kokoku," *Asahi Shimbun*, July 10, 1953, evening edition, 7.

47. Specifications, and transcript, 29–30, 41–43, case no. 14, *Philippines v. Harada Shimpei* et al., box 1690, UD 1323, RG 331, NACP.

48. Tsuji, *Montenrupa*, 122–23.

49. Ibid., 27–39, 120–21.

50. Kagao Shūnin to Hashimoto Ryogo, August 5, 1951, US Political Adviser, Tokyo cable no. 418, enclosure 2, September 17, 1951, decimal 694.9624/9-1751, Central Decimal File, 1950–54, box 3023, RG 59, NACP.

51. Kagao, *Montenrupa ni inoru*, 71–74, 103–31, 144–55, 168, 178; Tsuji, *Montenrupa*, 211–12; Okamoto, *Nokosareta hitobito*, letters and essays section, 6, 9–10; Kobayashi, *Ten ni tou tegami*, 132–33; Satō, *Onshū o koete*, 60–62, 75, 84–85.

52. Sugamo Isho Hensankai, *Seiki no isho*, 592, 607, 612–14.

53. Okamoto, *Nokosareta hitobito*, letters and essays section, 3–4, 17, 46, 49, 61, 107.

54. Ibid., 220–39.

55. Murata Shōzō, "Wakai no baishō o kataru," *Ekonomisto* 20, no. 30 (October 1951): 17–18; Kuroda, "Montenrupa," 133.

56. Kobayashi, *Ten ni tou tegami*, 152–54.

57. Dower, *Embracing Defeat*, 513.

58. John W. Dower, "'An Aptitude for Being Unloved': War and Memory in Japan," in *Crimes of War: Guilt and Denial in the Twentieth Century*, ed. Omer Bartov, Atina Grossmann, and Mary Nolan (New York: New Press, 2002), 228–30.

59. R. John Pritchard, ed., *The Tokyo Major War Crimes Trial: The Records of the International Military Tribunal for the Far East*, vols. 27 and 28, *The Case for the Prosecution* (Lewiston, NY: Edwin Mellon Press, 1998), 12,345–12,845.

60. Editorial, "Feeling toward Japan," *Manila Bulletin*, July 1, 1953, 12.

61. Hanna, "Japan's Return," 2. The American Universities Field Staff, organized in 1951, billed itself as an academic foreign service, and its staff members lived in foreign areas and provided periodic firsthand reports of local developments.

62. Note verbale, July 6, 1953, 1:438–39, disclosure 14, D'130 3-1-1, JDRO.

63. US Embassy Manila cable no. 1041, July 31, 1947, decimal 740.00116 PW/7-3147, Central Decimal File, 1945–49, box 3632, RG 59, NACP.

64. Press release, Office of the President of the Philippines, July 6, 1953, decimal 694.9624/7-653, Central Decimal File, 1950–54, box 3023, RG 59, NACP; note verbale, June 29, 1953, 1:481; cable no. 334, Nakagawa to Okazaki, June 29, 1953, 1:527, disclosure 14, D'130 3-1-1, JDRO.

65. US Embassy Manila cable no. 10, July 1, 1953, decimal 694.9624/7-153, Central Decimal File, 1950–54, box 3023, RG 59, NACP.

66. David Joel Steinberg, "The Philippine 'Collaborators': Survival of an Oligarchy," in *Southeast Asia in World War II: Four Essays*, ed. Joseph Silverstein (New Haven, CT: Yale University Press, 1966), 74.

67. "Tokusha wa seiron no koe datta," *Mainichi Shimbun*, July 17, 1953, evening edition, 3.

68. Saitō Masami, "Firippin no tai-Nichi kanjō," *Sekai Shūhō* 34, no. 26 (September 9, 1953): 44–45.

69. "Manira no sono goro," *Asahi Shimbun*, February 3, 1952, 2.

70. There were on occasion hints that money could or might have changed hands. For example, Quirino's biographer noted that in 1948 the idea of obtaining payment from the Japanese in exchange for release of the war criminals had been bruited about but claimed that Quirino had rejected the idea. Quirino, *Apo Lakay*, 117.

71. Santos, "Conquerors No More."

72. Editorial, "Sublimely Gratuitous," *Manila Times*, July 12, 1953, 4.

73. "FP Readers Reject Appeal for Jap Prisoners," *Philippines Free Press*, May 26, 1951, 47.

74. Letter, September 1, 1953, 2:70–72, disclosure 14, D'130 3-1-1, JDRO.

75. Yanase was bitterly resented by those who did stand trial. Fujita Takefumi, for example, testified at his own trial that he was indignant that Yanase, the man responsible for the atrocities at Fort Santiago, had been able to go home while others were made to assume responsibility for his crimes. In fact, the Philippine government had requested that Yanase be returned to the Philippines to stand trial, but the Americans deflected the request because Yanase had provided critical testimony for prosecutors in numerous US trials. Transcript, 416, case no. 1, *Philippines v. Fujita Takefumi*, box 1728, UD 1328, RG 331, NACP; teletype conference, FEC item no. 4, and PHILRYCOM item no. 70, September 25, 1947, Radio Messages, 1945–51, SCAP Legal Section, Administrative Division, box 1353, UD 1268, RG 331, NACP.

76. US Embassy Manila cable no. 645, February 12, 1957, decimal 694.96/2-1257, Central Decimal File, 1955–59, box 2722, RG 59, NACP; transcript, 247, 367–69, case no. 8, *Philippines v. Kita Heiji* et al., box 1688, UD 1323, RG 331, NACP; postsentence

review file, bundle no. 22, *Philippines v. Kita* et al., Japanese War Crime Records, Case Files, NAP; "Over a Cup of Coffee," *Manila Times*, February 8, 1957, 4.

77. Susan Dwyer, "Reconciliation for Realists," *Ethics & International Affairs* 13 (1999): 89.

78. Tsuji, *Montenrupa*, 197.

79. Nakano Satoshi, "Lost in Memorialization? Unmaking of 'History Issues' in Postwar Philippines-Japan Relations," in *Proceedings of the Symposium: The Philippines-Japan Relationship in an Evolving Paradigm* (Manila: Yuchengo Center, 2006), 76–77.

Conclusion

1. Gary Jonathan Bass, *Stay the Hand of Vengeance: The Politics of War Crimes Tribunals* (Princeton, NJ: Princeton University Press, 2000), 304; David A. Crocker, "Reckoning with Past Wrongs: A Normative Framework," *Ethics & International Affairs* 13 (1999): 56.

2. See, for example, Helena Cobban, *Amnesty after Atrocity? Healing Nations after Genocide and War Crimes* (Boulder, CO: Paradigm Publishers, 2007).

3. Bass, *Stay the Hand*, 24.

4. Ricardo Trota Jose, "The Philippine War Crimes Trials, 1947–1949," in *Remembering World War II in the Philippines: Proceedings of the Conference "World War II in the Philippines: Remembering 60 Years After"* (Manila: National Historical Institute, 2007), 2:78.

5. Bass, *Stay the Hand*, 16. Bass argues that it is not enough to simply dismiss such trials as "victors' justice"; what really matters is who the victors are and, therefore, which justice they attempt to dispense.

6. See, for example, Futamura, *War Crimes Tribunals*, 116.

7. Quoted in Ishida, *Remains of War*, 53–54.

8. Ibid., 237.

9. Nakano, "The Politics of Mourning," 342.

Epilogue

1. Kobayashi, *Ten ni tou tegami*, 282.

2. Ibid., 282–83; Itō et al., *Monten*, 91, 142.

3. Itō et al., *Monten*.

4. Ibid., 103–5, 116–17; Kobayashi, *Ten ni tou tegami*, 285–86.

5. Mineo, *Uminari ga kikoeru*, 1–13.

6. Satō, *Onshu o koete*, i–iv.

7. Itō et al., *Monten*, 2 and preface.

8. Kobayashi, *Ten ni tou tegami*, 293; "Shirota Gintarō," *Asahi Shimbun*, June 8, 2006, 19; "Aa Montenrupa," *Asahi Shimbun*, June 16, 2009, 13.

9. Kobayashi, *Ten ni tou tegami*, 286, 291; Itō et al., *Monten*, 133; memo of conversation, Department of State, June 8, 1956, subject "Request for Clemency for Remaining

Japanese War Criminals," decimal 694.0026/6-856, Central Decimal File, 1955–59, box 2719, RG 59, NACP.

10. Onoda Hiroo, *No Surrender: My Thirty-Year War*, trans. Charles S. Terry (Tokyo: Kodansha International Ltd., 1974), 100–101; "Tsuji Yutaka-san," *Asahi Shimbun*, November 18, 2008, 35; Nakamata Tomisaburō, "Watakushi no sengo 60 nen: Senpan shikeishu / Chūgoku tokuha-in," Japan National Press Club, November 2005, accessed June 21, 2009, www.jnpc.or.jp/cgi-bin/pb/article.php?id=476.

11. Kobayashi, *Ten ni tou tegami*, 281–85.

Bibliography

Archival Collections Consulted

Japan

Diplomatic Record Office, Japanese Ministry of Foreign Affairs, Tokyo
National Diet Library, Tokyo

The Philippines

Jorge C. Bocobo Papers, University of the Philippines, Diliman
Jose P. Laurel Papers (microform)
National Archives of the Philippines, Manila
Camilo Osias Papers, Filipiniana Division, National Library of the Philippines, Manila
Sergio Osmeña Papers, Filipiniana Division, National Library of the Philippines, Manila
People's Court Papers, University of the Philippines, Diliman
Elpidio Quirino Papers, Filipinas Heritage Museum, Manila
Carlos P. Romulo Papers, University of the Philippines, Diliman
Jorge Vargas Papers, Jorge Vargas Library and Archive, Jorge Vargas Museum, Diliman

United States

National Archives and Records Administration II, College Park, Maryland
Gordon Prange Collection, University of Maryland, College Park, Maryland
Harry S. Truman Presidential Library, Independence, Missouri

Published Government Materials

Awaya Kentarō, ed. *Shiryō Nihon gendaishi 2: Haisen chokugo no seiji to shakai*. Tokyo: Otsuki Shoten, 1981.

Japan National Diet. House of Councilors, Special Committee on Overseas Repatriation. Hearing, March 13, 1951, Testimony of Jimbō Nobuhiko.

———. House of Councilors, Committee on Welfare. Hearing, November 13, 1952, Testimony of Kobayashi Yusaku.

Office of the Resident Commissioner of the Philippines to the United States. *Report on the Destruction of Manila and Japanese Atrocities*. Washington, DC, 1945.

Republic of the Philippines, *Official Gazette*.

Supreme Commander for the Allied Powers. Monograph 5, "Trials of Class 'B' and 'C' War Criminals." In *History of the Nonmilitary Activities of the Occupation of Japan*. Wilmington, DE: Scholarly Resources, 1989. Microform.

United Nations War Crimes Commission. *History of the United Nations War Crimes Commission and the Development of the Laws of War*. London: HMSO, 1948.

US Department of State. *Foreign Relations of the United States, 1958–1960*. Vol. 18. Washington, DC: US Government Printing Office, 1994.

Diaries, Letters, Memoirs, Oral Histories, Speeches

Fujita Takefumi. "Hitō no shikeishū bochi." *Bungei Shunjū* 29, no. 13 (October 1951): 126–34.

Ishida Jintarō. *The Remains of War: Apology and Forgiveness—the Testimonies of the Japanese Imperial Army and Its Filipino Victims*. Quezon City: Megabooks Company, 2001.

Itō Masayasu et al., eds. *Monten: Kikoku 30 shūnen tokushūgo*. Tokyo: Montenrupa no Kai, 1983.

Kagao Shūnin. "Ikite iru Hitō senpan." *Kaizō* 32, no. 7 (June 1951): 132–39.

———. *Montenrupa ni inoru: Nippi senpan shikeishū to tomo ni*. Tokyo: Fuji Shoen, 1953.

———. "Montenrupa no namida." *Daihōrin* 20, no. 3 (March 1953): 6–13.

———. "Montenrupa no senpan to tomo ni." *Fujin Kōron* 39:10, no. 437 (September 1953): 204–7.

———. "Montenrupa shikei no ichiya." *Daihōrin* 20, no. 10 (October 1953): 6–15.

Kanegae Seitarō. *The Path to Friendship: A Tale of a Japanese Immigrant in the Philippines*. Translated by Kaoru Shimamura and Teruyoshi Mizuno. Tokyo: Keisō Shobō Publishing Company, 1987.

Kuroda Shigenori. "Montenrupa: Hitō senpan gokusha no taikenki." *Daiyamondo* 40, no. 17 (May 1952): 130–33.

Laurel, Jose P. *War Memoirs of Dr. Jose P. Laurel*. Manila: Jose P. Laurel Memorial Foundation, Inc., 1962.

Mineo Shisuhiko. *Uminari ga kikoeru: Hitō senpan shikeishū kaigun seinen shōkō no ikan*. Tokyo: Fuesu Shuppan, 1966.

Nakajima Shōhei. "Shikeishū no inori." *Sunday Mainichi*, August 19, 1951, 3–8.

Nihon no Firipin Senryōki ni Kansuru Shiryō Chōsa Fōramu, ed. *Nihon no Firipin senryō: Intabyū kiroku*. Tokyo: Ryūkei Shosha, 1994.

Okamoto Torao, ed. *Nokosareta hitobito: Hitō senpan shikeishū no shuki*. Tokyo: Sumashobō, 1952.

Onoda, Hiroo. *No Surrender: My Thirty-Year War*. Translated by Charles S. Terry. Tokyo: Kodansha International Ltd., 1974.

Osawa, Kiyoshi. *The Japanese Community in the Philippines before, during, and after the War*. Manila: Joshu Bunko Library / Kalayaan Press, 1994.

Osias, Camilo. *The Story of a Long Career of Varied Tasks*. Quezon City: Manila Paz Publishing Company, 1971.
Quirino, Elpidio. *The Memoirs of Elpidio Quirino*. Manila: National Historical Institute, 1990.
Roxas, Manuel A. *Speeches, Messages, and Other Pronouncements of President Manuel Roxas*. Manila: Bureau of Print, 1947.
Satō Sō. *Onshū o koete: Hitō B-kyū senpan no shuki*. Tokyo: Nihon Kōgyō Shinbunsha, 1981.
Shirota Kichiroku. *Davao imin no eikō to zasetsu: Ichi zairyū hōjin no shuki yori*. Nagasaki: Nagasaki Shuppan Bunka Kyōkai, 1980.
Sugamo Isho Hensankai, ed. *Seiki no isho*. Tokyo: Sugamo Isho Hensankai Kanko Jimusho, 1953.
Tsuji Chōichi. *Yūhei Montenrupa*. Tokyo: Senshi Kankōkai, Hatsubai Seiunsha, 1984.
Tsuji Yutaka, ed. *Montenrupa: Hitō yūshū no kiroku*. Tokyo: Asahi Shimbun Co., 1952.
Tsushima Hoto. *Manira in omou hitobito*. Tokyo: Hoto Kankokai, 1963.
Yokoyama Shizuo. "Sono goro no gokusō seikatsu o kataru." *Shūkyō Kōron* 23, no. 6 (August 1953): 3–6.

Newspapers

Asahi Shimbun, 1945–57
Evening Herald, 1946–48
Evening News, 1948, 1953
Mainichi Shimbun, 1946–57
Manila Bulletin, 1948–53
Manila Chronicle, 1947–53
Manila Times, 1947–54
Nihon Keizai Shimbun, 1951–54
Nippon Times, 1953
Philippines Free Press, 1946–57
Yomiuri Shimbun, 1945–48

Articles and Books

Abinales, Patricio N. "Davao-kuo: The Political Economy of a Japanese Settler Zone in Philippine Colonial Society." *Journal of American–East Asian Relations* 6, no. 1 (Spring 1997): 59–82.
Agoncillo, Teodoro A. *The Burden of Proof: The Vargas-Laurel Collaboration Case*. Manila: University of the Philippines Press, 1984.
———. *The Fateful Years: Japan's Adventure in the Philippines, 1941–45*. 2 vols. Quezon City: R. P. Garcia Publishing Company, 1965.
———. *A Short History of the Philippines*. New York: Mentor Books, 1969.

Agpalo, Remigio, et al., eds. *The Philippine Senate*. Manila: Dick Baldovino Enterprises, 1997.

Alam, Bachtiar, and Wifrido V. Villacorta. *Perceptions of Japan and the Japanese by Filipinos and Indonesians: An Intergenerational Study*. Manila: De La Salle University Yuchengco Center, 2002.

Arai Emiko. "Montenrupa no atsui kaze." *Shio* 475 (September 1998): 248–55.

Aszkielowicz, Dean. *The Australian Pursuit of Japanese War Criminals, 1943–1957: From Foe to Friend*. Hong Kong: Hong Kong University Press, 2017.

Banlaoi, Rommel C., and Clarita R. Carlos. *Political Parties in the Philippines: From 1900 to the Present*. Makati City, Philippines: Konrad Adenauer Foundation, 1996.

Bass, Gary Jonathan. *Stay the Hand of Vengeance: The Politics of War Crimes Tribunals*. Princeton, NJ: Princeton University Press, 2000.

Bengzon, Jose P. *The Philippine Judicial System*. Manila: G. Rangel & Sons, 1968.

Boister, Neil, and Robert Cryer. *The Tokyo International Military Tribunal: A Reappraisal*. Oxford: Oxford University Press, 2008.

Buruma, Ian. *Wages of Guilt: Memories of War in Germany and Japan*. New York: Farrar, Straus and Giroux, 1994.

Castro, Fred Ruiz, and Guillermo S. Santos. "A Report on War Crimes Trials in the Philippines." *Lawyers' Journal* 15, no. 10 (October 1950): 470–72.

Cheah Wui Ling. "The Superior Orders Defence at the Post-war Trials in Singapore." In *Trials for International Crimes in Asia*, edited by Kirsten Sellars, 100–120. New York: Cambridge University Press, 2016.

Chaen Yoshio, ed. *BC-kyū senpan Beigun Manira saiban shiryō*. Tokyo: Fuji Shuppan, 1986.

———. *BC-kyū senpan Firipin saiban shiryō*. Tokyo: Fuji Shuppan, 1987.

Churchill, Bernardita. "The Japanese-Sponsored National Assembly & Post Liberation Congress, 1943–1946." In *The Philippine Senate*, edited by Remigio Agpalo et al., 101–17. Manila: Dick Baldovino Enterprises, 1997.

Chuter, David. *War Crimes: Confronting Atrocity in the Modern World*. Boulder, CO: Lynne Rienner Publishers, 2003.

Cobban, Helena. *Amnesty after Atrocity? Healing Nations after Genocide and War Crimes*. Boulder, CO: Paradigm Publishers, 2007.

Cohen, David J. "Beyond Nuremberg: Individual Responsibility for War Crimes." In *Human Rights in Political Transitions: Gettysburg to Bosnia*, edited by Carla Hesse and Robert Post, 53–92. New York: Zone Books, 1999.

———. "The Singapore War Crimes Trials and Their Relevance Today." *Singapore Law Review* 31 (2013): 3–38.

Coquia, Jorge R. *The Philippine Presidential Election of 1953*. Manila: University Publishing Co., 1955.

Crocker, David A. "Reckoning with Past Wrongs: A Normative Framework." *Ethics & International Affairs* 13 (1999): 43–64.

———. "Transitional Justice and International Civil Society." In *War Crimes and Collective Wrongdoing: A Reader*, edited by Aleksandar Jokić, 270–300. Malden, MA: Blackwell Publishers Inc., 2001.

Crowe, David M. *War Crimes, Genocide, and Justice: A Global History*. New York: Palgrave Macmillan, 2014.

Delgado, Francisco A. "Collaborators of the Japanese." *Lawyers' Journal* 10, no. 2 (October 1945): 50–60.

Doromal, Jose. *The War in Panay: A Documentary History of the Resistance Movement in Panay during World War II*. Manila: Diamond Historical Publications, 1952.

Dower, John W. "'Aptitude for Being Unloved': War and Memory in Japan." In *Crimes of War: Guilt and Denial in the Twentieth Century*, edited by Omer Bartov, Atina Grossman, and Mary Nolan, 217–41. New York: New Press, 2002.

———. *Embracing Defeat: Japan in the Wake of World War II*. New York: W. W. Norton & Company, Inc., 1999.

———. *War without Mercy: Race and Power in the Pacific War*. New York: Pantheon Books, 1986.

Duran, Pio. *Philippine Independence and the Far Eastern Question*. Manila: Community Publishers Inc., 1935.

Dwyer, Susan. "Reconciliation for Realists." *Ethics & International Affairs* 13 (1999): 81–98.

Fernando, Enrique M. *The American Constitutional Influence in Asia: Its Impact on the Philippine Legal System*. Manila: Supreme Court, 1976.

Fitzpatrick, Georgina, Timothy L. H. McCormack, and Narrelle Morris, eds. *Australia's War Crimes Trials 1945–51*. Leiden: Brill Nijhoff, 2016.

Friend, Theodore. *Between Two Empires: The Ordeal of the Philippines, 1929–1946*. New Haven, CT: Yale University Press, 1965.

———. *The Blue-Eyed Enemy: Japan against the West in Java and Luzon, 1942–1945*. Princeton, NJ: Princeton University Press, 1988.

Futamura, Madoka. *War Crimes Tribunals and Transitional Justice: The Tokyo Trial and the Nuremburg Legacy*. London: Routledge Taylor & Francis Group, 2008.

Goodman, Grant K. "Consistency Is the Hobgoblin: Manuel L. Quezon and Japan, 1899–1934." *Journal of Southeast Asian Studies* 14, no. 1 (March 1983): 79–94.

———. *Davao: A Case Study in Japanese-Philippine Relations*. Lawrence: University of Kansas Center for East Asian Studies, 1967.

———. "The Japanese Occupation of the Philippines: Commonwealth Sustained." *Philippine Studies* 36 (1988): 98–104.

———. "The Japanese Occupation of the Philippines: Successful Collaboration of Invading and Indigenous Power Elites." *Journal of International Studies* (Sophia University) 5, no. 2 (December 1982): 30–39.

———. "Philippine Bushido." In *Nitobe Inazo: Japan's Bridge across the Pacific*, edited by John F. Howes, 119–32. Boulder, CO: Westview Press, 1995.

———. "President Harry S. Truman and the Problem of Philippine 'Collaborators.'" *Pilipinas* 28 (Spring 1997): 131–36.

Gupit, Fortunato, Jr., and Daniel T. Martinez. *A Guide to Philippine Legal Materials: A Text on Philippine Legal Bibliography, Philippine Legal History, Philippine Legal System, Legal Philosophy, Methods of Legal Research*. Manila: Rex Book Store, 1993.

Hanna, Willard A. "Japan's Return to the Philippines." *AUFS Reports: East Asia Series* (Japan) 4, no. 12 (1955).

Hartendorp, A. V. H. *History of Industry and Trade of the Philippines*. Manila: American Chamber of Commerce of the Philippines, Inc., 1958.

———. *The Japanese Occupation of the Philippines*. 2 vols. Manila: Bookmark, 1967.

Hayase, Shinzo. "The Japanese Residents of 'Dabao-kuo.'" In *The Philippines under Japan: Occupation Policy and Reaction*, edited by Ikehata Setsuho and Ricardo Trota Jose, 247–87. Manila: Ateneo de Manila University Press, 1999.

Hayashi Hirofumi. *BC-kyū senpan saiban*. Tokyo: Iwanami Shoten, 2005.

———. "British War Crimes Trials of Japanese." *Nature-People-Society: Science and the Humanities* 31 (July 2001): 79–102.

———. *Sabakareta sensō hanzai: Igirisu no tai-Nichi senpan saiban*. Tokyo: Iwanami Shoten, 1998.

———. *Senpan saiban no kenkyū: Senpan saiban seisaku no keisei kara Tōkyō saiban, BC-kyū saiban made*. Tokyo: Shohan Bensei Shuppan, 2010.

Hayden, Joseph Ralston. *The Philippines: A Study in National Development*. New York: Macmillan Company, 1950.

Ikehata Setsuho. *The Japanese Military Administration in the Philippines and the Tragedy of General Artemio Ricarte*. Translated by Elpidio R. Sta. Romana. Singapore: National University of Singapore, 1991.

Ikehata Setsuho, and Ricardo Trota Jose, eds. *The Philippines under Japan: Occupation Policy and Reaction*. Manila: Ateneo de Manila University Press, 2003.

Ikehata Setsuho, and Lydia N. Yu-Jose, eds. *Philippines-Japan Relations*. Manila: Ateneo de Manila University Press, 2003.

Iwakura Takashi. *Kōto no tsuchi to narutomo: BC-kyū senpan saiban*. Tokyo: Kōdansha, 1995.

Jia, Bing Bing. "The Plea of Superior Orders in the Hong Kong Trials." In *Hong Kong's War Crimes Trials*, edited by Suzannah Linton, 169–98. Oxford: Oxford University Press, 2013.

Jose, Ricardo Trota. "The Philippines: From Occupation and Japanese 'Independence' to Independence." In *1945 in Europe and Asia: Reconsidering the End of World War II and the Change of the World Order*, edited by Gerhard Krebs and Christian Oberländer, 271–81. Munich: Iudicium, 1997.

———. "The Philippine War Crimes Trials, 1947–1949." *Social Science Information* 33, no. 1 (January–June 2005): 33–44.

———. "The Philippine War Crimes Trials, 1947–1949." In *Remembering World War II in the Philippines: Proceedings of the Conference "World War II in the Philippines: Remembering 60 Years After,"* 2:65–80. Manila: National Historical Institute, 2007.

———. "War Memorials and Commemorations in the Philippines: An Exploratory Look." In *The Past, Love, Money and Much More: Philippines-Japan Relations since the End of the Second World War*, edited by Lydia N. Yu-Jose, 15–37. Quezon City: Japanese Studies Program, 2008.

Kobayashi Hirotada. *Ten ni tou tegami: Mujitsu no senpan kyūsai ni hansei o sasageta Ueki Shinkichi*. Tokyo: Mainichi Shinbunsha, 2008.

Kumai, Toshimi. *The Blood and Mud in the Philippines: Anti-Guerrilla Warfare on Panay Island*. Translated by Yukako Ibuki. Iloilo City, Philippines: Malones Press and Publishing House, 2009.

Kushner, Barak. *Men to Devils and Devils to Men: Japanese War Crimes and Chinese Justice*. Cambridge, MA: Harvard University Press, 2016.

Lael, Richard L. *The Yamashita Precedent: War Crimes and Command Responsibility*. Wilmington, DE: SR Scholarly Resources Inc., 1982.

Lapham, Robert, and Bernard Norling. *Lapham's Raiders: Guerrillas in the Philippines, 1942–1945*. Lexington: University Press of Kentucky, 1996.

Lawson, Konrad. "Wartime Atrocities and the Politics of Treason in the Ruins of the Japanese Empire, 1936–1953." PhD diss., Harvard University, 2012.

Linton, Suzannah, ed. *Hong Kong's War Crimes Trials*. Oxford: Oxford University Press, 2013.

Loftus, Elizabeth F. *Eyewitness Testimony*. Cambridge, MA: Harvard University Press, 1979.

Mainichi Shimbun Seijibu, ed. *Shimbun shiryō ni miru Tōkyō saiban, BC-kyū saiban*. Tokyo: Gendai Shiryō Shuppan, 2000.

McCoy, Alfred W., ed. *An Anarchy of Families: State and Family in the Philippines*. Madison: University of Wisconsin Center for Southeast Asian Studies, 1993.

———. "'Politics by Other Means': World War II in the Western Visayas, Philippines." In *Southeast Asia under Japanese Occupation*, edited by Alfred W. McCoy, 158–203. New Haven, CT: Yale University Southeast Asia Studies, 1980.

Meloni, Chantal. "Command Responsibility: Mode of Liability for the Crimes of Subordinates or Separate Offence of the Superior?" *Journal of International Criminal Law* 5 (2007): 619–37.

Miller, Robert W. "War Crimes Trials at Yokohama." *Brooklyn Law Review* 15, no. 2 (April 1949): 191–209.

Minear, Richard H. *Victors' Justice: The Tokyo War Crimes Trial*. Princeton, NJ: Princeton University Press, 1971.

Minow, Martha. *Between Vengeance and Forgiveness: Facing History after Genocide and Mass Violence*. Boston: Beacon Press, 1998.

Montenrupa no Kai. "Aa, Montenrupa." *Seiron* 414 (September 2006): 23–29.

Morris, Narrelle, and Tim McCormack. "Were the Australian Trials Fair?" In *Australia's War Crimes Trials 1945–51*, edited by Georgina Fitzpatrick, Timothy L. H. McCormack, and Narrelle Morris, 781–809. Leiden: Brill Nijhoff, 2016.

Morton, Lewis. *The Fall of the Philippines*. Washington, DC: Office of the Chief of Military History, United States Army, 1996.

Murata Shōzō. "Wakai no baishō o kataru." *Ekonomisto* 20, no. 30 (October 1951): 17–20.

Nagai Hitoshi. *Firipin BC-Kyū senpan saiban*. Tokyo: Kōdansha, 2013.

———. *Firipin to tai-Nichi senpan saiban: 1945–1953-nen*. Tokyo: Iwanami Shoten, 2010.

———. "Kyokutō kokusai gunji saiban ni okeru 'shokoku' no tachiba: Firipin no baai." In *Toinaosu Tokyo saiban*, edited by Ajia Minshu Hōtei Junbikai, 77–99. Tokyo: Ryofuku Shuppan, 1995.

———. "The Tokyo War Crimes Trial." In *Philippines-Japan Relations*, edited by Ikehata Setsuho and Lydia N. Yu-Jose, 261–98. Manila: Ateneo de Manila University Press, 2003.

Nakagawa, Toru. "Japan-Philippine Relations." *Fookien Times Yearbook*, 1953, 73–74, 80.

Nakano Satoshi. "Appeasement and Coercion." In *The Philippines under Japan: Occupation Policy and Reaction*, edited by Ikehata Setsuho and Ricardo Trota Jose, 21–58. Manila: Ateneo de Manila University Press, 1999.

———. "Lost in Memorialization? Unmaking of 'History Issues' in Postwar Philippines-Japan Relations." In *Proceedings of the Symposium: The Philippines-Japan Relationship in an Evolving Paradigm*, 74–84. Manila: Yuchengo Center, 2006.

———. "The Politics of Mourning." In *Philippines-Japan Relations*, edited by Ikehata Setsuho and Lydia N. Yu-Jose, 337–76. Manila: Ateneo de Manila University Press, 2003.

Nishimura Kanichi. "Montenrupa no dōfuku o tazunete." *Nyū Eiji* 5, no. 4 (April 1954): 60–64.

Ohno Takushi. *War Reparations and Peace Settlement: Philippines-Japan Relations, 1945–1956*. Manila: Solidaridad Publishing House, 1986.

Piccigallo, Philip R. *The Japanese on Trial: Allied War Crimes Operations in the East, 1945–1951*. Austin: University of Texas Press, 1979.

Pritchard, R. John. "Historical Experience of British War Crimes Courts in the Far East, 1946–1948." *International Relations* 6, no. 1 (1978): 311–26.

———. "Lessons from British Proceedings against Japanese War Criminals." *Human Rights Review* 3, no. 2 (Summer 1978): 104–21.

———. "The Nature and Significance of British Post-war Trials of Japanese War Criminals, 1945–1948." *Proceedings of the British Association for Japanese Studies* 2 (1977): 189–219.

———, ed. *The Tokyo Major War Crimes Trial: The Records of the International Military Tribunal for the Far East*. Vols. 27 and 28, *The Case for the Prosecution*. Lewiston, NY: Edwin Mellon Press, 1998.

Quiason, Seraphin D. "The Japanese Colony on Davao, 1904–1941." *Philippine Social Sciences and Humanities Review* 23, no. 2–4 (June–December 1958): 215–30.

———. "The Japanese Community in Manila: 1898–1941." *Philippine Historical Review* 3 (1970): 184–222.

Quirino, Carlos. *Apo Lakay: The Biography of President Elpidio Quirino of the Philippines*. Manila: Total Book World, 1987.

Rafael, Vicente L. *White Love and Other Events in Filipino History*. Durham, NC: Duke University Press, 2000.

Recto, Claro M. *The Law of Belligerent Occupation and the Effect of Change of Sovereignty on the Commonwealth Treason Law*. Manila, 1946.

———. *Three Years of Enemy Occupation: The Issue of Political Collaboration in the Philippines*. Manila: People's Publishers, 1946.

Reel, A. Frank. *The Case of General Yamashita*. New York: Octagon Books, 1971.

Remolona, Ilde. "Hitō no Nihonjin senpantachi: Sono seikatsu to kokoro no hi." *Nyū Eiji* 3, no. 8 (August 1951): 16–20.

Romana, Elpidio R. Sta., and Ricardo T. Jose. "'Never Imagine Yourself to Be Otherwise . . .': Filipino Images of Japan over the Centuries." *Asian Studies* (Quezon City) 29 (1991): 65–94.

Ryan, Allan A. *Yamashita's Ghost: War Crimes, MacArthur's Justice, and Command Accountability*. Lawrence: University Press of Kansas, 2012.

Saitō Masami. "Firippin no tai-Nichi kanjō." *Sekai Shūhō* 34, no. 26 (September 9, 1953): 44–45.

Santos, Enrique B. "Conquerors No More." *This Week Magazine* (*Manila Chronicle*), December 3, 1950, 9–12.

Schaller, Michael. *The Origins of the Cold War in Asia: The American Occupation of Japan*. New York: Oxford University Press, 1985.

Schouten, Lisette. "Colonial Justice in the Netherlands Indies War Crimes Trials." In *Trials for International Crimes in Asia*, edited by Kirsten Sellars, 75–99. New York: Cambridge University Press, 2016.

Seraphim, Franziska. *War Memory and Social Politics in Japan, 1945–2005*. Cambridge, MA: Harvard University Asia Center, 2006.

Shiraishi, Saya, and Takashi Shiraishi, eds. *The Japanese in Colonial Southeast Asia*. Ithaca, NY: Cornell Southeast Asia Program, 1993.

Smith, Robert Ross. *Triumph in the Philippines*. Washington, DC: Office of the Chief of Military History, Department of the Army, 1963.

"Special Feature: After the Trials—Repatriation and Release of Japanese War Criminals, 1946–1958," *Japanese Studies* 31, no. 2 (September 2011): 141–228.

Spector, Ronald H. *Eagle against the Sun: The American War with Japan*. New York: Vintage Books, 1985.

Steinberg, David Joel. "An Ambiguous Legacy: Years at War in the Philippines." *Pacific Affairs* 45, no. 2 (Summer 1972): 165–90.

———. "Jose P. Laurel: A 'Collaborator' Misunderstood." *Journal of Asian Studies* 24, no. 4 (August 1965): 651–65.

———. *Philippine Collaboration in World War II*. Ann Arbor: University of Michigan Press, 1967.

———. "The Philippine 'Collaborators': Survival of an Oligarchy." In *Southeast Asia in World War II: Four Essays*, edited by Josef Silverstein, 67–86. New Haven, CT: Yale University Press, 1966.

Taylor, Lawrence. *A Trial of Generals: Homma, Yamashita, MacArthur*. South Bend, IN: Icarus Press, 1981.

Terami-Wada, Motoe. "Cultivating Goodwill between Japan and the Philippines in the 1930s." In *Philippines-Japan Relations*, edited by Ikehata Setsuho and Lydia N. Yu-Jose, 155–84. Manila: Ateneo de Manila University Press, 2003.

———. "The Manila Japanese (1888–1942)." *Bulletin of the American Historical Collection* 17, no. 1 (January–March 1989): 84–101.

Tōjima Kazuko. "Nippi yūkō no ishizue ni: 'Montenrupa no yo wa fukete.'" *Energy Review* 20:2, no. 229 (February 2000): 32–37.

Totani, Yuma. *Justice in Asia and the Pacific Region, 1945–1952: Allied War Crimes Prosecutions*. New York: Cambridge University Press, 2015.

———. *The Tokyo War Crimes Trial: The Pursuit of Justice in the Wake of World War II*. Cambridge, MA: Harvard University Asia Center, 2008.

Trefalt, Beatrice. "Hostages to International Relations? The Repatriation of Japanese War Criminals from the Philippines." *Japanese Studies* 31, no. 2 (2011): 191–209.

———. *Japanese Army Stragglers and Memories of the War in Japan, 1950–1975*. London: Routledge-Curzon, 2003.

Tuazon, Bobby M., ed. *Oligarchic Politics: Elections and the Party-List System in the Philippines*. Quezon City: CenPEG Books, 2007.

Utsumi Aiko. "Changing Japanese Views of the Allied Occupation of Japan and the War Crimes Trials." *Journal of the Australian War Memorial* 30 (April 1997). www.awm.gov.au/journal/j30/utsumi.htm.

Veloso, Jose M. "Collaboration as a National Issue: A Grave Government Problem." *Lawyers' Journal* 10, no. 3 (November 30, 1945): 114–21.

———. "Collaboration as a National Issue: A Grave Government Problem." *Lawyers' Journal* 10, no. 4 (December 31, 1945): 170–78.

Wilson, Sandra. "War, Soldier and Nation in 1950s Japan." *International Journal of Asian Studies* 5, no. 2 (2008): 187–218.

Wilson, Sandra, Robert Cribb, Beatrice Trefalt, and Dean Aszkielowicz. *Japanese War Criminals: The Politics of Justice after the Second World War*. New York: Columbia University Press, 2017.

Yokoyama Bengoshikai. *Hōtei no seijōki: BC-kyū senpan Yokohama no kiroku*. Tokyo: Nihon Hyōronsha, 2004.

Yokoyama Misayo. "Kansha no kotoba." In *Nokosareta hitobito: Hitō senpan shikeishū no shuki*, edited by Okamoto Torao, 1–4. Tokyo: Sumashobō, 1952.

Yoshikawa Yōko. "Jose M. Tagawa and the Japanese Commercial Sector in Manila, 1898–1920." *Philippine Studies* 43, no. 2 (1995): 182–85.

———. *Nippi baishō gaikō kōshō no kenkyū, 1949–1956*. Tokyo: Keisō Shobō, 1991.

———. "War Reparations Implementation, Reparations-Secured Loans and a Treaty of Commerce." In *Philippines-Japan Relations*, edited by Ikehata Setsuho and Lydia N. Yu-Jose, 377–442. Manila: Ateneo de Manila University Press, 2003.

Yu-Jose, Lydia. *Japan Views the Philippines, 1900–1944*. Manila: Ateneo de Manila University Press, 1992.

———. "Philippine, American, and Japanese Relations as Seen through the Issue of Neutralization." In *Philippines-Japan Relations*, edited by Ikehata Setsuho and Lydia N. Yu-Jose, 63–69. Manila: Ateneo de Manila University Press, 2003.

———. "World War II and the Japanese in the Prewar Philippines." *Journal of Southeast Asian Studies* 27, no. 1 (March 1996): 64–81.

Zahar, Alexander. "Trial Procedure at the British Military Courts, Hong Kong, 1946–1948." In *Hong Kong's War Crimes Trials*, edited by Suzannah Linton, 13–69. Oxford: Oxford University Press, 2013.

Index

Page numbers in italics refer to illustrations. Page numbers followed by t *indicate tables.*

NEW PERSPECTIVES IN SOUTHEAST ASIAN STUDIES

The Burma Delta: Economic Development and Social Change on an Asian Rice Frontier, 1852–1941
Michael Adas

Of Beggars and Buddhas: The Politics of Humor in the "Vessantara Jataka" in Thailand
Katherine A. Bowie

Voices from the Plain of Jars: Life under an Air War, second edition
Edited by Fred Branfman with essays and drawings by Laotian villagers

A Reckoning: Philippine Trials of Japanese War Criminals
Sharon W. Chamberlain

From Rebellion to Riots: Collective Violence on Indonesian Borneo
Jamie S. Davidson

Feeding Manila in Peace and War, 1850–1945
Daniel F. Doeppers

The Floracrats: State-Sponsored Science and the Failure of the Enlightenment in Indonesia
Andrew Goss

In Plain Sight: Impunity and Human Rights in Thailand
Tyrell Haberkorn

Revolution Interrupted: Farmers, Students, Law, and Violence in Northern Thailand
Tyrell Haberkorn

Amazons of the Huk Rebellion: Gender, Sex, and Revolution in the Philippines
Vina A. Lanzona

Dreams of the Hmong Kingdom: The Quest for Legitimation in French Indochina, 1850–1960
Mai Na M. Lee

The Government of Mistrust: Illegibility and Bureaucratic Power in Socialist Vietnam
Ken MacLean

Policing America's Empire: The United States, the Philippines, and the Rise of the Surveillance State
Alfred W. McCoy

An Anarchy of Families: State and Family in the Philippines
Edited by Alfred W. McCoy

The Hispanization of the Philippines: Spanish Aims and Filipino Responses, 1565–1700
John Leddy Phelan

Pretext for Mass Murder: The September 30th Movement and Suharto's Coup d'État in Indonesia
John Roosa

Hamka's Great Story: A Master Writer's Vision of Islam for Modern Indonesia
James R. Rush

Dead in the Water: Global Lessons from the World Bank's Hydropower Project in Laos
Edited by Bruce Shoemaker and William Robichaud

The Social World of Batavia: Europeans and Eurasians in Colonial Indonesia, second edition
Jean Gelman Taylor

Everyday Economic Survival in Myanmar
Ardeth Maung Thawnghmung

Việt Nam: Borderless Histories
Edited by Nhung Tuyet Tran and Anthony Reid

Thailand's Political Peasants: Power in the Modern Rural Economy
Andrew Walker

Modern Noise, Fluid Genres: Popular Music in Indonesia, 1997–2001
Jeremy Wallach

www.ingramcontent.com/pod-product-compliance
Ingram Content Group UK Ltd.
Pitfield, Milton Keynes, MK11 3LW, UK
UKHW031906170425
457510UK00007B/167

9 780299 318604